Table o

Appetizers, Dips & Snacks

Beverages

Soups

Beef

Fish & Seafood

Pork & Lamb

Poultry

Vegetarian

Sides

Breads

Desserts

The Company's Coming Story

Jean Paré (pronounced "jeen PAIR-ee") grew up understanding that the combination of family, friends and home cooking is the best recipe for a good life. From her mother, she learned to appreciate good cooking, while her father praised even her earliest attempts in the kitchen. When Jean left home, she took with her a love of cooking, many family recipes and an intriguing desire to read cookbooks as if they were novels!

When her four children had all reached school age, Jean volunteered to cater the 50th anniversary celebration of the Vermilion School of Agriculture, now Lakeland College, in Alberta, Canada. Working out of her home, Jean prepared a dinner for more than 1,000 people, launching a flourishing catering operation that continued for over 18 years. During that time, she had countless opportunities to test new ideas with immediate feedback—resulting in empty plates and contented customers! Whether preparing cocktail sandwiches for a house party or serving a hot meal for 1,500 people, Jean Paré earned a reputation for great food, courteous service and reasonable prices.

"Never share a recipe you wouldn't use yourself."

As requests for her recipes increased, Jean was often asked the question, "Why don't you write a cookbook?" Jean responded by teaming up with her son, Grant Lovig, in the fall of 1980 to form Company's Coming Publishing Limited. The publication of *150 Delicious Squares* on April 14, 1981 marked the debut of what would soon become one of the world's most popular cookbook series.

The company has grown since those early days when Jean worked from a spare bedroom in her home. Nowadays every Company's Coming recipe is *kitchen-tested* before it is approved for publication.

Company's Coming cookbooks are distributed in Canada, the United States, Australia and other world markets. Bestsellers many times over in English, Company's Coming cookbooks have also been published in French and Spanish.

Familiar and trusted in home kitchens around the world, Company's Coming cookbooks are offered in a variety of formats. Highly regarded as kitchen workbooks, the softcover Original Series, with its lay-flat plastic comb binding, is still a favourite among readers.

Jean Paré's approach to cooking has always called for *quick and easy recipes* using *everyday ingredients*. That view has served her well. The recipient of many awards, including the Queen Elizabeth Golden Jubilee Medal, Jean was appointed Member of the Order of Canada, her country's highest lifetime achievement honour.

Jean continues to share what she calls The Golden Rule of Cooking: *Never share a recipe you wouldn't use yourself.* It's an approach that has worked—*millions of times over!*

Foreword

Life is so hectic for people and families these days. Too often it becomes tempting to stop for fast food or call for takeout instead of making dinner. Eating this way is fine as an occasional treat, but if we do it too often, it can end up just shrinking our wallets and expanding our waistlines. Luckily, the solution to this dinner-time dilemma can be found in your very own kitchen: the slow cooker.

Many of the recipes in this collection focus on basic, fresh and nutritious ingredients to provide you and your family with easy, healthy meal options that don't sacrifice flavour. We've used healthier fats, lower-sodium and higher-fibre ingredients, and we've packed in the fruit and vegetables wherever we could. It's a much healthier—and more economical—alternative to fast food!

Other recipes focus on rustling up just a few simple ingredients to make a delicious, filling meal for your family every night—and you don't even have to be in the kitchen to do it! These recipes feature readily available convenience products to save you time and effort. Ingredients run from the everyday, such as frozen meatballs, canned tomatoes and condensed soup mixes, to the more exotic, like grape leaves, sambal oelek, okra and quinoa.

There are a number of ways that slow cookers make meal preparation more convenient. With a little advance planning, you and your family will be greeted with a warm, delicious meal when you arrive home

from school or work. Try preparing the ingredients for your meal the night before. Additionally, slow cooker recipes often make large batches. You can freeze leftovers for future meals, or take them to work for lunch the following day. To remove the guesswork, we have provided storage information for those recipes that freeze particularly well.

This book does not focus on main courses alone; we've also developed recipes for appetizers, sides, soups and even breads and desserts. As usual, we've come up with delicious, kitchen tested combinations that will make your dishes a hit with family and friends.!

Jean Paré

Nutrition Information Guidelines

Each recipe is analyzed using the most current versions of the Canadian Nutrient File from Health Canada, and the United States Department of Agriculture (USDA) Nutrient Database for Standard Reference.

- If more than one ingredient is listed (such as "butter or hard margarine"), or if a range is given (1 – 2 tsp., 5 – 10 mL), only the first ingredient or first amount is analyzed.
- For meat, poultry and fish, the recommended serving size per person is 4 oz. (113 g) uncooked weight (without bone), which is 2 – 3 oz. (57 – 85 g) cooked weight (without bone)—approximately the size of a deck of playing cards.
- Milk used is 1% M.F. (milk fat), unless otherwise stated.
- Cooking oil used is canola oil, unless otherwise stated.
- Ingredients indicating "sprinkle," "optional" or "for garnish" are not included in the nutrition information.
- The fat in recipes and combination foods can vary greatly depending upon the sources and types of fats used in each specific ingredient. For these reasons, the amount of saturated, monounsaturated and polyunsaturated fats may not add up to the total fat content.

Slow Cooker Basics

A slow cooker uses only a small amount of electricity, making slow cooking a cost-effective way to cook. It can be a versatile tool in your kitchen. Besides being a great way to prepare a variety of dishes, it can serve as an extra pot any time you cook; it won't heat up your kitchen and it won't dry out your food the way your oven might. Slow cooking also allows you to prepare more economical cuts of meat, leaving them moist and tender.

Our recipes have been written to represent the most common sizes of slow cookers on the market, and each recipe has been tested to ensure great results. You may need to adjust a recipe to fit your particular slow cooker. Consult your owner's manual for particular guidelines. It will outline how to get the most from your particular brand of cooker, how cooking times can vary between different brands and how high altitude and power fluctuations can affect your slow cooker. Once you've read the manual and prepared a few meals, you'll get to know your slow cooker well enough to anticipate how it will respond to any given recipe.

General Guidelines

In addition to the specific cooking tips included in the recipes, we also offer these general guidelines, which you can apply any time you use your slow cooker:

- Cooking times can vary with different makes and models of slow cookers, and some cookers can be forgiving if you go over the specified time in the recipe. However, for best results, follow the cooking times provided in our recipes, as they have all been thoroughly tested.

- Fill your slow cooker at least halfway, but no more than three-quarters full, for the most even heat distribution. (Ingredients will typically cook down in volume.) Note that some of our recipes, such as dips, deviate from this general principle because we are simply heating the ingredients, not cooking them. We've tested the recipes to make sure they work, but if you happen to have a smaller slow cooker—such as a 1 1/2 quart (1.5 L) size—it would work well.

- When using your slow cooker to heat dips, transfer the warmed dip to a fondue pot, on lowest heat, for a more pleasing presentation.

- Thaw frozen food before cooking to ensure accurate cooking times.

- Don't lift the lid while food is cooking because heat and moisture will escape, adding 20 to 30 extra minutes of cooking time to the recipe each time the lid is raised.

- Layer foods in this order for best results: root vegetables (carrots, onions, beets, potatoes) at the bottom, then meats, seasonings and, lastly, non-root vegetables (beans, peas, corn). Generally, the ingredients that take longest to cook should be at the bottom, and those that cook most quickly should be near the top.

- To adapt one of your own recipes for a slow cooker, you may have to reduce the liquid in the recipe by up to 50 per cent and add more herbs and spices. Slow cooking foods at a lower temperature can produce a fair amount of liquid, which dilutes the herbs or spices that enhance flavour.

- Use dried herbs while the dish is cooking, and add fresh herbs to the pot in the final moments, or just before serving for an extra dash of flavour.

- Trim meat of all visible fat before adding it to the slow cooker.

- Pre-brown meat and ingredients such as onions and garlic to add a more robust flavour and colour to a dish.

Safety Tips

If you've never used a slow cooker before, these safety tips should ensure safe cooking:

- Follow manufacturer's instructions for processing hot liquids.

- Always cook large pieces of meat such as roasts on High, unless they have been pre-browned first, to get the temperature up more quickly and into a safe zone.

- Keep ingredients, especially raw meat, refrigerated and in separate containers until you are ready to assemble the recipe.

- Partially cooking meat and refrigerating it can lead to bacterial growth. Our make-ahead instructions keep food safety in mind, so follow them as they are written.

- Test the doneness of large pieces of meat with a thermometer to ensure the correct temperature has been reached.

- Don't reheat leftover food in a slow cooker because it doesn't reach the necessary high temperature quickly enough to eliminate potential bacterial growth.

- Chill all cooked food within two hours of cooking.

- When adding liquids to a hot slow cooker, make sure liquid is at least room temperature, as cold liquids could cause the liner to crack.

Chili Dip and Chips

A rich, high-fibre chili dip with delicious homemade
tortilla crisps—great for a satisfying snack.

BEEF CHILI DIP
Canola oil	1/2 tsp.	2 mL
Lean ground beef	1/2 lb.	225 g
Finely chopped celery	1/2 cup	125 mL
Finely chopped onion	1/2 cup	125 mL
Finely chopped fresh jalapeño pepper (see Tip, page 167)	1 tbsp.	15 mL
All-purpose flour	1 tbsp.	15 mL
Chili powder	1 tbsp.	15 mL
Evaporated milk	1 cup	250 mL
Chopped tomato	2 cups	500 mL
Tomato paste (see Tip, page 83)	1 tbsp.	15 mL
Brown sugar, packed	2 tsp.	10 mL
Can of black beans, (19 oz., 540 mL) rinsed and drained	1	1
Grated sharp Cheddar cheese	1 cup	250 mL
Lime juice	1 tbsp.	15 mL

BAKED CHIPS
Canola oil	3 tbsp.	45 mL
Chili powder	2 tsp.	10 mL
Salt	1/8 tsp.	0.5 mL
Whole wheat flour tortillas (10 inch, 25 cm, diameter)	5	5

Beef Chili Dip: Heat canola oil in large frying pan on medium-high. Add next 4 ingredients. Scramble-fry for about 5 minutes until beef is no longer pink. Drain.

Add flour and chili powder. Heat and stir for 1 minute. Slowly add evaporated milk, stirring constantly, until boiling and thickened. Remove from heat.

Add next 3 ingredients. Stir. Transfer to greased 3 1/2 to 4 quart (3.5 to 4 L) slow cooker.

Mash 1 cup (250 mL) beans in small bowl. Add to beef mixture with remaining beans. Stir. Cook, covered, on Low for 3 to 4 hours or on High for 1 1/2 to 2 hours.

Add cheese and lime juice. Stir until cheese is melted. Makes about 4 1/3 cups (1.1 L).

Baked Chips: Combine first 3 ingredients in small cup. Brush over tortillas. Cut into 8 wedges each. Arrange in single layer on 2 ungreased baking sheets. Bake on separate racks in 375°F (190°C) oven for about 10 minutes, turning wedges and switching position of baking sheets at halftime, until browned and crisp. Serve with Beef Chili Dip. Makes 40 chips.

1 tbsp. (15 mL) chili dip with 1 chip: 76 Calories; 3.5 g Total Fat (1.0 g Mono, 0.5 g Poly, 1.3 g Sat); 9 mg Cholesterol; 8 g Carbohydrate; 1 g Fibre; 4 g Protein; 121 mg Sodium

Sun-dried Tomato Bean Dip

Serve this rustic, creamy-textured dip with whole wheat pita bread and fresh vegetables. Store leftover Slow-cooked Beans in an airtight container in the freezer for up to three months.

SLOW-COOKED BEANS (see Note, below)		
Water	5 cups	1.25 L
Dried navy beans, soaked in water overnight, rinsed and drained	2 cups	500 mL
DIP		
Chopped sun-dried tomatoes, softened in boiling water for 10 minutes before chopping	3 tbsp.	45 mL
Chopped fresh basil	2 tbsp.	30 mL
Chopped walnuts	2 tbsp.	30 mL
Grated Asiago cheese	2 tbsp.	30 mL
Balsamic vinegar	4 tsp.	20 mL
Finely chopped onion	1 tbsp.	15 mL
Olive (or canola) oil	1 tbsp.	15 mL
Tomato paste (see Tip, page 83)	1 tsp.	5 mL
Garlic clove, minced (or 1/4 tsp., 1 mL, powder)	1	1
Salt	1/8 tsp.	0.5 mL
Coarsely ground pepper	1/4 tsp.	1 mL

Slow-cooked Beans: Put water and beans in 3 1/2 to 4 quart (3.5 to 4 L) slow cooker. Cook, covered, on High for 4 1/2 to 5 hours until tender. Drain. Rinse with cold water. Drain well. Makes about 5 cups (1.25 mL).

Dip: Process all 11 ingredients in food processor until combined. Add 2 cups (500 mL) Slow-cooked Beans. Process until smooth. Makes about 1 3/4 cups (425 mL).

1/4 cup (60 mL): 123 Calories; 4.8 g Total Fat (2.0 g Mono, 1.4 g Poly, 0.9 g Sat); 2 mg Cholesterol; 15 g Carbohydrate; 6 g Fibre; 5 g Protein; 70 mg Sodium

Note: You can use the Slow-cooked Beans recipe as a base for cooking other dried beans. Kidney beans require a 10-minute boil before being slow-cooked, while some beans, such as chickpeas (garbanzo beans), may require more than 5 hours of cooking before they are tender.

Artichoke Spinach Dip

Lovely wine and pesto flavours give this rich dip a real bistro feel—it tastes fabulous served with fresh baguette slices.

Jar of marinated artichoke hearts (12 oz., 340 mL), drained and chopped	1	1
Herb and garlic cream cheese	1 cup	250 mL
Dry (or alcohol-free) white wine	1/2 cup	125 mL
Pepper, sprinkle		
Coarsely chopped fresh spinach leaves, lightly packed	4 cups	1 L
Basil pesto	1/4 cup	60 mL

Combine first 4 ingredients in 3 1/2 to 4 quart (3.5 to 4 L) slow cooker. Cook, covered, on Low for 4 to 5 hours or on High for 2 to 2 1/2 hours. Stir until smooth.

Add spinach and pesto. Stir. Makes about 2 1/2 cups (625 mL).

1/4 cup (60 mL): 113 Calories; 8.8 g Total Fat (0 g Mono, trace Poly, 4.1 g Sat); 26 mg Cholesterol; 4 g Carbohydrate; trace Fibre; 3 g Protein; 256 mg Sodium

Pictured on page 17.

Baba Ganoush

Cooking up this exotic favourite is easy with the slow cooker. Try it hot or cold and serve with fresh pita or pita chips.

Chopped, peeled Asian eggplant	5 cups	1.25 L
Garlic cloves, minced	2	2
Ground cumin	1 tsp.	5 mL
Olive oil	2 tbsp.	30 mL
Water	1/4 cup	60 mL
Salt	1/4 tsp.	1 mL
Pepper	1/4 tsp.	1 mL
Lemon juice	1 tbsp.	15 mL
Olive oil	1 tbsp.	15 mL

Combine first 7 ingredients in 3 1/2 to 4 quart (3.5 to 4 L) slow cooker. Cook, covered, on Low for 4 to 6 hours or on High for 2 to 3 hours, stirring once at halftime, until soft and fragrant.

Transfer to blender or food processor. Add lemon juice and second amount of olive oil. Process until smooth (see Safety Tip, page 9). Makes about 1 3/4 cups (425 mL).

1/3 cup (75 mL): 88 Calories; 7.9 g Total Fat (5.5 g Mono, 1.2 g Poly, 1.1 g Sat); 0 mg Cholesterol; 5 g Carbohydrate; 3 g Fibre; 1 g Protein; 214 mg Sodium

Pictured on page 17.

Hot Crab Dip

This tomato-topped, cheesy crab dip will be a hit at any gathering. Scoop up tasty mouthfuls with toasted baguette rounds, pita crisps or crackers.

Cream cheese, softened	1 1/2 cups	375 mL
Cans of crabmeat (6 oz., 170 g, each), drained, cartilage removed, flaked	2	2
Grated Asiago (or Parmesan) cheese	1 cup	250 mL
Diced seeded Roma (plum) tomato	1 cup	250 mL
Finely chopped green onion	2 tbsp.	30 mL
Salt, sprinkle		

Combine first 3 ingredients in 3 1/2 to 4 quart (3.5 to 4 L) slow cooker. Cook, covered, on Low for about 2 hours or on High for about 1 hour, stirring twice, until heated through. Transfer to serving dish.

Combine tomato, onion and salt in small bowl. Spoon over crab mixture. Makes about 3 1/2 cups (875 mL).

1/4 cup (60 mL): 144 Calories; 7.5 g Total Fat (0.1 g Mono, 0.1 g Poly, 7.5 g Sat); 54 mg Cholesterol; 2 g Carbohydrate; trace Fibre; 9 g Protein; 286 mg Sodium

Pictured on page 17.

Spicy Black-eyed Pea Dip

This hot and spicy dip may be topped with chopped green onion and grated Monterey Jack cheese. It's perfect for dipping fresh vegetables or spooning onto slices of ciabatta bread or taco chips. Serve warm from the slow cooker because it will thicken as it cools.

Cans of black-eyed peas (19 oz., 540 mL, each), rinsed and drained	2	2
Process cheese loaf, chopped	16 oz.	450 g
Hot chunky salsa	1 cup	250 mL
Taco seasoning mix, stir before measuring	1 tbsp.	15 mL
Canned sliced jalapeño peppers, finely chopped	2 tsp.	10 mL

Combine all 5 ingredients in 3 1/2 to 4 quart (3.5 to 4 L) slow cooker. Cook, covered, on Low for 2 to 3 hours or on High for 1 to 1 1/2 hours, stirring twice, until heated through. Break up mixture with potato masher. Makes about 5 cups (1.25 L).

1/4 cup (60 mL): 100 Calories; 4.8 g Total Fat (0 g Mono, 0 g Poly, 3.2 g Sat); 16 mg Cholesterol; 10 g Carbohydrate; 2 g Fibre; 6 g Protein; 703 mg Sodium

White Bean and Garlic Spread

For garlic lovers! Spread over crostini slices or melba toast. Leave one clove out if you prefer a milder flavour.

Dried navy beans	1 1/2 cups	375 mL
Italian seasoning	2 tbsp.	30 mL
Water	3 cups	750 mL
Large lemon	1	1
Olive oil	2 tbsp.	30 mL
Garlic cloves, minced (or 1/2 tsp., 2 mL, powder)	2	2
Salt	1/4 tsp.	1 mL
Pepper	1/4 tsp.	1 mL

Put beans into medium bowl. Add water until 2 inches (5 cm) above beans. Let stand overnight (see Tip, below). Drain. Rinse beans. Drain. Transfer to 3 1/2 to 4 quart (3.5 to 4 L) slow cooker.

Add Italian seasoning and water. Cook, covered, on High for 3 1/2 to 4 hours until beans are tender (see Note). Drain, reserving 1/4 cup (60 mL) cooking liquid. Transfer beans and liquid to food processor.

Grate 1 tsp. (5 mL) lemon zest into bean mixture. Squeeze in 2 tbsp. (30 mL) lemon juice. Add olive oil, garlic, salt and pepper. Carefully process until smooth (see Safety Tip, page 9). Makes about 3 1/2 cups (875 mL).

1/3 cup (75 mL): 67 Calories; 2.8 g Total Fat (1.9 g Mono, 0.5 g Poly, 0.4 g Sat); 0 mg Cholesterol; 8 g Carbohydrate; 2 g Fibre; 3 g Protein; 279 mg Sodium

Note: Cooking this spread on Low is not recommended, as it may not fully cook the beans.

 If you would like a quicker method for soaking the beans, place them in a heatproof dish, cover with boiling water and let stand for at least one hour until cool.

Lemony Vine Leaves

These Greek-style grape leaves are a great summertime appetizer to serve with purchased tzatziki dip.

Long-grain white rice	2 cups	500 mL
Roasted red pepper cream cheese	1 cup	250 mL
Greek seasoning	2 tbsp.	30 mL
Salt, sprinkle		
Pepper, sprinkle		
Grape leaves, rinsed and drained, tough stems removed	60	60
Lemon juice	1/3 cup	75 mL
Water	4 cups	2 L

Mix first 5 ingredients in medium bowl until no dry rice remains.

Arrange 38 to 40 grape leaves on work surface, vein-side up, stem end closest to you. Spoon about 1 tbsp. (15 mL) rice mixture onto leaf about 1/2 inch (12 mm) from stem end of leaf. Fold bottom of leaf over rice mixture. Fold in sides. Roll up from bottom to enclose filling (see Note 1). Repeat with remaining leaves and rice mixture. Cover bottom of greased 3 1/2 to 4 quart (3.5 to 4 L) slow cooker with 4 to 5 grape leaves. Arrange rolls, seam-side down, close together in single layer over leaves. Cover with 4 to 5 grape leaves. Repeat with remaining rolls and leaves.

Add lemon juice and water. Do not stir. Place a heatproof plate on top to keep rolls submerged during cooking (see Note 2). Cook, covered, on Low for 7 to 8 hours or on High for 3 1/2 to 4 hours until rice is tender. Let stand, covered, for 20 minutes. Makes 38 to 40 stuffed grape leaves.

1 stuffed grape leaf: 57 Calories; 1.6 g Total Fat (trace Mono, 0.1 g Poly, 1.0 g Sat); 6 mg Cholesterol; 9 g Carbohydrate; trace Fibre; 1 g Protein; 44 mg Sodium

Note 1: Leaves should be rolled securely, but not too tightly, as the filling will expand during cooking.

Note 2: If you have an oval slow cooker that will not fit a round plate, use two smaller, heatproof plates that will fit.

Variation: Try with herb and garlic cream cheese instead of the red pepper cream cheese.

Green Goddess Fondue

Serve this tangy dip with whole wheat bread cubes and raw or blanched vegetables, and be sure to try it with cooked shrimp for a special treat!

Coarsely chopped fresh parsley	1 1/2 cups	375 mL
Coarsely chopped fresh chives	2/3 cup	150 mL
White wine vinegar	1/3 cup	75 mL
Block cream cheese (8 oz., 250 g, each), diced	2	2
Evaporated milk	1 1/2 cups	375 mL
Salt	1/4 tsp.	1 mL
Pepper	1/4 tsp.	1 mL

Process first 3 ingredients in blender or food processor until paste forms.

Add remaining 4 ingredients. Process with on/off motion until smooth. Pour into 3 1/2 to 4 quart (3.5 to 4 L) slow cooker. Cook, covered, on Low for 1 1/2 hours, stirring every 30 minutes, until heated through. Makes about 4 cups (1 L).

1/4 cup (60 mL): 127 Calories; 11.0 g Total Fat (0.3 g Mono, 0.1 g Poly, 7.8 g Sat); 36 mg Cholesterol; 4 g Carbohydrate; trace Fibre; 4 g Protein; 157 mg Sodium

1. Baba Ganoush, page 12
2. Hot Crab Dip, page 13
3. Artichoke Spinach Dip, page 12

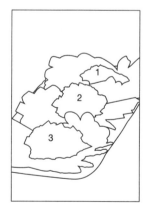

Nacho Cheese Fondue

Hungry kids, teenagers and adults alike will devour this Mexican-themed cheese fondue! Serve with cubed bread or tortilla chips straight from the slow cooker on the lowest setting, or transfer to a serving bowl.

Process cheese spread	2 cups	500 mL
Roasted red pepper cream cheese	1 cup	250 mL
Salsa	1 cup	250 mL
Finely chopped red pepper	1/2 cup	125 mL
Can of diced green chilies (4 oz., 113 g)	1	1

Combine all 5 ingredients in 3 1/2 to 4 quart (3.5 to 4 L) slow cooker. Cook, covered, on Low for 2 to 3 hours or on High for 1 to 1 1/2 hours until heated through. Makes about 5 cups (1.25 L).

1/4 cup (60 mL): 106 Calories; 8.4 g Total Fat (0 g Mono, trace Poly, 4.2 g Sat); 28 mg Cholesterol; 4 g Carbohydrate; trace Fibre; 4 g Protein; 291 mg Sodium

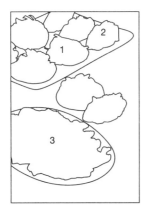

1. Pork Pita Sliders, page 27
2. Mushroom Trio Toasts, page 21
3. Buffalo Chicken Bites, page 24

French Onion Canapés

These small toasts include all the popular flavours of French onion soup—with far less fat and calories! A sweet onion topping and a sprinkle of Gruyère cheese make for tasty appetizers from your slow cooker.

Thinly sliced onion	6 cups	1.5 L
Canola oil	3 tbsp.	45 mL
Dried thyme	1/2 tsp.	2 mL
Dry sherry	2 tbsp.	30 mL
Dijon mustard	1 tsp.	5 mL
Salt, sprinkle		
Pepper, sprinkle		
Round Melba toasts	60	60
Grated Gruyère cheese	1/2 cup	125 mL

Combine first 3 ingredients in 3 1/2 to 4 quart (3.5 to 4 L) slow cooker. Cook, covered, on High for 4 1/2 to 5 hours, stirring at halftime, until onion is caramelized. Transfer to medium bowl.

Add next 4 ingredients. Stir. Makes about 1 1/2 cups (375 mL).

Spoon onion mixture onto Melba toasts. Sprinkle with cheese. Makes 60 canapés.

1 canapé: 27 Calories; 1.1 g Total Fat (0.5 g Mono, 0.3 g Poly, 0.2 g Sat); 1 mg Cholesterol; 4 g Carbohydrate; trace Fibre; 1 g Protein; 32 mg Sodium

Mexi Meatballs

Serve these tasty appetizer meatballs with toothpicks. Choose your own level of heat by using mild, medium or hot salsa. Frozen meatballs should be thawed overnight in the refrigerator.

Box of frozen cooked meatballs, thawed	2 lbs.	900 g
Salsa	2 cups	500 mL
Sour cream	1/2 cup	125 mL
Lime juice	2 tbsp.	30 mL
Chopped fresh cilantro (or parsley)	1 tbsp.	15 mL

Combine meatballs and salsa in 3 1/2 to 4 quart (3.5 to 4 L) slow cooker. Cook, covered, on Low for 3 to 4 hours or on High for 1 1/2 to 2 hours.

Combine remaining 3 ingredients in small bowl. Add to meatball mixture. Stir. Serves 12.

1 serving: 274 Calories; 19.4 g Total Fat (0 g Mono, 0 g Poly, 8.3 g Sat); 42 mg Cholesterol; 10 g Carbohydrate; 2 g Fibre; 4 g Protein; 824 mg Sodium

Mushroom Trio Toasts

A tasty appetizer for mushroom lovers! An onion and mushroom mixture tops toasty baguette slices, with Parmesan cheese adding a nice, sharp bite.

Chopped portobello mushrooms	3 cups	750 mL
Sliced fresh white mushrooms	3 cups	750 mL
Thinly sliced red onion	1 cup	250 mL
Package of dried porcini mushrooms (3/4 oz., 22 g), coarsely chopped	1	1
Butter	1 tbsp.	15 mL
Dried tarragon	1/4 tsp.	1 mL
Dry mustard	1/4 tsp.	1 mL
Garlic clove, minced (or 1/4 tsp., 1 mL, powder)	1	1
Salt	1/8 tsp.	0.5 mL
Pepper	1/4 tsp.	1 mL
Chopped fresh parsley (or 3/4 tsp., 4 mL, flakes)	2 tbsp.	30 mL
Grated Parmesan cheese	2 tbsp.	30 mL
White wine vinegar	1 tsp.	5 mL
Whole wheat baguette bread loaf, cut into 3/4 inch (2 cm) slices	1	1

Combine first 10 ingredients in greased 3 1/2 to 4 quart (3.5 to 4 L) slow cooker. Cook, covered, on Low for 6 to 7 hours or on High for 3 to 3 1/2 hours.

Add next 3 ingredients. Stir. Makes about 1 2/3 cups (400 mL).

Arrange bread slices on ungreased baking sheet. Broil on top rack in oven for about 1 minute per side until golden. Spoon mushroom mixture over top. Makes about 25 toasts.

1 toast: 40 Calories; 1.1 g Total Fat (0.3 g Mono, 0.1 g Poly, 0.5 g Sat); 2 mg Cholesterol; 6 g Carbohydrate; 1 g Fibre; 2 g Protein; 77 mg Sodium

Pictured on page 18.

Garlic Mushrooms

Enjoy these creamy, flavourful mushrooms with crostini or baguette slices—or serve them alongside a steak dinner!

Fresh small white mushrooms	2 lbs.	900 g
Alfredo pasta sauce	1/2 cup	125 mL
Dry (or alcohol-free) white wine	1/4 cup	60 mL
Garlic cloves, minced	4	4
(or 1 tsp., 5 ml, powder)		
Pepper, sprinkle		
Lemon juice	2 tsp.	10 mL

Arrange mushrooms on large greased baking sheet with sides. Broil on top rack in oven for about 15 minutes, stirring once, until starting to brown. Drain and discard any liquid. Transfer to 3 1/2 to 4 quart (3.5 to 4 L) slow cooker.

Add next 4 ingredients. Stir. Cook, covered, on Low for 5 to 6 hours or on High for 2 1/2 to 3 hours.

Add lemon juice. Stir. Makes about 3 cups (750 mL).

1/3 cup (75 mL): 54 Calories; 2.4 g Total Fat (0 g Mono, 0 g Poly, 0.8 g Sat); 6 mg Cholesterol; 5 g Carbohydrate; trace Fibre; 2 g Protein; 83 mg Sodium

Honey Garlic Wings

These tender wings are a real crowd-pleaser with their classic honey garlic flavour. Set them out hot on a platter and watch everyone gather 'round.

Split chicken wings, tips discarded	3 lbs.	1.4 kg
Pepper, sprinkle		
Liquid honey	1 cup	250 mL
Soy sauce	1/2 cup	125 mL
Garlic cloves, minced	2	2
(or 1/2 tsp., 2 mL, powder)		
Ground ginger	1/4 tsp.	1 mL

Arrange wings on greased baking sheet with sides. Sprinkle with pepper. Broil on top rack in oven for about 6 minutes per side until browned. Transfer to 4 to 5 quart (4 to 5 L) slow cooker.

Combine remaining 4 ingredients in small bowl. Pour over chicken. Stir until coated. Cook, covered, on Low for 4 to 5 hours or on High for 2 to 2 1/2 hours. Discard liquid from slow cooker. Makes about 32 wings.

1 wing: 114 Calories; 6.7 g Total Fat (0 g Mono, 0 g Poly, 1.8 g Sat); 32 mg Cholesterol; 5 g Carbohydrate; trace Fibre; 8 g Protein; 196 mg Sodium

Appetizers, Dips & Snacks

Rosemary Steak Bites

Dig into these tasty, tender steak bites seasoned with savoury rosemary and coarse pepper.

Canola oil	2 tsp.	10 mL
Boneless beef blade steak, trimmed of fat, cut into 1 inch (2.5 cm) pieces	3 lbs.	1.4 kg
Seasoned salt	1/8 tsp.	0.5 mL
Dry (or alcohol-free) red wine	1/2 cup	125 mL
Prepared beef broth	1 cup	250 mL
All-purpose flour	4 tsp.	20 mL
Coarsely ground pepper	1 1/4 tsp.	6 mL
Chopped fresh rosemary	1/4 tsp.	1 mL

Heat canola oil in large frying pan on medium-high. Sprinkle beef with seasoned salt. Cook beef, in 3 batches, for about 5 minutes, stirring occasionally, until browned. Transfer with slotted spoon to greased 3 1/2 to 4 quart (3.5 to 4 L) slow cooker.

Add wine to same frying pan. Heat and stir, scraping any brown bits from bottom of pan, until boiling.

Whisk next 3 ingredients in small bowl until smooth. Add to pan. Heat and stir until boiling and thickened. Add to beef. Stir. Cook, covered, on Low for 5 to 6 hours or on High for 2 1/2 to 3 hours. Skim and discard fat.

Add rosemary. Stir. Serve with wooden picks. Makes about 4 cups (1 L).

1/4 cup (60 mL): 207 Calories; 14.9 g Total Fat (6.5 g Mono, 0.7 g Poly, 5.7 g Sat); 57 mg Cholesterol; 1 g Carbohydrate; trace Fibre; 15 g Protein; 96 mg Sodium

Buffalo Chicken Bites

Enjoy this updated pub favourite with less fat and sodium than the original! Blue cheese adds richness and pairs well with spicy tomato sauce. Serve these bites with cucumber and celery sticks.

Canola oil	1 tsp.	5 mL
Boneless, skinless chicken breast halves, cut into 1 inch (2.5 cm) pieces	2 lbs.	900 g
Can of tomato paste (5 1/2 oz., 156 mL)	1	1
Prepared chicken broth	1/2 cup	125 mL
Bourbon whiskey	1/4 cup	60 mL
Louisiana hot sauce	1/4 cup	60 mL
Butter, melted	1 tbsp.	15 mL
Dried oregano	1 tsp.	5 mL
Pepper	1/4 tsp.	1 mL
Crumbled blue cheese (optional)	1/4 cup	60 mL

Heat canola oil in large frying pan on medium-high. Cook chicken, in 2 batches, for about 5 minutes, stirring occasionally, until browned. Transfer with slotted spoon to greased 3 1/2 to 4 quart (3.5 to 4 L) slow cooker.

Combine next 7 ingredients in small bowl. Pour over chicken. Stir. Cook, covered, on Low for 3 to 4 hours or on High for 1 1/2 to 2 hours. Transfer chicken with slotted spoon to serving plate. Discard remaining cooking liquid.

Sprinkle with cheese. Serve with wooden picks. Makes about 4 cups (1 L).

1/4 cup (60 mL): 85 Calories; 1.5 g Total Fat (0.5 g Mono, 0.3 g Poly, 0.6 g Sat); 34 mg Cholesterol; 1 g Carbohydrate; trace Fibre; 14 g Protein; 138 mg Sodium

Pictured on page 18.

Mango Turkey Meatballs

Turkey meatballs make for fun party fare when you add a bright curry mango sauce with a hint of spicy heat! These have lower fat and salt content than you'd expect in cocktail party meatballs.

Chopped frozen mango pieces, thawed	2 cups	500 mL
Prepared chicken broth	1/2 cup	125 mL
Chopped onion	1/4 cup	60 mL
Mango chutney, larger pieces chopped	1/4 cup	60 mL
Hot curry paste	2 tsp.	10 mL
Large egg, fork-beaten	1	1
Quick-cooking rolled oats	1/2 cup	125 mL
Finely chopped onion	3 tbsp.	45 mL
Chili paste (sambal oelek)	1 tsp.	5 mL
Finely grated ginger root	1 tsp.	5 mL
(or 1/4 tsp., 1 mL, ground ginger)		
Garlic clove, minced	1	1
(or 1/4 tsp., 1 mL, powder)		
Salt	1/2 tsp.	2 mL
Pepper	1/4 tsp.	1 mL
Lean ground turkey	1 1/2 lbs.	680 g
Lime juice	2 tbsp.	30 mL

Combine first 5 ingredients in greased 3 1/2 to 4 quart (3.5 to 4 L) slow cooker.

Combine next 8 ingredients in large bowl.

Add turkey. Mix well. Roll into balls, using 1 tbsp. (15 mL) for each. Arrange on greased baking sheet with sides. Broil on top rack in oven for about 7 minutes until browned and no longer pink inside. Makes about 38 meatballs. Transfer with slotted spoon to slow cooker. Stir gently. Cook, covered, on Low for 4 to 5 hours or on High for 2 to 2 1/2 hours.

Add lime juice. Stir gently. Serve with wooden picks. Makes about 5 cups (1.25 L).

1/2 cup (125 mL): 159 Calories; 5.8 g Total Fat (0.3 g Mono, 0.1 g Poly, 1.4 g Sat); 60 mg Cholesterol; 13 g Carbohydrate; 1 g Fibre; 15 g Protein; 315 mg Sodium

Pork and Guacamole Tostadas

Serve this easy, crowd-pleasing appetizer at your next party. About half of the pork mixture will be left over— freeze it or make it into fajitas for lunch!

Boneless pork shoulder butt roast, trimmed of fat	2 lbs.	900 g
Salt, sprinkle		
Pepper, sprinkle		
Hot salsa	1 1/2 cups	375 mL
Hot salsa	1/2 cups	125 mL
Tortilla chips	9 oz.	250 g
Prepared guacamole	1 1/2 cups	375 mL
Grated jalapeño Monterey Jack cheese	1 1/2 cups	375 mL

Place roast in 3 1/2 to 4 quart (3.5 to 4 L) slow cooker. Sprinkle with salt and pepper. Pour first amount of salsa over top. Cook, covered, on High for 4 1/2 to 5 hours.

Transfer roast to large plate. Skim and discard fat from sauce. Shred pork with 2 forks. Return to sauce. Add second amount of salsa. Stir. Spoon pork mixture over each tortilla chip. Top with guacamole. Sprinkle with cheese. Makes 48 tostadas.

1 tostada: 79 Calories; 4.4 g Total Fat (0.8 g Mono, 0.2 g Poly, 1.4 g Sat); 14 mg Cholesterol; 5 g Carbohydrate; 1 g Fibre; 5 g Protein; 155 mg Sodium

Pictured on page 125.

Red-peppered Chorizo

This creamy sausage and cheese mixture tastes great on crisp crackers or crostini slices.

Chorizo (or hot Italian) sausage, casing removed	1 1/2 lbs.	680 g
Jar of roasted red peppers (12 oz., 340 mL), drained, chopped	1	1
Balsamic vinaigrette dressing	2 tbsp.	30 mL
Frozen concentrated orange juice, thawed	2 tbsp.	30 mL
Goat (chèvre) cheese	1/3 cup	75 mL

Scramble-fry sausage in large frying pan on medium-high for about 12 minutes until no longer pink. Drain. Transfer to 3 1/2 to 4 quart (3.5 to 4 L) slow cooker.

Add next 3 ingredients. Stir. Cook, covered, on Low for 3 to 4 hours or on High for 1 1/2 to 2 hours.

Add cheese. Stir until melted. Makes about 2 1/2 cups (625 mL).

1/4 cup (60 mL): 304 Calories; 20.2 g Total Fat (8.5 g Mono, 2.3 g Poly, 7.6 g Sat); 42 mg Cholesterol; 11 g Carbohydrate; trace Fibre; 16 g Protein; 1191 mg Sodium

Pictured on page 125.

Appetizers, Dips & Snacks

Pork Pita Sliders

Mini pitas are topped with pulled pork and a fresh, shredded salad for a fun appetizer. About half of the pork mixture will be left over—freeze it for later, or use it in wraps for lunches.

Boneless pork shoulder blade roast, trimmed of fat	2 lbs.	900 g
Can of crushed tomatoes (14 oz., 398 mL)	1	1
Balsamic vinegar	1/4 cup	60 mL
Greek seasoning	2 tbsp.	30 mL
Granulated sugar	2 tsp.	10 mL
Smoked (sweet) paprika	1 tsp.	5 mL
Pepper	1/2 tsp.	2 mL
Lemon juice	1 tbsp.	15 mL
Shredded romaine lettuce, lightly packed	1 cup	250 mL
Diced English cucumber (with peel)	1/2 cup	125 mL
Diced seeded tomato	1/2 cup	125 mL
Chopped fresh mint	2 tbsp.	30 mL
Finely chopped red onion	2 tbsp.	30 mL
Pita breads (3 inch, 7.5 cm, diameter)	24	24
Sliced red onion, for garnish		

Place roast in 3 1/2 to 4 quart (3.5 to 4 L) slow cooker.

Combine next 6 ingredients in medium bowl. Pour over roast. Cook, covered, on High for 4 1/2 to 5 hours. Transfer roast to large plate. Skim and discard fat from sauce. Shred pork using 2 forks. Remove and discard any fat. Return pork to slow cooker.

Add lemon juice. Stir.

Combine next 5 ingredients in medium bowl.

Arrange lettuce mixture over pitas. Top with pork mixture.

Garnish with red onion. Makes 24 sliders.

1 slider: 88 Calories; 2.2 g Total Fat (0.9 g Mono, 0.3 g Poly, 0.7 g Sat); 11 mg Cholesterol; 12 g Carbohydrate; 1 g Fibre; 5 g Protein; 126 mg Sodium

Pictured on page 18.

Mango Ribs

Mango gives these tender, tasty ribs a sweet and fruity flavour twist—perfect for a simple, hands-on appetizer at a casual get-together.

Frozen mango pieces, thawed	1 cup	250 mL
Prepared chicken broth	1 cup	250 mL
Mango chutney	1/2 cup	125 mL
Brown sugar, packed	1 tbsp.	15 mL
Sweet-and-sour-cut pork ribs, trimmed of fat and cut into 1-bone portions	3 1/2 lbs	1.6 kg
Salt, sprinkle		
Pepper, sprinkle		

Combine first 4 ingredients in 4 to 5 quart (4 to 5 L) slow cooker.

Arrange ribs on greased baking sheet with sides. Sprinkle with salt and pepper. Broil on top rack in oven for about 7 minutes per side until lightly browned. Drain and discard liquid. Add ribs to slow cooker. Stir. Cook, covered, on Low for 6 to 7 hours or on High for 3 to 3 1/2 hours. Transfer ribs with slotted spoon to medium bowl. Cover to keep warm. Skim and discard fat from cooking liquid. Carefully process in blender until smooth (see Safety Tip, page 9). Pour over ribs. Makes about 6 cups (1.5 L).

1/2 cup (125 mL): 567 Calories; 41.3 g Total Fat (17.9 g Mono, 3.7 g Poly, 14.7 g Sat); 160 mg Cholesterol; 8 g Carbohydrate; trace Fibre; 39 g Protein; 399 mg Sodium

Smokin' Smokies

A triple hit of smoky flavour with smoked sausages, chipotle peppers and smoked paprika— and some chili spice too! Serve from the slow cooker on lowest setting with a generous supply of toothpicks.

Cocktail-sized smokies (or regular smokies, cut diagonally into 1/2 inch, 12 mm, slices)	2 lbs.	900 g
Chili sauce	1 3/4 cups	425 mL
Brown sugar, packed	1 tbsp.	15 mL
Finely chopped chipotle peppers in adobo sauce (see Tip, page 56)	1 tbsp.	15 mL
Smoked sweet paprika	2 tsp.	10 mL

Combine all 5 ingredients in 3 1/2 to 4 quart (3.5 to 4 L) slow cooker. Cook, covered, on Low for 6 to 7 hours or on High for 3 to 3 1/2 hours. Makes about 5 cups (1.25 L).

1/3 cup (75 mL): 224 Calories; 16.7 g Total Fat (0 g Mono, 0 g Poly, 5.8 g Sat); 36 mg Cholesterol; 11 g Carbohydrate; trace Fibre; 7 g Protein; 1396 mg Sodium

Pictured on page 125.

Appetizers, Dips & Snacks

Creamy Seafood Filling

When you're in the mood to indulge, this elegant, delicious lobster and seafood appetizer is just the ticket. Serve over fresh puff pastry cups or points and garnish with sprigs of fresh dill.

Chive and onion cream cheese	2 cups	500 mL
Can of frozen lobster meat	1	1
(11 1/3 oz., 320 g), thawed, drained,		
larger pieces cut up		
Dry (or alcohol-free) white wine	1/3 cup	75 mL
Pepper, sprinkle		
Shrimp and scallop medley, thawed,	1 lb.	454 g
drained and blotted dry		
Chopped fresh dill	2 tsp.	10 mL
(or 1/2 tsp., 2 mL, dried)		

Combine first 4 ingredients in 3 1/2 to 4 quart (3.5 to 4 L) slow cooker. Cook, covered, on Low for 3 to 4 hours or on High for 1 1/2 to 2 hours. Stir until smooth.

Add shrimp and scallops. Stir. Cook, covered, on High for about 20 minutes until shrimp turn pink.

Add dill. Stir. Makes about 4 cups (1 L).

1/4 cup (60 mL): 168 Calories; 10.7 g Total Fat (0.1 g Mono, 0.3 g Poly, 7.1 g Sat); 72 mg Cholesterol; 3 g Carbohydrate; trace Fibre; 11 g Protein; 220 mg Sodium

Cajun-spiced Nuts

The spicy heat of Cajun seasoning pairs well with the roasted crunch of this flavourful, nutty snack.

Raw cashews	1 1/2 cups	375 mL
Whole natural almonds	1 1/2 cups	375 mL
Pecan halves	1 cup	250 mL
Butter (or hard margarine), melted	1/4 cup	60 mL
Cajun seasoning	2 tbsp.	30 mL
Salt, sprinkle		

Combine all 6 ingredients in 3 1/2 to 4 quart (3.5 to 4 L) slow cooker. Cook, covered, on Low for 2 hours. Stir well. Cook, covered, on High for about 1 hour, stirring occasionally, until nuts are browned. Spread on ungreased baking sheet to cool and crisp. Makes about 4 cups (1 L).

1/4 cup (60 mL): 217 Calories; 19.8 g Total Fat (10.9 g Mono, 4.0 g Poly, 4.0 g Sat); 8 mg Cholesterol; 8 g Carbohydrate; 2 g Fibre; 5 g Protein; 262 mg Sodium

Sugar and Spice Pecans

These sweet, toasted treats won't stay in the candy dish for long.

Pecan halves	4 cups	1 L
Butter	1/3 cup	75 mL
Brown sugar, packed	1/2 cup	125 mL
Ground cinnamon	1 1/2 tsp.	7 mL
Ground allspice	1/4 tsp.	1 mL

Put pecans into 3 1/2 to 4 quart (3.5 to 4 L) slow cooker.

Stir butter and sugar in small saucepan on medium until butter is melted. Stir. Pour over pecans. Stir until coated. Cook, covered, on High for 30 minutes. Stir. Reduce heat to Low. Cook, covered, for about 2 hours, stirring every 30 minutes, until pecans are glazed and golden.

Combine cinnamon and allspice in small cup. Sprinkle over nuts. Stir. Spread evenly on ungreased baking sheet to cool. Makes about 4 cups (1 L).

1/4 cup (60 mL): 247 Calories; 23.2 g Total Fat (12.0 g Mono, 6.0 g Poly, 4.1 g Sat); 10 mg Cholesterol; 11 g Carbohydrate; 3 g Fibre; 3 g Protein; 30 mg Sodium

Chili Snack Mix

This crunchy treat balances sweet and spicy flavours and will disappear fast when snack time arrives!

"O"-shaped toasted oat cereal	2 cups	500 mL
Small pretzels	2 cups	500 mL
Butter (or hard margarine), melted	1/4 cup	60 mL
Chili seasoning mix, stir before measuring	2 tbsp.	30 mL
Trail mix	2 cups	500 mL

Combine first 4 ingredients in 3 1/2 to 4 quart (3.5 to 4 L) slow cooker. Cook, covered, on High for 30 minutes. Stir. Cook, covered, on Low for 1 to 1 1/2 hours, stirring every 20 minutes, until crisp and golden. Spread on ungreased baking sheet to cool. Transfer to large bowl.

Add trail mix. Stir. Makes about 6 cups (1.5 mL).

1/3 cup (75 mL): 133 Calories; 7.9 g Total Fat (2.9 g Mono, 1.8 g Poly, 2.6 g Sat); 7 mg Cholesterol; 14 g Carbohydrate; 1 g Fibre; 174 mg Sodium

Spiced Granola

Add your favourite dried fruits, toasted nuts or seeds after the granola cools. Pour in some milk or stir it up with yogurt for a nutritious breakfast.

Brown sugar, packed	1/4 cup	60 mL
Cooking oil	1/4 cup	60 mL
Liquid honey	1/4 cup	60 mL
Pumpkin pie spice	1/4 tsp.	1 mL
Large flake rolled oats	5 cups	1.25 L

Combine first 4 ingredients in 3 1/2 to 4 quart (3.5 to 4 L) slow cooker.

Add oats. Stir until coated. Lay double layer of tea towels over slow cooker liner. Cover with lid. Cook on High for 1 hour. Stir. Lay double layer of tea towel over slow cooker liner. Cover with lid. Cook on Low for about 30 minutes until golden. Spread evenly on ungreased baking sheet to cool and crisp. Makes about 5 cups (1.25 L).

1/2 cup (125 mL): 263 Calories; 8.6 g Total Fat (3.2 g Mono, 1.6 g Poly, 0.4 g Sat); 0 mg Cholesterol; 41 g Carbohydrate; 5 g Fibre; 6 g Protein; 2 mg Sodium

Allspice Mulled Wine

The flavours of cinnamon and orange stand out in this spicy beverage. Sipping some around the fireplace will warm you right down to your toes.

Dry (or alcohol-free) red wine	6 cups	1.5 L
Can of frozen concentrated cranberry cocktail (9 1/2 oz., 275 mL)	1	1
Water	2 cups	500 mL
Medium orange, sliced	1	1
Cinnamon sticks (4 inches, 10 cm, each)	2	2
Whole allspice	6	6

Combine wine, cranberry cocktail and water in 3 1/2 to 4 quart (3.5 to 4 L) slow cooker.

Put remaining 3 ingredients onto 12 inch (30 cm) square piece of cheesecloth. Draw up corners and tie with butcher's string. Submerge in wine mixture. Cook, covered, on Low for 5 to 6 hours or on High for 2 1/2 to 3 hours. Remove and discard cheesecloth bag. Makes about 9 1/3 cups (2.4 L).

1 cup (250 mL): 185 Calories; 0 g Total Fat (0 g Mono, 0 g Poly, 0 g Sat); 0 mg Cholesterol; 18 g Carbohydrate; trace Fibre; trace Protein; 7 mg Sodium

Chocolate Peanut Delight

This hot-chocolatey drink is topped with whipped cream and peanuts, for all the chocolate-with-peanut butter lovers out there—kids will love it too!

Chocolate milk powder	1 cup	250 mL
Smooth peanut butter	1/2 cup	125 mL
Milk	8 cups	2 L
Whipped cream (or whipped topping)	1 cup	250 mL
Finely chopped unsalted peanuts	2 tsp.	10 mL

Stir first 3 ingredients in 3 1/2 to 4 quart (3.5 to 4 L) slow cooker until milk powder is dissolved. Cook, covered, on Low for 4 to 5 hours or on High for 2 to 2 1/2 hours until heated through and peanut butter is melted. Whisk until combined. Makes about 9 1/2 cups (2.4 L)

Pour into 8 mugs. Spoon whipped cream over top. Sprinkle with peanuts. Serves 8.

1 serving: 417 Calories; 22.8 g Total Fat (4.4 g Mono, 0.5 g Poly, 10.2 g Sat); 56 mg Cholesterol; 41 g Carbohydrate; 1 g Fibre; 16 g Protein; 289 mg Sodium

Pictured on page 287.

Coconut Rum Mocha

This delightful chocolate coffee has a hint of coconut and rum—a grown-up treat after a sleigh-ride.

Chocolate milk	6 cups	1.5 L
Strong prepared coffee	6 cups	1.5 L
Coconut rum	1 1/4 cups	300 mL
Whipped cream (or whipped topping)	1 1/2 cups	375 mL
Medium sweetened coconut, toasted (see Tip, page 267)	2 tbsp.	30 mL

Combine chocolate milk and coffee in 3 1/2 to 4 quart (3.5 to 4 L) slow cooker. Cook, covered, on Low for 4 to 5 hours or on High for 2 to 2 1/2 hours.

Add coconut rum. Stir. Makes about 13 1/4 cups (3.3 L)

Pour into 12 large mugs. Spoon whipped cream over top. Sprinkle with coconut. Serves 12.

1 serving: 266 Calories; 13.8 g Total Fat (3.2 g Mono, 0.4 g Poly, 8.6 g Sat); 53 mg Cholesterol; 18 g Carbohydrate; 1 g Fibre; 5 g Protein; 141 mg Sodium

Variation: Omit coconut rum and sweetened coconut. Substitute same amount of vanilla liqueur and vanilla sugar or cocoa.

Variation: Omit coconut rum and sweetened coconut. Substitute same amount of hazelnut liqueur and sprinkle with flaked hazelnuts or cocoa.

Ginger Citrus Tonic

This mixture of tea, calming ginger and antibacterial, throat-soothing honey works wonders on a cold. Rooibos tea is antioxidant-rich and caffeine-free, but mint tea also works well. Remove the solids, and keep a batch hot on Low for up to 12 hours.

Lemon slices (1/4 inch, 6 mm, thick)	1 cup	250 mL
Orange slices (1/4 inch, 6 mm, thick)	1 cup	250 mL
Liquid honey	1/3 cup	75 mL
Sliced ginger root (1/4 inch, 6 mm, thick)	1/4 cup	60 mL
Vanilla rooibos teabags	4	4
Water	8 cups	2 L

Combine first 5 ingredients in 3 1/2 to 4 quart (3.5 to 4 L) slow cooker. Add water. Cook, covered, on Low for 5 to 6 hours or on High for 2 1/2 to 3 hours. Remove and discard solids with slotted spoon. Makes about 8 cups (2 L).

1 cup (250 mL): 45 Calories; 0 g Total Fat (0 g Mono, 0 g Poly, 0 g Sat); 0 mg Cholesterol; 11 g Carbohydrate; 0 g Fibre; 0 g Protein; 0 mg Sodium

Hot Fruit Punch

Treat the kids to a mug of this warming winter beverage after they've finished shoveling the snow off the sidewalk!

Apple juice	4 cups	1 L
Cranberry cocktail	4 cups	1 L
Pineapple juice	4 cups	1 L
Cinnamon stick (4 inches, 10 cm), broken up	1	1
Whole allspice	1 tsp.	5 mL

Combine first 3 ingredients in 3 1/2 to 4 quart (3.5 to 4 L) slow cooker.

Put cinnamon stick pieces and allspice onto 6 inch (15 cm) square piece of cheesecloth. Draw up corners and tie with butcher's string. Submerge in juice mixture. Cook, covered, on Low for 4 to 6 hours or on High for 2 to 3 hours. Remove and discard cheesecloth bag. Makes about 12 cups (3 L).

1 cup (250 mL): 127 Calories; 0 g Total Fat (0 g Mono, 0 g Poly, 0 g Sat); 0 mg Cholesterol; 32 g Carbohydrate; 0 g Fibre; 0 g Protein; 2 mg Sodium

Pictured on page 35.

1. Mulled Blackcurrant Sipper, page 38
2. Warm and Fuzzy Navel, page 41
3. Hot Fruit Punch, above

Hazelnut Hot Chocolate

This silky, rich hot chocolate has a hint of hazelnut for a European flair. Liqueur-scented whipped cream transforms it into an adult treat, but omit the liqueur for a kid-friendly winter warmer.

Milk	12 cups	3 L
Chocolate hazelnut spread	2 cups	500 mL
Whipping cream	1 cup	250 mL
Hazelnut liqueur	2 tbsp.	30 mL
Granulated sugar	2 tbsp.	30 mL

Combine milk and chocolate hazelnut spread in 4 to 5 quart (4 to 5 L) slow cooker. Cook, covered, on Low for 4 to 5 hours or on High for 2 to 2 1/2 hours until heated through. Stir until smooth. Makes about 14 cups (3.5 L). Pour into 12 large mugs.

Beat remaining 3 ingredients in medium bowl until stiff peaks form. Spoon over milk mixture. Serves 12.

1 serving: 399 Calories; 21.1 g Total Fat (9.3 g Mono, 2.8 g Poly, 8.1 g Sat); 42 mg Cholesterol; 40 g Carbohydrate; 2 g Fibre; 11 g Protein; 153 mg Sodium

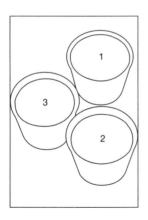

1. Chipotle Black Bean Soup, page 46
2. Asparagus Corn Soup, page 42
3. Edamame Vegetable Soup, page 58

Hot Mulled Cider

The classic flavours of spiced hot cider will warm everyone up on a blustery winter day.

Sweet apple cider	8 cups	2 L
Brown sugar, packed	1/4 cup	60 mL
Large orange, cut into 1/4 inch (6 mm) slices	1	1
Cinnamon sticks (4 inches, 10 cm, each)	2	2
Whole allspice	1 tsp.	5 mL

Combine cider and brown sugar in 3 1/2 to 4 quart (3.5 to 4 L) slow cooker.

Put remaining 3 ingredients onto 12 inch (30 cm) square piece of cheesecloth. Draw up corners and tie with butcher's string. Submerge in cider mixture. Cook, covered, on Low for 5 to 6 hours or on High for 2 1/2 to 3 hours. Remove and discard cheesecloth bag. Makes about 6 1/2 cups (1.6 L).

1 cup (250 mL): 180 Calories; 0 g Total Fat (0 g Mono, 0 g Poly, 0 g Sat); 0 mg Cholesterol; 45 g Carbohydrate; 0 g Fibre; 0 g Protein; 34 mg Sodium

Mulled Blackcurrant Sipper

While cinnamon, cloves and allspice are typically used for mulling, aniseed and star anise impart a lovely hint of licorice that pairs well with blackcurrant.

White cranberry juice	10 cups	2.5 L
Concentrated blackcurrant nectar	2 cups	500 mL
Aniseed	1 tbsp.	15 mL
Star anise	2	2
Brown sugar, packed (optional)	1 tbsp.	15 mL

Combine juice and nectar in 4 to 5 quart (4 to 5 L) slow cooker.

Put aniseed and star anise onto 5 inch (12.5 cm) square piece of cheesecloth. Draw up corners and tie with butcher's string. Submerge in cranberry juice mixture. Cook, covered, on Low for 6 to 8 hours or on High for 3 to 4 hours. Remove and discard cheesecloth bag.

Add brown sugar. Stir. Makes about 12 cups (3 L).

1 cup (250 mL): 115 Calories; 0 g Total Fat (0 g Mono, 0 g Poly, 0 g Sat); 0 mg Cholesterol; 27 g Carbohydrate; 0 g Fibre; trace Protein; 15 mg Sodium

Pictured on page 35.

Sweet Spiced Coffee

This sweet coffee was inspired by Vietnamese coffee, which is strong French roasted coffee with sweetened condensed milk. The added dimension of aromatic spices gives this an exotic flair. It's delicious served over ice, too!

Whole green cardamom, bruised (see Tip, page 41)	5	5
Cinnamon sticks (4 inches, 10 cm, each)	2	2
Star anise	1	1
Water	8 cups	2 L
Instant coffee granules	1 cup	250 mL
Cans of sweetened condensed milk (11 oz., 300 mL, each)	2	2

Combine first 4 ingredients in 3 1/2 to 4 quart (3.5 to 4 L) slow cooker. Cook, covered, on Low for 3 to 4 hours or on High for 1 1/2 to 2 hours. Remove and discard spices with slotted spoon.

Add coffee granules. Stir until dissolved. Add condensed milk. Stir until smooth. Makes about 11 cups (2.75 L).

1 cup (250 mL): 203 Calories; 4.5 g Total Fat (0 g Mono, trace Poly, 3.0 g Sat); 15 mg Cholesterol; 34 g Carbohydrate; 0 g Fibre; 5 g Protein; 69 mg Sodium

Pomegranate Cheer

This dark, jewel-toned beverage is ideal for entertaining during the holidays—try adding lemon vodka, vanilla liqueur or port for a grown-up twist.

Apple juice	4 cups	1 L
Pomegranate juice	4 cups	1 L
Orange juice	1 cup	250 mL
Brown sugar, packed	1/3 cup	75 mL
Slices of ginger root (about 1/4 inch, 6 mm, thick)	3	3

Combine all 5 ingredients in 3 1/2 to 4 quart (3.5 to 4 L) slow cooker. Cook, covered, on Low for 4 to 6 hours or on High for 2 to 3 hours. Remove and discard ginger with slotted spoon. Makes about 9 1/3 cups (2.4 L).

1 cup (250 mL): 149 Calories; 0.1 g Total Fat (trace Mono, trace Poly, trace Sat); 0 mg Cholesterol; 38 g Carbohydrate; trace Fibre; 1 g Protein; 16 mg Sodium

Peppermint Hot Chocolate

Pull a candy cane off the Christmas tree for this decadent holiday treat. Creamy chocolate and peppermint make a deliciously sweet pair!

Milk	6 cups	1.5 L
Chocolate-covered peppermint patties, chopped	2 cups	500 mL
Chocolate milk	2 cups	500 mL
Whipped cream (or whipped topping)	1 cup	250 mL
Finely crushed candy cane	2 tbsp.	30 mL

Combine first 3 ingredients in 3 1/2 to 4 quart (3.5 to 4 L) slow cooker. Cook, covered, on Low for 4 to 5 hours or on High for 2 to 2 1/2 hours. Stir. Makes about 8 cups (2 L).

Pour into 8 mugs. Spoon whipped cream over top. Sprinkle with crushed candy cane. Serves 8.

1 serving: 474 Calories; 18.3 g Total Fat (4.2 g Mono, 0.5 g Poly, 11.2 g Sat); 59 mg Cholesterol; 68 g Carbohydrate; 1 g Fibre; 11 g Protein; 197 mg Sodium

Vanilla Chai Temptation

This smooth and creamy treat is perfect with a plate of sweets at a meeting, or to unwind with after a family day of winter activities. Turn your slow cooker to the Low or Warm setting to maintain serving temperature.

Water	6 cups	1.5 L
Chai tea bags	10	10
Vanilla bean	1	1
Whole green cardamom, bruised (see Tip, page 41)	12	12
Canned evaporated milk	3 cups	750 mL
Honey	1/4 cup	60 mL

Pour water into 3 1/2 to 4 quart (3.5 to 4 L) slow cooker. Put next 3 ingredients onto 12 inch (25 cm) square piece of cheesecloth. Draw up corners and tie with butcher's string. Submerge in water. Cook, covered, on Low for 4 to 5 hours or on High for 2 to 2 1/2 hours. Remove and discard cheesecloth bag.

Add evaporated milk and honey. Stir. Cook, covered, on High for 30 minutes until heated through. Makes about 9 cups (2.25 L).

1 cup (250 mL): 137 Calories; 5.3 g Total Fat (1.1 g Mono, 0.2 g Poly, 4.0 g Sat); 27 mg Cholesterol; 16 g Carbohydrate; 0 g Fibre; 5 g Protein; 80 mg Sodium

Warm and Fuzzy Navel

Serve this welcoming cocktail in a punchbowl for a cozy winter brunch, or hand it out at a holiday party.

Apricot fruit juice blend	6 cups	1.5 L
Orange juice	6 cups	1.5 L
Grenadine syrup (optional)	1 tbsp.	15 mL
Orange liqueur	3/4 cup	175 mL
Peach schnapps	3/4 cup	175 mL

Combine first 3 ingredients in 3 1/2 to 4 quart (3.5 to 4 L) slow cooker. Cook, covered, on Low for 2 to 4 hours or on High for 1 to 2 hours.

Add liqueur and schnapps. Stir. Makes about 13 1/2 cups (3.4 L).

1 cup (250 mL): 183 Calories; 0.3 g Total Fat (0.1 g Mono, 0.1 g Poly, trace Sat); 0 mg Cholesterol; 35 g Carbohydrate; trace Fibre; 1 g Protein; 9 mg Sodium

Pictured on page 35.

 To bruise cardamom, pound the pods with a mallet or press them with the flat side of wide knife to "bruise," or crack them open slightly.

Asparagus Corn Soup

With its sweet corn flavour, this smooth asparagus soup makes a great starter for a summer meal. The best part is, you can make it in advance and store it in an airtight container in the freezer for up to three months—perfect for those days when it's just too hot to cook.

Low-sodium prepared chicken broth	6 cups	1.5 L
Chopped fresh asparagus (about 1 1/2 lbs., 680 g)	5 1/3 cups	1.4 L
Chopped peeled potato	3 cups	750 mL
Frozen kernel corn, thawed	2 cups	500 mL
Canola oil	2 tsp.	10 mL
Chopped fennel bulb (white part only)	1 1/2 cups	375 mL
Chopped onion	1 1/2 cups	375 mL
Salt	1/2 tsp.	2 mL
Pepper	1/2 tsp.	2 mL

Fresh asparagus spears, for garnish
Kernel corn, for garnish

Combine first 4 ingredients in 4 to 5 quart (4 to 5 L) slow cooker.

Heat canola oil in large frying pan on medium. Add remaining 4 ingredients. Cook for about 10 minutes, stirring often, until softened. Transfer to slow cooker. Cook, covered, on Low for 7 to 8 hours or on High for 3 1/2 to 4 hours. Carefully process with hand blender, or in blender in batches, until smooth (see Safety Tip, page 9).

Garnish with asparagus and corn. Makes about 12 cups (3 L).

1 cup (250 mL): 87 Calories; 1.1 g Total Fat (0.5 g Mono, 0.3 g Poly, 0.1 g Sat); 3 mg Cholesterol; 17 g Carbohydrate; 3 g Fibre; 4 g Protein; 408 mg Sodium

Pictured on page 36.

Ruby Beet Soup

The flavours of pears and beets complement each other in this velvety, beautifully coloured soup. Add a sour cream garnish, or serve chilled for a refreshing variation.

Chopped onion	3/4 cup	175 mL
Chopped fresh peeled beet (see Tip, below)	6 cups	1.5 L
Prepared vegetable broth	4 cups	1 L
Can of pear halves (28 oz., 796 mL), drained and juice reserved	1	1
Red wine vinegar	2 tbsp.	30 mL

Heat medium greased frying pan on medium. Add onion. Cook for about 5 minutes, stirring often, until softened. Transfer to 3 1/2 to 4 quart (3.5 to 4 L) slow cooker.

Add next 3 ingredients. Cook, covered, on Low for 8 to 9 hours or High for 4 to 4 1/2 hours until beet is tender.

Add vinegar and reserved pear juice. Stir. Carefully process with hand blender or in blender in batches until smooth (see Safety Tip, page 9). Makes about 9 1/2 cups (2.4 L).

1 cup (250 mL): 93 Calories; 0.9 g Total Fat (0.3 g Mono, 0.2 g Poly, 0.1 g Sat); 0 mg Cholesterol; 21 g Carbohydrate; 3 g Fibre; 2 g Protein; 383 mg Sodium

Pictured on page 53.

 tip Don't get caught red handed! Wear rubber gloves when handling beets.

Saigon Veggie Beef Soup

A colourful offering with noodles, lots of veggies and a fresh herb sprinkle. If you are watching your sodium intake, substitute a homemade beef stock for the prepared broth.

Low-sodium prepared beef broth	6 cups	1.5 L
Water	2 cups	500 mL
Diagonally sliced trimmed snow peas	1 cup	250 mL
Thinly sliced red pepper	1 cup	250 mL
Thinly sliced yellow pepper	1 cup	250 mL
Julienned carrot (see Tip, below)	3/4 cup	175 mL
Soy sauce	1 tbsp.	15 mL
Garlic cloves, thinly sliced	2	2
Piece of ginger root (1 inch, 2.5 cm, length)	1	1
Star anise	1	1
Dried crushed chilies	1/4 tsp.	1 mL
Beef strip loin steak, trimmed of fat, thinly sliced across the grain (about 1/8 inch, 3 mm, slices), see Tip, page 45	1/4 lb.	113 g
Medium rice stick noodles, broken in half	3 oz.	85 g
Sliced green onion	1/4 cup	60 mL
Lime juice	2 tbsp.	30 mL
Chopped fresh cilantro (or parsley)	2 tbsp.	30 mL
Chopped fresh mint	2 tbsp.	30 mL

Combine first 11 ingredients in 4 to 5 quart (4 to 5 L) slow cooker. Cook, covered, on Low for 6 to 7 hours or on High for 3 to 3 1/2 hours. Remove and discard ginger root and anise.

Add next 4 ingredients. Stir. Cook, covered, on High for about 15 minutes until noodles are tender but firm.

Sprinkle individual servings with cilantro and mint. Makes about 10 cups (2.5 L).

1 cup (250 mL): 97 Calories; 2.8 g Total Fat (1.2 g Mono, 0.3 g Poly, 1.0 g Sat); 6 mg Cholesterol;
12 g Carbohydrate; 1 g Fibre; 6 g Protein; 235 mg Sodium

 To julienne, cut into very thin strips that resemble matchsticks.

Taco Beef Soup

Serve this hearty meal soup with tortilla chips, a swirl of sour cream and a sprinkle of green onions—and dinner is made!

Stewing beef, trimmed of fat, cut into 1/2 inch (12 mm) pieces	1 lb.	454 g
Chopped onion	1 cup	250 mL
Diced peeled baking potato	3 cups	750 mL
Envelope of taco seasoning mix (1 1/4 oz., 35 g)	1	1
Water	4 cups	1 L
Frozen mixed vegetables, thawed	1 1/2 cups	375 mL

Heat large greased frying pan on medium-high. Add beef. Cook for about 5 minutes, stirring occasionally, until browned. Transfer to 3 1/2 to 4 quart (3.5 to 4 L) slow cooker.

Add onion to same greased frying pan on medium. Cook for about 5 minutes, stirring often, until softened. Add to slow cooker.

Add potato, seasoning mix and water. Stir. Cook, covered, on Low for 7 to 8 hours or on High for 3 1/2 to 4 hours. Mash mixture several times with potato masher to break up potato.

Add mixed vegetables. Stir. Cook, covered, on High for about 30 minutes until vegetables are tender. Makes about 8 cups (2 L).

1 cup (250 mL): 227 Calories; 9.4 g Total Fat (3.8 g Mono, 0.6 g Poly, 3.4 g Sat); 37 mg Cholesterol; 23 g Carbohydrate; 2 g Fibre; 12 g Protein; 532 mg Sodium

 To slice meat easily, place it in the freezer for about 30 minutes until it is just starting to freeze. If using meat from a frozen state, partially thaw it before cutting. Be certain the meat is fully thawed before adding it to slow cooker.

Chipotle Black Bean Soup

A rich, spicy black bean soup with plenty of beans and veggies. Fresh avocado and tomato add a refreshing contrast. Store leftovers in an airtight container in the freezer for up to three months, but only add the avocado and green onion after thawing and reheating.

Canola oil	2 tsp.	10 mL
Chopped onion	1 1/2 cups	375 mL
Chopped celery	1 cup	250 mL
Chili powder	1 tsp.	5 mL
Ground cumin	1 tsp.	5 mL
Garlic cloves, minced	2	2
(or 1/2 tsp., 2 mL, powder)		
Pepper	1/2 tsp.	2 mL
Prepared vegetable broth	7 cups	1.75 L
Dried black beans, soaked in water overnight, rinsed and drained	1 1/2 cups	375 mL
Grated peeled orange-fleshed sweet potato	1 cup	250 mL
Finely chopped chipotle peppers in adobo sauce (see Tip, page 56)	2 tsp.	10 mL
Chopped fresh spinach leaves, lightly packed	1 cup	250 mL
Chopped tomato	1 cup	250 mL
Lime juice	2 tbsp.	30 mL
Salt	1/4 tsp.	1 mL
Chopped avocado	3/4 cup	175 mL
Thinly sliced green onion	2 tbsp.	30 mL

Heat canola oil in large frying pan on medium. Add onion and celery. Cook for about 12 minutes, stirring often, until softened.

Add next 4 ingredients. Heat and stir for about 1 minute until fragrant. Transfer to 4 to 5 quart (4 to 5 L) slow cooker.

Add next 4 ingredients. Stir. Cook, covered, on High for 5 to 6 hours until beans are tender. Mash mixture several times with potato masher to break up beans.

Add next 4 ingredients. Stir.

Scatter avocado and green onion over individual servings. Makes about 12 cups (3 L).

1 cup (250 mL): 156 Calories; 2.6 g Total Fat (1.4 g Mono, 0.5 g Poly, 0.3 g Sat); 0 mg Cholesterol; 27 g Carbohydrate; 5 g Fibre; 6 g Protein; 340 mg Sodium

Pictured on page 36.

Butternut Cream Soup

The sweetness and rich texture of squash and pear blend perfectly with sour cream in this creamy, beautifully golden soup.

Chopped onion	1 1/2 cups	375 mL
Chopped butternut squash	8 cups	2 L
Can of pear halves in juice (with juice), (28 oz., 796 mL)	1	1
Salt	1/4 tsp.	1 mL
Water	2 1/2 cups	625 mL
Sour cream	1 cup	250 mL
Chopped fresh chives, for garnish		

Heat large greased frying pan on medium. Add onion. Cook, stirring often, for about 8 minutes until softened. Transfer to 4 to 5 quart (4 to 5 L) slow cooker.

Add squash, pears with juice, salt and water. Cook, covered, on Low for 8 to 10 hours or on High for 4 to 5 hours. Carefully process with hand blender or in blender in batches until smooth (see Safety Tip, page 9).

Add sour cream. Whisk until smooth. Garnish with chives. Makes about 12 cups (3 L).

1 cup (250 mL): 157 Calories; 3.9 g Total Fat (0.3 g Mono, 0.2 g Poly, 2.4 g Sat); 13 mg Cholesterol; 30 g Carbohydrate; 5 g Fibre; 3 g Protein; 113 mg Sodium

Pictured on page 53.

Apricot Red Lentil Soup

This simple vegetarian soup, Armenian in origin, is a lovely balance of sweet and peppery flavours. It's low-fat, high-fibre and thick, creamy and satisfying!

Chopped onion	2 cups	500 mL
Salt	1/4 tsp.	1 mL
Prepared vegetable broth	4 cups	1 L
Chopped carrot	2 cups	500 mL
Dried red split lentils	2 cups	500 mL
Chopped dried apricot	1 1/2 cups	375 mL
Water	5 cups	1.25 mL

Heat large greased frying pan on medium. Add onion and salt. Cook for about 15 minutes, stirring often, until onion is browned. Transfer to 5 to 7 quart (5 to 7 L) slow cooker.

Add remaining 5 ingredients and water. Stir. Cook, covered, on Low for 10 to 12 hours or on High for 5 to 6 hours. Carefully process with hand blender or in blender in batches until smooth (see Safety Tip, page 9). Makes about 11 cups (2.75 L).

1 cup (250 mL): 206 Calories; 1.4 g Total Fat (0.3 g Mono, 0.2 g Poly, trace Sat); 0 mg Cholesterol; 39 g Carbohydrate; 8 g Fibre; 11 g Protein; 306 mg Sodium

Carrot Parsnip Coriander Soup

A thick, smooth and spicy soup with a smattering of fresh cilantro—vibrant, aromatic and warming. Packed with flavour and a good dose of healthy vegetables!

Canola oil	2 tsp.	10 mL
Chopped onion	1 1/2 cups	375 mL
Ground coriander	1 1/2 tsp.	7 mL
Finely grated ginger root	1 tsp.	5 mL
(or 1/2 tsp., 2 mL, ground ginger)		
Salt	1/2 tsp.	2 mL
Pepper	1/2 tsp.	2 mL
Prepared vegetable broth	5 cups	1.25 L
Chopped carrot	3 cups	750 mL
Chopped parsnip	2 cups	500 mL
Chopped fresh cilantro (or parsley)	1/4 cup	60 mL

Heat canola oil in large frying pan on medium. Add onion. Cook for about 8 minutes, stirring often, until softened.

Add next 4 ingredients. Heat and stir for about 1 minute until fragrant. Transfer to 3 1/2 to 4 quart (3.5 to 4 L) slow cooker.

Add next 3 ingredients. Cook, covered, on Low for 7 to 8 hours or on High for 3 1/2 to 4 hours. Carefully process with hand blender, or in blender in batches, until smooth (see Safety Tip, page 9).

Add cilantro. Stir. Makes about 7 cups (1.75 L).

1 cup (250 mL): 99 Calories; 2.0 g Total Fat (0.8 g Mono, 0.5 g Poly, 0.1 g Sat); 0 mg Cholesterol; 19 g Carbohydrate; 5 g Fibre; 2 g Protein; 538 mg Sodium

Coconut Carrot Soup

Try this fragrant, velvety smooth soup with a splash of lime juice—any way you serve it, it's sweet, spicy and delicious.

Chopped onion	1 1/2 cups	375 mL
Thai red curry paste	2 tsp.	10 mL
Sliced carrot	6 cups	1.5 L
Prepared vegetable broth	5 cups	1.25 L
Salt, sprinkle		
Can of coconut milk	14 oz.	398 mL

(continued on next page)

Soups

Heat large greased frying pan on medium. Add onion. Cook for about 8 minutes, stirring often, until onion is softened.

Add curry paste. Heat and stir for 1 minute. Transfer to 3 1/2 to 4 quart (3.5 to 4 L) slow cooker.

Add carrot, broth and salt. Stir. Cook, covered, on Low for 8 to 10 hours or on High for 4 to 5 hours.

Add coconut milk. Stir. Carefully process with hand blender or in blender in batches until smooth (see Safety Tip, page 9). Makes about 10 cups (2.5 L).

1 cup (250 mL): 142 Calories; 9.6 g Total Fat (0.6 g Mono, 0.3 g Poly, 7.6 g Sat); 0 mg Cholesterol; 14 g Carbohydrate; 3 g Fibre; 2 g Protein; 383 mg Sodium

---

Chicken Stock

Nothing beats a homemade broth! This versatile stock contains only a few calories and a small amount sodium and can be used as a base in recipes calling for chicken stock. Store portions in airtight containers in the freezer for up to six months.

Chicken necks and backs, trimmed of fat, organs removed (see Note 1)	4 lbs.	1.8 kg
Water	12 cups	3 L
Coarsely chopped onion	2 cups	500 mL
Coarsely chopped carrot	1 cup	250 mL
Coarsely chopped celery ribs, with leaves	1 cup	250 mL
Bunch of fresh parsley stems (see Note 2)	1	1
Whole black peppercorns	2 tsp.	10 mL
Bay leaves	2	2

Combine all 8 ingredients in 7 quart (7 L) slow cooker. Cook, covered, on High for 6 to 8 hours. Remove and discard bones with slotted spoon. Carefully strain through fine sieve into large bowl. Discard solids. Skim and discard fat. Makes about 10 cups (2.5 L).

Note 1: If you can't find chicken necks and backs in the freezer or cooler of your grocer's meat department, ask the butcher to order them for you. Alternatively, you can substitute the same weight with other chicken bones.

Note 2: Be sure to remove all the leaves from the parsley stems. The leaves can colour your stock green, and they have a less intense flavour than the stems.

1 cup (250 mL): 15 Calories; 0 g Total Fat (0 g Mono, 0 g Poly, 0 g Sat); 0 mg Cholesterol; 1.5 g Carbohydrate; 0 g Fibre; 1.5 g Protein; 95 mg Sodium

Chicken Pesto Pea Soup

Wild rice, chicken and vegetables offer plenty of texture, and bold pesto punches up the flavour. Serve with lemon wedges for a dash of freshness. Store in an airtight container in the freezer for up to three months.

Low-sodium prepared chicken broth	8 cups	2 L
Diced celery	1 cup	250 mL
Diced onion	1 cup	250 mL
Diced zucchini (with peel)	1 cup	250 mL
Wild rice	1/2 cup	125 mL
Garlic cloves, minced (or 1/2 tsp., 2 mL, powder)	2	2
Bay leaves	2	2
Pepper	1/2 tsp.	2 mL
Finely chopped cooked chicken (see Tip, below)	3 cups	750 mL
Frozen tiny peas, thawed	1 1/2 cups	375 mL
Basil pesto	1 tbsp.	15 mL
Chopped fresh spinach leaves, lightly packed	2 cups	500 mL
Chopped fresh basil	2 tbsp.	30 mL
Chopped fresh parsley	1 tbsp.	15 mL

Combine first 8 ingredients in 4 to 5 quart (4 to 5 L) slow cooker. Cook, covered, on Low for 6 to 8 hours or on High for 3 to 4 hours. Remove and discard bay leaves.

Add next 3 ingredients. Stir. Cook, covered, on High for about 10 minutes until heated through.

Add remaining 3 ingredients. Stir. Makes about 13 cups (3.25 L).

1 cup (250 mL): 120 Calories; 2.0 g Total Fat (0.4 g Mono, 0.3 g Poly, 0.5 g Sat); 31 mg Cholesterol; 11 g Carbohydrate; 2 g Fibre; 14 g Protein; 445 mg Sodium

 No leftover chicken? Start with 3 boneless, skinless chicken breast halves (4 – 6 oz., 113 – 117 g, each). Place them in a large frying pan with 1 1/2 cups (375 mL) water or chicken broth. Simmer, covered, for 12 to 14 minutes until no longer pink inside. Drain. Chop. Makes about 3 cups (750 mL) of cooked chicken.

Chicken Vegetable Gumbo

A thick, hearty gumbo filled with healthy brown rice and vegetables. Sausage adds a nice, smoky flavour. This is truly comfort food at its best!

Boneless, skinless chicken thighs, trimmed of fat, cut into 1 inch (2.5 cm) pieces	1 lb.	454 g
Sliced fresh (or frozen, thawed) okra (1/2 inch, 12 mm, pieces)	2 cups	500 mL
Sliced kielbasa (or other spiced cooked lean sausage), 1/4 inch (6 mm) pieces	1 cup	250 mL
Canola oil	3 tbsp.	45 mL
All-purpose flour	3 tbsp.	45 mL
Chopped celery	1 1/2 cups	375 mL
Chopped green pepper	1 1/2 cups	375 mL
Chopped onion	1 1/2 cups	375 mL
Dried oregano	1 tsp.	5 mL
Dried thyme	1 tsp.	5 mL
Dry mustard	1/2 tsp.	2 mL
Garlic powder	1/2 tsp.	2 mL
Pepper	1/4 tsp.	1 mL
Low-sodium prepared chicken broth	4 cups	1 L
Tomato juice	1 cup	250 mL
Bay leaves	2	2
Cooked long-grain brown rice (about 2/3 cup, 150 mL, uncooked)	2 cups	500 mL
Chopped seeded tomato	1 cup	250 mL
Hot pepper sauce	1 tbsp.	15 mL

Combine first 3 ingredients in 4 to 5 quart (4 to 5 L) slow cooker.

Heat canola oil in large frying pan on medium. Add flour. Heat and stir for about 9 minutes until browned.

Add next 11 ingredients. Heat and stir until boiling and thickened. Add to slow cooker. Stir. Cook, covered, on Low for 7 to 8 hours or on High for 3 1/2 to 4 hours. Skim and discard fat. Remove and discard bay leaves.

Add remaining 3 ingredients. Stir. Cook, covered, on High for about 15 minutes until heated through. Makes about 11 1/2 cups (2.9 L).

1 cup (250 mL): 194 Calories; 9.3 g Total Fat (4.4 g Mono, 2.2 g Poly, 2.0 g Sat); 36 mg Cholesterol; 17 g Carbohydrate; 2 g Fibre; 12 g Protein; 488 mg Sodium

Meaty Chicken Soup

This simple, feel-good soup is great for when you're under the weather. The broth is very tasty and can be used in other dishes—it also freezes well. Add egg noodles or cooked rice for an even heartier soup.

Chicken legs, back attached (11 oz., 310 g, each), skin removed	4	4
Chopped onions	2 1/2 cups	625 mL
Chopped celery (with leaves)	1 cup	250 mL
Sprig of fresh rosemary	1	1
Water	8 cups	2 L
Salt	1/4 tsp.	1 mL
Pepper	1/4 tsp.	1 mL
Chopped carrot	1 1/2 cups	375 mL

Put chicken into 5 to 7 quart (5 to 7 L) slow cooker. Add next 6 ingredients. Cook, covered, on Low for 6 hours or on High for 3 hours.

Add carrot. Cook, covered, on High for about 2 hours until chicken and carrot are tender. Remove and discard rosemary. Transfer chicken and bones with slotted spoon to cutting board. Let stand until cool enough to handle. Remove chicken from bones. Discard bones. Coarsely chop chicken. Skim and discard fat from broth. Return chicken to broth. Sprinkle generously with salt and pepper. Stir. Makes about 13 cups (3.25 L).

1 cup (250 mL): 124 Calories; 4.7 g Total Fat (1.7 g Mono, 1.1 g Poly, 1.3 g Sat); 49 mg Cholesterol; 5 g Carbohydrate; 1 g Fibre; 15 g Protein; 245 mg Sodium

1. Ruby Beet Soup, page 43
2. Orange Sweet Potato Soup, page 66
3. Easy Tomato Soup, page 68
4. Butternut Cream Soup, page 47

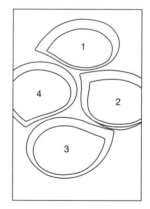

Favourite Clam Chowder

Here is everyone's favourite seafood soup with only five ingredients! This version is rich and creamy with the delicious flavours of potatoes, clams and dill.

Cans of minced clams (3 oz., 85 g, each), drained and liquid reserved (see Tip, page 59)	3	3
Can of condensed cream of mushroom (10 oz., 284 mL)	1	1
Water	1 cup	250 mL
Diced peeled potato	3 cups	750 mL
Dried dillweed	1/2 tsp.	2 mL
Homogenized milk	1 1/2 cups	375 mL

Combine clam liquid, soup and water in 3 1/2 to 4 quart (3.5 to 4 L) slow cooker. Stir until smooth. Chill clams.

Add potato and dill to slow cooker. Stir. Cook, covered, on Low for 6 to 8 hours or on High for 3 to 4 hours.

Add milk and reserved clams. Cook, covered, on High for about 15 minutes until heated through. Makes about 7 cups (1.75 L).

1 cup (250 mL): 185 Calories; 5.2 g Total Fat (0.5 g Mono, 0.2 g Poly, 2.0 g Sat); 38 mg Cholesterol; 26 g Carbohydrate; 2 g Fibre; 10 g Protein; 739 mg Sodium

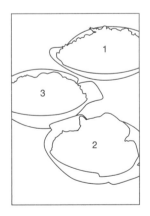

1. Cranberry Chickpea Curry, page 207
2. Coconut Beef Curry, page 81
3. Coconut Curry Pork, page 137

Creamy Clam Chowder

A lower-fat version with plenty of flavour—you don't even need to give up the bacon!

Chopped unpeeled baking potato	3 1/2 cups	875 mL
Prepared vegetable broth	3 cups	750 mL
Thinly sliced leek (white part only)	1 1/2 cups	375 mL
Thinly sliced celery	1 cup	250 mL
Grated carrot	1/2 cup	125 mL
Bay leaf	1	1
Dried thyme	1/2 tsp.	2 mL
Pepper	1/4 tsp.	1 mL
Reserved liquid from clams	2/3 cup	150 mL
All-purpose flour	3 tbsp.	45 mL
Can of skim evaporated milk (13 oz., 370 mL)	1	1
Can of whole baby clams (5 oz., 142 g), drained and liquid reserved (see Tip, page 59)	1	1
Bacon slices, cooked crisp and crumbled	2	2
Chopped fresh parsley (or 3/4 tsp., 4 mL, flakes)	1 tbsp.	15 mL

Combine first 8 ingredients in 3 1/2 to 4 quart (3.5 to 4 L) slow cooker.

Stir clam liquid into flour in small bowl until smooth. Add to slow cooker. Stir. Chill clams. Cook, covered, on Low for 6 to 7 hours or on High for 3 to 3 1/2 hours. Remove and discard bay leaf. Mash mixture several times with potato masher to break up potato.

Add evaporated milk and clams. Stir. Cook, covered, on High for about 15 minutes until heated through.

Add bacon and parsley. Stir. Makes about 9 cups (2.25 L).

1 cup (250 mL): 133 Calories; 1.4 g Total Fat (0.3 g Mono, 0.1 g Poly, 0.4 g Sat); 14 mg Cholesterol; 23 g Carbohydrate; 2 g Fibre; 8 g Protein; 341 mg Sodium

 tip Chipotle chili peppers are smoked jalapeño peppers. Be sure to wash your hands after handling them. Divide leftover chipotle chili peppers into recipe-friendly portions and freeze, with sauce, in airtight containers for up to one year.

Chipotle Corn Chowder

The sweet aroma of this soup will bring a southwestern feel to your kitchen! Enjoy the richness of creamed corn and the flavour of smoky bacon and chipotle peppers.

Chopped onion	1 cup	250 mL
Bacon slices, diced	6	6
Cans of cream-style corn (14 oz., 398 mL, each)	3	3
Can of red kidney beans (14 oz., 398 mL), rinsed and drained	1	1
Finely chopped chipotle peppers in adobo sauce (see Tip, page 56)	1 tbsp.	15 mL
Water	2 1/2 cups	625 mL

Heat medium frying pan on medium-high. Add onion and bacon. Cook for about 5 minutes, stirring often, until onion is softened. Transfer to 3 1/2 to 4 quart (3.5 to 4 L) slow cooker.

Add remaining 4 ingredients. Stir. Cook, covered, on Low for 6 to 7 hours or on High for 3 to 3 1/2 hours. Makes about 8 1/2 cups (2.1 L).

1 cup (250 mL): 198 Calories; 2.7 g Total Fat (0.8 g Mono, 0.2 g Poly, 0.6 g Sat); 5 mg Cholesterol; 36 g Carbohydrate; 6 g Fibre; 7 g Protein; 586 mg Sodium

Curry Corn Soup

This rich, smooth soup blends the flavours of mild curry, sweet coconut and creamed corn.

Chopped onion	1 1/2 cups	375 mL
Hot curry paste	1 tbsp.	15 mL
Granulated sugar	1 tsp.	5 mL
Can of coconut milk (14 oz., 398 mL)	1	1
Frozen kernel corn, thawed	4 cups	1 L
Water	2 cups	500 mL
Salt	1/4 tsp.	1 mL

Heat large greased frying pan on medium. Add onion. Cook for about 8 minutes, stirring often, until softened.

Add curry paste and sugar. Heat and stir for 1 minute. Add coconut milk. Stir. Transfer to 4 to 5 quart (4 to 5 L) slow cooker.

Add corn, water and salt. Stir. Cook, covered, on Low for 5 to 6 hours or on High for 2 1/2 to 3 hours. Carefully process with hand blender or in blender in batches until smooth (see Safety Tip, page 9). Makes about 6 cups (1.5 L).

1 cup (250 mL): 244 Calories; 15.9 g Total Fat (1.1 g Mono, 0.4 g Poly, 12.7 g Sat); 0 mg Cholesterol; 24 g Carbohydrate; 4 g Fibre; 5 g Protein; 352 mg Sodium

Edamame Vegetable Soup

A delicately flavoured Asian-inspired soup with baby corn, edamame (eh-dah-MAH-meh) beans and shiitake mushrooms. Edamame beans are loaded with protein, which makes this vegetable soup a complete meal.

Prepared vegetable broth	8 cups	2 L
Frozen shelled edamame (soybeans), thawed	2 cups	500 mL
Sliced fresh shiitake mushrooms	2 cups	500 mL
Can of cut baby corn, drained (14 oz., 398 mL)	1	1
Can of shoestring-style bamboo shoots (8 oz., 227 mL), drained	1	1
Piece of ginger root (1 inch, 2.5 cm, length), halved	1	1
Sliced trimmed sugar snap peas	1 cup	250 mL
Sliced water chestnuts	1/2 cup	125 mL
Sliced green onion	1/4 cup	60 mL
Soy sauce	1 tbsp.	15 mL
Sesame oil (for flavour)	2 tsp.	10 mL
Pepper	1/4 tsp.	1 mL

Combine first 6 ingredients in 3 1/2 to 4 quart (3.5 to 4 L) slow cooker. Cook, covered, on Low for 5 to 6 hours or on High for 2 1/2 to 3 hours.

Add remaining 6 ingredients. Stir. Cook, covered, on High for about 15 minutes until peas are tender-crisp. Remove and discard ginger root. Makes about 12 cups (3 L).

1 cup (250 mL): 98 Calories; 2.5 g Total Fat (0.1 g Mono, 0.2 g Poly, 0.2 g Sat); 0 mg Cholesterol; 15 g Carbohydrate; 4 g Fibre; 5 g Protein; 435 mg Sodium

Pictured on page 36.

Spicy Goulash Soup

Spice is nice, especially when you're enjoying this hearty, satisfying soup filled with spicy sausage and plenty of tasty seasonings and tender veggies.

Chopped onion	1 1/2 cups	375 mL
Hot Italian sausage, casing removed	1/2 lb.	225 g
Garlic cloves, minced (or 1/2 tsp., 2 mL, powder)	2	2
Low-sodium prepared beef broth	3 cups	750 mL
Chopped seeded tomato	2 cups	500 mL
Diced peeled potato	1 1/2 cups	375 mL
Chopped red pepper	1 cup	250 mL
Diced carrot	1 cup	250 mL
Diced zucchini (with peel)	1 cup	250 mL
Tomato paste (see Tip, page 83)	1 tbsp.	15 mL
Paprika	2 tsp.	10 mL
Caraway seed	1/2 tsp.	2 mL
Pepper	1/4 tsp.	1 mL

Scramble-fry first 3 ingredients in large frying pan on medium for about 8 minutes until sausage is no longer pink. Drain. Transfer to 3 1/2 to 4 quart (3.5 to 4 L) slow cooker.

Add remaining 10 ingredients. Stir. Cook, covered, on Low for 6 to 7 hours or on High for 3 to 3 1/2 hours. Skim and discard fat. Makes about 7 1/2 cups (1.9 L).

1 cup (250 mL): 185 Calories; 9.2 g Total Fat (3.9 g Mono, 1.3 g Poly, 3.1 g Sat); 17 mg Cholesterol; 17 g Carbohydrate; 3 g Fibre; 10 g Protein; 414 mg Sodium

 Clams can spoil quickly, so be sure to keep them refrigerated until adding to the slow cooker.

Kielbasa Potato Soup

This wholesome soup is thick with cooked-down potato and makes a meal when served with crusty bread. The longer it stands, the more the flavours blend.

Chopped peeled potato	6 cups	1.5 L
Prepared vegetable broth	4 cups	1 L
Kielbasa (or other spiced cooked lean sausage), thinly sliced	3/4 lb.	340 g
Garlic and herb no-salt seasoning	1/2 tsp.	2 mL
Water	2 cups	500 mL
Salt	1/4 tsp.	1 mL
Pepper	1/4 tsp.	1 mL
Frozen cut green beans, thawed	1 1/2 cups	375 mL

Combine first 5 ingredients in 5 to 7 quart (5 to 7 L) slow cooker. Sprinkle with salt and pepper. Cook, covered, on Low for 10 to 11 hours or on High for 5 to 5 1/2 hours.

Add green beans. Stir. Cook, covered, on High for about 30 minutes until tender. Break up with potato masher. Makes about 11 cups (2.75 L).

1 cup (250 mL): 161 Calories; 1.1 g Total Fat (0 g Mono, 0.1 g Poly, 0.3 g Sat); 11 mg Cholesterol; 31 g Carbohydrate; 1 g Fibre; 7 g Protein; 853 mg Sodium

Lobster Chowder

This thick, creamy chowder makes an elegant starter for a dinner party when you want something extra-special for your guests.

Chopped onion	2 cups	500 mL
Salt	1/4 tsp.	1 mL
Pepper	1/4 tsp.	1 mL
Diced peeled baking potato	4 cups	1 L
Prepared vegetable broth	4 cups	1 L
Can of frozen lobster meat (with liquid) (11 1/3 oz., 320 g), thawed, larger pieces cut up	1	1
Evaporated milk (or half-and-half cream)	1 1/2 cups	375 mL

Heat large greased frying pan on medium. Add onion, salt and pepper. Cook for about 10 minutes, stirring often, until softened. Transfer to 4 to 5 quart (4 to 5 L) slow cooker.

Add next 3 ingredients to slow cooker. Stir. Cook, covered, on Low for 6 to 7 hours or on High for 3 to 3 1/2 hours. Break up mixture with potato masher.

Add evaporated milk. Stir. Makes about 9 cups (2.25 L).

1 cup (250 mL): 213 Calories; 4.1 g Total Fat (1.0 g Mono, 0.5 g Poly, 2.2 g Sat); 38 mg Cholesterol; 31 g Carbohydrate; 3 g Fibre; 13 g Protein; 681 mg Sodium

Lamb and Barley Soup

Also known as Scotch broth, this warming soup is a centuries-old favourite.

Lamb shanks, trimmed of fat, cut into 1/2 inch (12 mm) pieces, bones reserved (see Note, page 152)	1 lb.	454 g
Water	1 1/2 cups	375 mL
Diced carrot (1/4 inch, 6mm, pieces)	1 cup	250 mL
Diced yellow turnip (rutabaga)	1 cup	250 mL
Pot barley	1/2 cup	125 mL
Envelope of onion soup mix	1 1/2 oz.	42 g
Water	5 cups	1.25 mL
Salt, sprinkle		
Pepper, sprinkle		

Heat large greased frying pan on medium-high. Add lamb. Cook for about 8 minutes, stirring occasionally, until browned. Transfer to 4 to 5 quart (4 to 5 L) slow cooker. Add water to same frying pan. Heat and stir, scraping any brown bits from bottom of pan, until boiling. Pour over lamb.

Add next 7 ingredients and reserved bones. Stir. Cook, covered, on Low for 8 to 10 hours or on High for 4 to 5 hours. Remove and discard bones. Makes about 7 1/2 cups (1.9 L).

1 cup (250 mL): 131 Calories; 3.9 g Total Fat (1.7 g Mono, 0.4 g Poly, 1.2 g Sat); 21 mg Cholesterol; 16 g Carbohydrate; 3 g Fibre; 8 g Protein; 631 mg Sodium

Pictured on page 71.

Minestrone Soup

This lovely Italian soup is super easy to make. Serve it with crusty bread and a salad.

Prepared vegetable broth	3 cups	750 mL
Frozen mixed vegetables, thawed	2 cups	500 mL
Vegetable cocktail juice	2 cups	500 mL
Italian seasoning	2 tsp.	10 mL
Water	1 cup	250 mL
Salt, sprinkle		
Pepper, sprinkle		
Rotini pasta	1 1/2 cups	375 mL

Combine first 7 ingredients in 3 1/2 to 4 quart (3.5 to 4 L) slow cooker. Cook, covered, on Low for 4 to 5 hours or on High for 2 to 2 1/2 hours.

Add pasta. Stir. Cook, covered, on High for 20 to 30 minutes until pasta is tender but firm. Makes about 6 cups (1.5 L).

1 cup (250 mL): 123 Calories; 2.4 g Total Fat (trace Mono, trace Poly, 0.8 g Sat); 3 mg Cholesterol; 22 g Carbohydrate; 2 g Fibre; 4 g Protein; 517 mg Sodium

Sweet Onion Soup

An easy take on onion soup—and no need to caramelize the onions on the stove! For a real treat, serve this delicious soup with slices of toast topped with melted smoked cheddar or havarti.

Thinly sliced sweet onion	6 cups	1.5 L
Olive (or cooking) oil	3 tbsp.	45 mL
Prepared beef broth (see Note, below)	6 cups	1.5 L
Dark beer	1 1/2 cups	375 mL
Sprig of fresh thyme	1	1
(or 1/2 tsp., 2 mL, dried)		
Salt, sprinkle		
Pepper, sprinkle		

Combine onion and olive oil in 3 1/2 to 4 quart (3.5 to 4 L) slow cooker. Cook, covered, on High for about 6 hours, stirring once at halftime, until onion is caramelized.

Add next 5 ingredients. Cook, covered, on High for about 45 minutes until heated through. Remove and discard thyme sprig. Makes about 8 3/4 cups (2.2 L).

1 cup (250 mL): 122 Calories; 5.4 g Total Fat (3.6 g Mono, 0.7 g Poly, 0.9 g Sat); 0 mg Cholesterol; 15 g Carbohydrate; 1 g Fibre; 2 g Protein; 1017 mg Sodium

Note: When adding liquid to a hot slow cooker, make sure the liquid is at least room temperature, as cold liquids could cause the liner to crack.

Curried Pumpkin Soup

This thick, creamy soup has apple cider sweetness and a touch of curry heat. With a dollop of sour cream, it's an attractive starter for a holiday meal.

Finely chopped onion	1 1/2 cups	375 mL
Cans of pure pumpkin (no spices),	2	2
14 oz. (398 mL) each		
Prepared chicken broth	2 cups	500 mL
Sweet apple cider	2 cups	500 mL
Mild curry paste	2 tsp.	10 mL
Salt, sprinkle		
Pepper, sprinkle		

Heat large greased frying pan on medium. Add onion. Cook for about 8 minutes, stirring often, until softened. Transfer to 3 1/2 to 4 quart (3.5 to 4 L) slow cooker.

Add next 4 ingredients. Stir. Cook, covered, on Low for 5 to 6 hours or on High for 2 1/2 to 3 hours. Sprinkle with salt and pepper. Carefully process with hand blender or in blender in batches until smooth (see Safety Tip, page 9). Makes about 8 cups (2 L).

1 cup (250 mL): 90 Calories; 1.4 g Total Fat (0.5 g Mono, 0.3 g Poly, 0.3 g Sat); 0 mg Cholesterol; 19 g Carbohydrate; 3 g Fibre; 2 g Protein; 500 mg Sodium

Mushroom Dill Soup

A light and refreshing combination. Earthy mushrooms blend with the tanginess of dill in a wine-accented broth.

Chopped assorted fresh mushrooms (see Note)	6 cups	1.5 L
Dry (or alcohol-free) white wine	1 cup	250 mL
Salt	1/4 tsp.	1 mL
Pepper	1/4 tsp.	1 mL
Prepared vegetable broth	4 cups	1 L
Grated peeled potato	1 1/2 cups	375 mL
Dried dillweed	2 tsp.	10 mL

Heat large greased frying pan or Dutch oven on medium-high. Add mushrooms. Cook for about 10 minutes, stirring occasionally, until mushrooms start to brown.

Add wine, salt and pepper. Heat and stir for 2 minutes. Transfer to 3 1/2 to 4 quart (3.5 to 4 L) slow cooker.

Add remaining 3 ingredients. Stir. Cook, covered, on Low for 4 to 5 hours or on High for 2 to 2 1/2 hours. Makes about 7 cups (1.75 L).

1 cup (250 mL): 109 Calories; 1.2 g Total Fat (0.4 g Mono, 0.2 g Poly, 0.1 g Sat); 0 mg Cholesterol; 16 g Carbohydrate; 2 g Fibre; 3 g Protein; 553 mg Sodium

Note: If using portobello mushrooms, remove gills before chopping.

Smoked Pork and Bean Soup

Enjoy this hearty soup with a slice of multi-grain bread for dipping. Buy a packaged bean mix or create your own custom mixture. Make sure about a third of it is split peas and/or red lentils because these legumes break up during cooking, giving the soup a great texture.

Dried mixed beans and lentils	1 1/2 cups	375 mL
Smoked pork hock (or meaty ham bone)	1 1/2 lbs.	680 g
Chopped onion	1 cup	250 mL
Water	9 cups	2.25 mL
Can of diced tomatoes (with juice), (14 oz., 398 mL)	1	1
Envelope of vegetable soup mix (1 1/4 oz., 40 g)	1	1
Salt, sprinkle		
Pepper, sprinkle		

Measure beans and lentils into medium bowl. Add water until 2 inches (5 cm) above beans. Let stand overnight (see Tip, page 14). Drain. Rinse beans. Drain. Transfer to 5 to 7 quart (5 to 7 L) slow cooker.

Add pork hock, onion and water. Cook, covered, on High for 4 to 5 hours until beans are tender. Remove pork hock. Let stand until cool enough to handle. Remove and discard skin, bones and fat. Chop meat. Return to slow cooker.

Add tomatoes, soup mix, salt and pepper. Stir. Cook, covered, on High for about 45 minutes until vegetables are tender. Makes about 13 1/2 cups (3.4 L).

1 cup (250 mL): 219 Calories; 12.1 g Total Fat (5.2 g Mono, 1.2 g Poly, 4.4 g Sat); 55 mg Cholesterol; 10 g Carbohydrate; 3 g Fibre; 17 g Protein; 304 mg Sodium

Pictured on page 71.

Paprika Potato Soup

No one would expect such a thick, smooth soup to be so low in fat! This soup boasts an appealing orange colour and a surprisingly spicy aftertaste from smoked paprika.

Chopped peeled potato	6 cups	1.5 L
Low-sodium prepared chicken broth	4 cups	1 L
Chopped onion	1 cup	250 mL
Chopped celery	1/2 cup	125 mL
Smoked (sweet) paprika	1 1/2 tsp.	7 mL
Paprika	1 tsp.	5 mL
Salt	1/2 tsp.	2 mL
Pepper	1/2 tsp.	2 mL
Milk	1 cup	250 mL

(continued on next page)

Combine first 8 ingredients in 3 1/2 to 4 quart (3.5 to 4 L) slow cooker. Cook, covered, on Low for 6 to 7 hours or on High for 3 to 3 1/2 hours. Carefully process with hand blender, or in blender in batches, until smooth (see Safety Tip, page 9).

Add milk. Stir. Cook, covered, on High for about 15 minutes until heated through. Makes about 8 1/2 cups (2.1 L).

1 cup (250 mL): 113 Calories; 0.5 g Total Fat (0.1 g Mono, 0.1 g Poly, 0.2 g Sat); 4 mg Cholesterol; 23 g Carbohydrate; 3 g Fibre; 4 g Protein; 447 mg Sodium

Smoky Salmon Potato Soup

This smooth, smoky-tasting soup was inspired by Cullen Skink, a soup from the Scottish village of Cullen. It is traditionally made with smoked haddock, and has kept generations of people warm on cold, rainy nights. Sprinkle with chopped fresh parsley just before serving.

Finely chopped onion	1 1/2 cups	375 mL
Diced, peeled baking potato	4 cups	1 L
Prepared vegetable broth	3 cups	750 mL
Milk	2 cups	500 mL
Thinly sliced smoked salmon, chopped	4 oz.	113 g
Salt	1/4 tsp.	1 mL
Pepper	1/4 tsp.	1 mL

Heat large greased frying pan on medium. Add onion. Cook for about 8 minutes, stirring often, until softened. Transfer to 3 1/2 to 4 quart (3.5 to 4 L) slow cooker.

Add potato and broth. Cook, covered, on Low for 5 to 6 hours or on High for 2 1/2 to 3 hours until potato is tender.

Carefully process with hand blender or in blender in batches until smooth (see Safety Tip, page 9). Add milk and smoked salmon. Cook, covered, on High for about 15 minutes until heated through. Sprinkle with salt and pepper. Stir. Makes about 8 cups (2 L).

1 cup (250 mL): 171 Calories; 2.2 g Total Fat (0.9 g Mono, 0.4 g Poly, 0.6 g Sat); 7 mg Cholesterol; 31 g Carbohydrate; 3 g Fibre; 7 g Protein; 735 mg Sodium

Sausage Kale Soup

This hearty and flavourful soup is great on a chilly winter's evening. For added aroma, look for Italian sausage with fennel seeds or add 2 tsp. (10 mL) whole fennel seeds to the sausage while it's browning for a delicious, licorice-like flavour.

Hot (or mild) Italian sausage, casing removed	3/4 lb.	340 g
Chopped kale leaves, lightly packed (see Tip, page 223)	4 cups	1 L
Can of diced tomatoes (with juice), (28 oz., 796 mL)	1	1
Can of black-eyed peas (or navy beans), with liquid (19 oz., 540 mL)	1	1
Water	4 cups	1 L
Basil pesto	1/4 cup	60 mL

Scramble-fry sausage meat in large frying pan on medium for about 10 minutes until no longer pink. Drain. Transfer to 4 to 5 quart (4 to 5 L) slow cooker.

Add next 4 ingredients. Stir. Cook, covered, on Low for 9 to 10 hours or on High for 4 1/2 to 5 hours. Break up mixture with potato masher.

Add pesto. Stir. Makes about 9 3/4 cups (2.4 L).

1 cup (250 mL): 212 Calories; 12.9 g Total Fat (4.2 g Mono, 1.2 g Poly, 3.9 g Sat); 21 mg Cholesterol; 15 g Carbohydrate; 3 g Fibre; 12 g Protein; 958 mg Sodium

Orange Sweet Potato Soup

Serve this thick, creamy and vibrant soup either warm or chilled. Cilantro lovers will enjoy a sprinkle of this fresh herb in their bowls.

Chopped, peeled orange-fleshed sweet potatoes	3 lbs.	1.4 kg
Prepared vegetable broth	4 cups	1 L
Chopped onion	1 cup	250 mL
Large oranges	2	2
Plain yogurt	1 cup	250 mL

Combine sweet potato and broth in 3 1/2 to 4 quart (3.5 to 4 L) slow cooker.

(continued on next page)

Heat medium greased frying pan on medium. Add onion. Cook for about 5 minutes, stirring often, until softened. Add to slow cooker. Cook, covered, on Low for 6 to 7 hours or on High for 3 to 3 1/2 hours.

Grate 1/2 tsp. (2 mL) orange zest into small bowl. Squeeze orange juice into same bowl. Add to slow cooker. Carefully process with hand blender or in blender in batches until almost smooth (see Safety Tip, page 9).

Add yogurt. Stir. Makes about 10 cups (2.5 L).

1 cup (250 mL): 158 Calories; 1.1 g Total Fat (0.3 g Mono, 0.2 g Poly, 0.3 g Sat); 2 mg Cholesterol; 33 g Carbohydrate; 5 g Fibre; 4 g Protein; 276 mg Sodium

Pictured on page 53.

Chili Shrimp Vegetable Soup

With its cheery, colourful vegetables and tender shrimp, this flavourful, chili-spiced soup makes a great lunch on a cold day.

Frozen Oriental mixed vegetables, thawed, larger pieces halved	4 cups	1 L
Prepared vegetable broth	4 cups	1 L
Dried crushed chilies	1/2 tsp.	2 mL
Salt	1/4 tsp.	1 mL
Pepper	1/4 tsp.	1 mL
Uncooked medium shrimp (peeled and deveined)	1/2 lb.	225 g
Lime juice	2 tbsp.	30 mL

Combine first 5 ingredients in 3 1/2 to 4 quart (3.5 to 4 L) slow cooker. Cook, covered, on Low for 2 to 3 hours or on High for 1 to 1 1/2 hours until vegetables are tender-crisp.

Add shrimp. Stir. Cook, covered, on High for about 15 minutes until shrimp turn pink. Add lime juice. Stir. Makes about 6 cups (1.5 L).

1 cup (250 mL): 88 Calories; 1.0 g Total Fat (0.1 g Mono, 0.3 g Poly, 0.1 g Sat); 57 mg Cholesterol; 9 g Carbohydrate; 3 g Fibre; 9 g Protein; 587 mg Sodium

Split Pea Soup

This simple, classic soup has lots of smoky sausage flavour and a hint of garlic. It can be cooked on Low, but it will take 12 hours or more for the peas to soften.

Chopped carrots	2 cups	500 mL
Yellow split peas, rinsed and drained	2 cups	500 mL
Diced kielbasa (or other spiced cooked lean sausage)	1 1/2 cups	375 mL
Chopped celery (with leaves)	3/4 cup	175 mL
Chopped onion	3/4 cup	175 mL
Water	8 cups	2 L
Salt	1/4 tsp.	1 mL
Pepper	1/4 tsp.	1 mL

Combine first 5 ingredients in 3 1/2 to 4 quart (3.5 to 4 L) slow cooker. Add water. Stir. Cook, covered, on High for 6 to 7 hours until peas are tender. Sprinkle with salt and pepper. Stir. Makes about 9 cups (2.25 L).

1 cup (250 mL): 223 Calories; 1.1 g Total Fat (trace Mono, 0.1 g Poly, 0.4 g Sat); 13 mg Cholesterol; 37 g Carbohydrate; 1 g Fibre; 17 g Protein; 480 mg Sodium

Pictured on page 71.

Easy Tomato Soup

This fresh, light-tasting tomato soup couldn't be easier to make! Try serving it in white bowls for a striking contrast.

Tomato juice	12 cups	3 L
Granulated sugar	2 tbsp.	30 mL
Worcestershire sauce	1 tbsp.	15 mL
Italian seasoning	2 tsp.	10 mL
Lime juice	1 tbsp.	15 mL

Combine first 4 ingredients in 4 to 5 quart (4 to 5 L) slow cooker. Cook, covered, on Low for 5 to 6 hours or on High for 2 1/2 to 3 hours.

Add lime juice. Stir. Makes about 12 cups (3 L).

1 cup (250 mL): 91 Calories; 0.1 g Total Fat (trace Mono, 0.1 g Poly, trace Sat); trace Cholesterol; 23 g Carbohydrate; 1 g Fibre; 4 g Protein; 1329 mg Sodium

Pictured on page 53.

Turkey Rice Soup

Rich and comforting like a turkey soup should be—this version includes a good dose of healthy brown rice, vegetables and tomatoes. Store in an airtight container in the freezer for up to three months.

Canola oil	1 tsp.	5 mL
Chopped onion	2 cups	500 mL
Sliced celery	2 cups	500 mL
Lean ground turkey	1 lb.	454 g
Low-sodium prepared chicken broth	7 cups	1.75 L
Chopped tomato	3 cups	750 mL
Sliced carrot	2 cups	500 mL
Long-grain brown rice	1/2 cup	125 mL
Parsley flakes	2 tsp.	10 mL
Dried thyme	1/2 tsp.	2 mL
Garlic clove, minced	1	1
(or 1/4 tsp., 1 mL, powder)		
Dried rosemary, crushed	1/4 tsp.	1 mL
Pepper	1/4 tsp.	1 mL

Heat canola oil in large frying pan on medium-high. Add next 3 ingredients. Scramble-fry for about 10 minutes until turkey is no longer pink. Transfer to 4 to 5 quart (4 to 5 L) slow cooker.

Add remaining 9 ingredients. Stir. Cook, covered, on Low for 7 to 8 hours or on High for 3 1/2 to 4 hours. Makes about 12 cups (3 L).

1 cup (250 mL): 123 Calories; 3.2 g Total Fat (0.4 g Mono, 0.3 g Poly, 0.8 g Sat); 25 mg Cholesterol; 14 g Carbohydrate; 2 g Fibre; 10 g Protein; 412 mg Sodium

Tortilla Soup

This creamy, cheesy soup has a nacho twist with crunchy tortilla chips in every bowl—a perfect starter for a casual or Mexican-themed party. Adjust the heat by choosing mild, medium or hot salsa.

Prepared chicken broth	4 cups	1 L
Chunky salsa	1 1/2 cups	375 mL
Can of condensed Cheddar cheese soup (10 oz., 284 mL)	1	1
Sour cream	2/3 cup	150 mL
Tortilla chips, broken up	1 cup	250 mL

Combine first 3 ingredients in 3 1/2 to 4 quart (3.5 to 4 L) slow cooker. Cook, covered, on Low for 4 to 6 hours or on High for 2 to 3 hours.

Add sour cream. Stir until smooth.

Put tortilla chips into 4 soup bowls. Ladle soup over chips. Serves 4.

1 serving: 260 Calories; 13.9 g Total Fat (1.4 g Mono, 1.5 g Poly, 6.8 g Sat); 32 mg Cholesterol; 27 g Carbohydrate; 1 g Fibre; 5 g Protein; 2834 mg Sodium

1. Lamb and Barley Soup, page 61
2. Smoked Pork and Bean Soup, page 64
3. Split Pea Soup, page 68

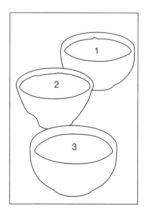

Vegetable Stock

Homemade stock is generally lower in sodium and fat than store-bought—and this one is virtually free of both! Nutritious vegetables are cooked right into this versatile broth. Freeze portions in airtight containers for up to six months.

Water	12 cups	3 L
Fresh brown (or white) mushrooms, halved	8	8
Sprigs of fresh parsley	4	4
Celery ribs, with leaves, coarsely chopped	3	3
Large carrots, coarsely chopped	2	2
Large onions, halved	2	2
Parsnips, coarsely chopped	2	2
Medium leek, coarsely chopped	1	1
Medium yellow turnip (rutabaga), coarsely chopped	1	1
Bay leaves	2	2
Garlic clove, halved	1	1
Sprig of fresh thyme	1	1
Whole black peppercorns	1/4 tsp.	1 mL

Combine all 13 ingredients in 7 quart (7 L) slow cooker. Cook, covered, on Low for 7 to 8 hours or on High for 3 1/2 to 4 hours. Carefully strain through fine sieve into large bowl. Discard solids. Makes about 10 cups (2.5 L).

1 cup (250 mL): 10 Calories; 0 g Total Fat (0 g Mono, 0 g Poly, 0 g Sat); 0 mg Cholesterol; 2 g Carbohydrate; <1 g Fibre; 0.3 g Protein; 50 mg Sodium

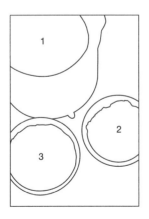

1. Cowboy Slim's Beef Stew, page 75
2. Mediterranean Chickpea Stew, page 222
3. Spanish Fisherman's Stew, page 122

Beef Bourguignon

Red wine adds a subtle, yet rich, note to this lower-sodium version of a French classic.
Delicate pearl onions and button mushrooms flavour the gravy.

All-purpose flour	1/4 cup	60 mL
Salt	1/4 tsp.	1 mL
Pepper	1/4 tsp.	1 mL
Boneless beef cross-rib roast, trimmed of fat, cut into 1 inch (2.5 cm) pieces	3 lbs.	1.4 kg
Canola oil	2 tbsp.	30 mL
Pearl onions	2 cups	500 mL
Small fresh white mushrooms	2 cups	500 mL
Italian seasoning	1 tbsp.	15 mL
Tomato paste (see Tip, page 83)	1 tbsp.	15 mL
Garlic clove, minced (or 1/4 tsp., 1 mL, powder)	1	1
Prepared beef broth	1 cup	250 mL
Dry (or alcohol-free) red wine	1/2 cup	125 mL
Chopped fresh parsley (or 1 1/2 tsp., 7 mL, flakes)	2 tbsp.	30 mL
Red wine vinegar	1 tbsp.	15 mL

Combine first 3 ingredients in large resealable freezer bag. Add half of beef. Seal bag. Toss until coated. Remove beef. Repeat with remaining beef. Discard any remaining flour mixture.

Heat canola oil in large frying pan on medium. Cook beef, in 2 batches, for about 8 minutes, stirring occasionally, until browned. Transfer with slotted spoon to 4 to 5 quart (4 to 5 L) slow cooker.

Add onions and mushrooms to same frying pan. Cook for about 5 minutes, stirring often, until onions start to soften.

Add next 3 ingredients. Heat and stir for 1 minute. Add broth and wine. Heat and stir, scraping any brown bits from bottom of pan, until boiling. Add to slow cooker. Stir. Cook, covered, on Low for 8 to 9 hours or on High for 4 to 4 1/2 hours. Skim and discard fat.

Add parsley and vinegar. Stir. Makes about 6 3/4 cups (1.7 L).

2/3 cup (150 mL): 327 Calories; 18.5 g Total Fat (8.4 g Mono, 1.4 g Poly, 6.4 g Sat); 8 mg Cholesterol; 9 g Carbohydrate; trace Fibre; 28 g Protein; 189 mg Sodium

Beef

Cowboy Slim's Beef Stew

An easy, hearty stew with baked-bean sweetness. A last-minute addition of tiny peas adds a fresh punch of colour and flavour to this family-friendly dish. Store in an airtight container in the freezer for up to three months.

Baby potatoes, larger ones halved	2 lbs.	900 g
Cans of baked beans in tomato sauce (14 oz., 398 mL, each)	2	2
Stewing beef, trimmed of fat	1 1/2 lbs.	680 g
Baby carrots	3 1/2 cups	875 mL
Water	1 cup	250 mL
Barbecue sauce	1/4 cup	60 mL
Pepper	1/4 tsp.	1 mL
Frozen tiny peas, thawed	1 1/2 cups	375 mL

Combine first 7 ingredients in 5 to 7 quart (5 to 7 L) slow cooker. Cook, covered, on Low for 9 to 10 hours or on High for 4 1/2 to 5 hours.

Add peas. Stir. Makes about 12 1/2 cups (3.1 L).

1 cup (250 mL): 254 Calories; 7.2 g Total Fat (3.0 g Mono, 0.3 g Poly, 2.7 g Sat); 33 mg Cholesterol; 31 g Carbohydrate; 6 g Fibre; 15 g Protein; 361 mg Sodium

Pictured on page 72.

Curry Beef Stew

This beef stew cooks up into a satisfying main course flavoured with a spicy-sweet sauce.

Boneless beef blade (or chuck) roast, trimmed of fat, cut into 1 inch (2.5 cm) pieces	3 lbs.	1.4 kg
Salt	1/4 tsp.	1 mL
Pepper	1/4 tsp.	1 mL
Prepared beef broth	1 1/2 cups	375 mL
Sweetened applesauce	1 1/2 cups	375 mL
Mixed dried fruit (such as raisins, apricot, apple and pineapple), chopped	1 cup	250 mL
Hot curry paste	2 tbsp.	30 mL

Heat large well-greased frying pan on medium-high. Cook beef, in 3 batches, for about 5 minutes, stirring occasionally, until browned. Transfer to 3 1/2 to 4 quart (3.5 to 4 L) slow cooker. Sprinkle with salt and pepper.

Add remaining 4 ingredients to same frying pan. Heat and stir for 1 minute, scraping any brown bits from bottom of pan. Pour over beef. Cook, covered, on Low for 6 to 8 hours or on High for 3 to 4 hours. Skim and discard fat. Makes about 7 cups (1.75 L).

3/4 cup (175 mL): 646 Calories; 41.6 g Total Fat (17.9 g Mono, 1.9 g Poly, 15.9 g Sat); 157 mg Cholesterol; 25 g Carbohydrate; 3 g Fibre; 42 g Protein; 588 mg Sodium

Greek Beef and Spinach Stew

Bright flavours of lemon and feta in a hearty beef and barley stew.

Boneless beef blade steak, trimmed of fat, cut into 1 1/2 inch (3.8 cm) pieces	1 1/2 lbs.	680 g
Chopped onion	2 cups	500 mL
Chopped tomato	2 cups	500 mL
Chopped parsnip (1 inch, 2.5 cm, pieces)	1 1/2 cups	375 mL
Chopped unpeeled potato (1 inch, 2.5 cm, pieces)	1 1/2 cups	375 mL
Pot barley	1/2 cup	125 mL
Prepared beef broth	1/2 cup	125 mL
Lemon juice	2 tbsp.	30 mL
Dried oregano	1 tsp.	5 mL
Dried rosemary, crushed	1 tsp.	5 mL
Garlic cloves, minced (or 1/2 tsp., 2 mL, powder)	2	2
Salt	1/8 tsp.	0.5 mL
Coarsely ground pepper	1/2 tsp.	2 mL
Chopped fresh spinach leaves, lightly packed	4 cups	1 L
Crumbled feta cheese	1/3 cup	75 mL

Combine first 6 ingredients in 4 to 5 quart (4 to 5 L) slow cooker.

Combine next 7 ingredients in small bowl. Pour over top. Cook, covered, on Low for 8 to 9 hours or on High for 4 to 4 1/2 hours.

Add spinach and cheese. Stir. Let stand, covered, for about 5 minutes until spinach is wilted. Makes about 8 cups (2 L).

1 cup (250 mL): 284 Calories; 10.9 g Total Fat (3.9 g Mono, 0.6 g Poly, 4.4 g Sat); 62 mg Cholesterol; 27 g Carbohydrate; 5 g Fibre; 21 g Protein; 247 mg Sodium

Mexican Beef Stew

This thick beef stew gets its deep, rich flavour from the cocoa and chipotle peppers. Try it with cornbread and a green salad to make a complete meal. Makes a big batch that can be stored in an airtight container in the freezer for up to three months.

Chopped butternut squash (1/2 inch, 12 mm, pieces)	4 cups	1 L
Can of crushed tomatoes (28 oz., 796 mL)	1	1
Chopped carrot (1/2 inch, 12 mm, pieces)	2 cups	500 mL
Chopped onion (1/2 inch, 12 mm, pieces)	1 1/2 cups	375 mL
Prepared beef broth	1 cup	250 mL
Cocoa, sifted if lumpy	3 tbsp.	45 mL
Minute tapioca	2 tbsp.	30 mL
Finely chopped chipotle peppers in adobo sauce (see Tip, page 56)	2 tsp.	10 mL
Dried oregano	1 tsp.	5 mL
Garlic cloves, minced (or 1/2 tsp., 2 mL, powder)	2	2
Granulated sugar	1/2 tsp.	2 mL
Ground cinnamon	1/2 tsp.	2 mL
Salt	1/4 tsp.	1 mL
Pepper	1/2 tsp.	2 mL
Ground allspice	1/8 tsp.	0.5 mL
Canola oil	1 tsp.	5 mL
Boneless beef blade (or chuck) roast, trimmed of fat, cut into 1 inch (2.5 cm) pieces	2 lbs.	900 g
Chopped fresh parsley (or 2 tsp., 10 mL, flakes)	1/4 cup	60 mL
Lime juice	3 tbsp.	45 mL
Roasted sesame seeds (optional)	1 tbsp.	15 mL

Combine first 15 ingredients in 5 to 7 quart (5 to 7 L) slow cooker.

Heat canola oil in large frying pan on medium-high. Cook beef, in 2 batches, for about 5 minutes, stirring occasionally, until browned. Transfer with slotted spoon to slow cooker. Stir. Cook, covered, on Low for 8 to 10 hours or on High for 4 to 5 hours. Skim and discard fat.

Add remaining 3 ingredients. Stir. Makes about 9 3/4 cups (2.4 L).

1 cup (250 mL): 325 Calories; 16.8 g Total Fat (7.2 g Mono, 0.9 g Poly, 6.5 g Sat); 63 mg Cholesterol; 27 g Carbohydrate; 5 g Fibre; 20 g Protein; 329 mg Sodium

Thai Red Curry Beef

This rich, mildly-spiced coconut curry features tender beef and baby potatoes. Spoon some of the sauce over rice, or dunk in some naan bread.

Baby potatoes, cut in half	2 lbs.	900 g
Boneless beef round steak, trimmed of fat, cut into 1 inch (2.5 cm) cubes	2 lbs.	900 g
Salt	1/4 tsp.	1 mL
Pepper	1/4 tsp.	1 mL
Chopped sweet onion	2 cups	500 mL
Thai red curry paste	2 tbsp.	30 mL
Water	1 cup	250 mL
Can of coconut milk (14 oz., 398 mL)	1	1
Salt	1/4 tsp.	1 mL

Put potatoes into 4 to 5 quart (4 to 5 L) slow cooker.

Heat large well-greased frying pan on medium-high. Cook beef, in 2 batches, for about 10 minutes, stirring occasionally, until browned. Transfer to slow cooker. Sprinkle with salt and pepper.

Add onion to same greased frying pan. Reduce heat to medium. Cook for about 10 minutes, stirring occasionally, until starting to brown.

Add curry paste and water. Heat and stir, scraping to remove any brown bits from bottom of pan, until boiling. Pour over beef. Cook, covered, on Low for 8 to 9 hours or on High for 4 to 4 1/2 hours.

Add coconut milk and a generous sprinkle of salt. Stir. Cook, covered, on High for 15 minutes. Makes about 8 cups (2 L).

1 cup (250 mL): 381 Calories; 17.3 g Total Fat (3.2 g Mono, 0.9 g Poly, 11.0 g Sat); 64 mg Cholesterol; 26 g Carbohydrate; 2 g Fibre; 30 g Protein; 472 mg Sodium

Mushroom Beef Barley

A hot bowl of this fibre-rich beef and barley dish will warm you to the core. Store leftovers in an airtight container in the freezer for up to three months.

All-purpose flour	2 tbsp.	30 mL
Pepper	1/4 tsp.	1 mL
Stewing beef, trimmed of fat	1 1/2 lbs.	680 g
Canola oil	1 tbsp.	15 mL
Low-sodium prepared beef broth	6 cups	1.25 L
Sliced fresh white mushrooms	4 cups	1 L
Chopped onion	2 cups	500 mL
Pot barley	1 1/2 cups	375 mL
Chopped carrot	1 cup	250 mL
Sliced celery	1 cup	250 mL
Package of dried porcini mushrooms (3/4 oz., 22 g)	1	1
Worcestershire sauce	1 tbsp.	15 mL
Salt	1/8 tsp.	0.5 mL

Combine flour and pepper in large resealable freezer bag. Add beef. Seal bag. Toss until coated. Remove beef. Discard any remaining flour mixture.

Heat canola oil in large frying pan on medium-high. Cook beef, in 2 batches, for about 5 minutes, stirring occasionally, until browned. Transfer with slotted spoon to 4 to 5 quart (4 to 5 L) slow cooker.

Add remaining 9 ingredients. Stir. Cook, covered, on Low for 7 to 8 hours or on High for 3 1/2 to 4 hours. Makes about 12 1/2 cups (3.1 L).

1 cup (250 mL): 244 Calories; 8.8 g Total Fat (3.7 g Mono, 0.6 g Poly, 3.0 g Sat); 33 mg Cholesterol; 26 g Carbohydrate; 5 g Fibre; 15 g Protein; 113 mg Sodium

Potato Beef Curry

Enjoy curry heat in a thick, saucy beef and potato stew. This lightened version is ideal for serving with brown rice or whole wheat naan bread.

Baby potatoes, larger ones halved	1 lb.	454 g
Stewing beef, trimmed of fat	2 lbs.	900 g
Canola oil	1 tsp.	15 mL
Chopped onion	1 cup	250 mL
Finely grated ginger root	1 tsp.	5 mL
(or 1/4 tsp., 1 mL, ground ginger)		
Garlic cloves, minced	2	2
(or 1/2 tsp., 2 mL, powder)		
Curry powder	2 tsp.	10 mL
Dried crushed chilies	1 tsp.	5 mL
Ground coriander	1 tsp.	5 mL
Ground cumin	1 tsp.	5 mL
Can of light coconut milk	1	1
(14 oz., 398 mL)		
Tomato paste (see Tip, page 83)	2 tbsp.	30 mL
Whole green cardamom, bruised	6	6
(see Tip, page 41)		
Cinnamon stick (4 inches, 10 cm)	1	1
Salt	1/2 tsp.	2 mL

Layer potatoes and beef, in order given, in 4 to 5 quart (4 to 5 L) slow cooker.

Heat canola oil in medium frying pan on medium. Add next 3 ingredients. Cook for about 5 minutes, stirring often, until onion is softened.

Add next 4 ingredients. Heat and stir for about 1 minute until fragrant. Remove from heat.

Add remaining 5 ingredients. Stir. Add to slow cooker. Do not stir. Cook, covered, on Low for 8 to 9 hours or on High for 4 to 4 1/2 hours. Stir. Remove and discard cardamom and cinnamon stick. Makes about 6 cups (1.5 L).

1 cup (250 mL): 442 Calories; 26.6 g Total Fat (8.8 g Mono, 1.0 g Poly, 13.8 g Sat); 93 mg Cholesterol; 20 g Carbohydrate; 2 g Fibre; 29 g Protein; 261 mg Sodium

Coconut Beef Curry

If you love a creamy curry with a lingering spicy heat but aren't interested in all the sodium that often comes with it, this recipe is for you. Serve with pappadums or over brown rice.

Stewing beef, trimmed of fat	2 lbs.	900 g
Cubed peeled potato (3/4 inch, 2 cm, pieces)	2 1/2 cups	625 mL
Chopped peeled orange-fleshed sweet potato (1 inch, 2.5 cm, pieces)	1 cup	250 mL
Thinly sliced onion	1 cup	250 mL
Prepared beef broth	1/2 cup	125 mL
Sweet chili sauce	2 tbsp.	30 mL
Thai red curry paste	1 tbsp.	15 mL
Brown sugar, packed	1 tsp.	5 mL
Finely grated ginger root (or 1/4 tsp., 1 mL, ground ginger)	1 tsp.	5 mL
Grated lime zest	1 tsp.	5 mL
Soy sauce	1 tsp.	5 mL
Can of coconut milk (14 oz., 398 mL)	1	1
Cornstarch	1 tbsp.	15 mL
Chopped fresh cilantro (or parsley)	2 tbsp.	30 mL

Combine first 4 ingredients in 4 to 5 quart (4 to 5 L) slow cooker.

Combine next 7 ingredients in small bowl. Add to slow cooker. Stir. Cook, covered, on Low for 8 to 10 hours or on High for 4 to 5 hours.

Stir coconut milk into cornstarch in small bowl until smooth. Add to slow cooker. Stir gently. Cook, covered, on High for about 15 minutes until boiling and thickened.

Sprinkle with cilantro. Makes about 7 1/2 cups (1.9 L).

3/4 cup (175 mL): 308 Calories; 20.3 g Total Fat (5.3 g Mono, 0.5 g Poly, 12.0 g Sat); 56 mg Cholesterol; 14 g Carbohydrate; 2 g Fibre; 18 g Protein; 253 mg Sodium

Pictured on page 54.

Taco Beef Hash

A one-dish meal with Mexican flair! It makes a satisfying brunch or lunch for the whole family.

Lean ground beef	1 lb.	454 g
Diced cooked potato	4 cups	1 L
Taco seasoning mix, stir before measuring	2 tbsp.	30 mL
Pepper	1/4 tsp.	1 mL
Large eggs	6	6
Can of condensed cheddar cheese (10 oz., 285 g), (or condensed cream of onion) soup	1	1

Scramble-fry ground beef in large greased frying pan on medium-high for about 5 minutes until no longer pink. Transfer to large bowl.

Add potato, taco seasoning and pepper. Stir well. Transfer to well-greased 3 1/2 to 4 quart (3.5 to 4 L) slow cooker.

Whisk eggs and soup in medium bowl until smooth. Pour over beef mixture. Stir. Cook, covered, on High for about 2 hours until set. Serves 6.

1 serving: 346 Calories; 14.7 g Total Fat (0.5 g Mono, 0.3 g Poly, 5.5 g Sat); 268 mg Cholesterol; 28 g Carbohydrate; 3 g Fibre; 24 g Protein; 1077 mg Sodium

Variation: To spice up this dish, replace taco seasoning with 2 tsp. (10 mL) finely chopped chipotle peppers in adobo sauce (see Tip, page 56). Add a generous sprinkle of salt to the potato mixture.

Beef Vegetable Pasta Sauce

This beefy tomato sauce offers a great alternative to the expected ground beef! Asiago adds a nice, sharp flavour. Serve over your favourite whole-wheat pasta, and store in an airtight container in the freezer for up to three months.

Canola oil	2 tsp.	10 mL
Beef inside round steak, trimmed of fat, cut into 3/4 inch (2 cm) pieces	1 lb.	454 g
Canola oil	1 tsp.	5 mL
Chopped fennel bulb (white part only)	1 1/2 cups	375 mL
Chopped onion	1 1/2 cups	375 mL
Prepared beef broth	1 cup	250 mL
Chopped tomato	2 cups	500 mL
Chopped zucchini (with peel)	2 cups	500 mL
Chopped carrot	1 cup	250 mL

(continued on next page)

Chopped sun-dried tomatoes, softened in boiling water for 10 minutes before chopping	1/4 cup	60 mL
Tomato paste (see Tip, below)	3 tbsp.	45 mL
Brown sugar, packed	1 tsp.	5 mL
Dried thyme	1 tsp.	5 mL
Bay leaf	1	1
Garlic clove, minced (or 1/4 tsp., 1 mL, powder)	1	1
Dried rosemary, crushed	1/2 tsp.	2 mL
Salt	1/8 tsp.	0.5 mL
Pepper	1/2 tsp.	2 mL
Grated Asiago cheese	1/4 cup	60 mL
Chopped fresh parsley (or 3/4 tsp., 4 mL, flakes)	1 tbsp.	15 mL
Balsamic vinegar	1 tsp.	5 mL

Heat first amount of canola oil in large frying pan on medium-high. Add beef. Cook, in 2 batches, for about 5 minutes, stirring occasionally, until browned. Transfer with slotted spoon to 3 1/2 to 4 quart (3.5 to 4 L) slow cooker. Discard any remaining drippings. Reduce heat to medium.

Heat second amount of canola oil in same frying pan. Add fennel and onion. Cook for about 8 minutes, stirring often, until onion is softened.

Add broth. Heat and stir, scraping any brown bits from bottom of pan, until boiling. Pour over beef.

Add next 12 ingredients. Stir. Cook, covered, on Low for 7 to 8 hours or on High for 3 1/2 to 4 hours. Remove and discard bay leaf.

Add remaining 3 ingredients. Stir. Makes about 7 1/2 cups (1.9 L).

1 cup (250 mL): 179 Calories; 7.6 g Total Fat (2.7 g Mono, 0.9 g Poly, 2.3 g Sat); 38 mg Cholesterol; 13 g Carbohydrate; 3 g Fibre; 16 g Protein; 282 mg Sodium

 tip If a recipe calls for less than an entire can of tomato paste, freeze the unopened can for 30 minutes. Open both ends and push the contents through one end. Slice off only what you need. Freeze the remaining paste in a resealable freezer bag or plastic wrap for future use.

Beef Mushroom Lasagna

You couldn't find a better tasting lasagna made in the slow cooker—and it's nutritious too! Unlike regular lasagna recipes, this recipe doesn't make a huge batch—so you won't be eating leftovers all week.

Canola oil	1 tsp.	5 mL
Lean ground beef	1/2 lb.	225 g
Chopped fresh white mushrooms	3 cups	750 mL
Chopped onion	1 cup	250 mL
Chopped tomato	2 cups	500 mL
Orange juice	1/4 cup	60 mL
Tomato paste (see Tip, page 83)	2 tbsp.	30 mL
Dried thyme	1 tsp.	5 mL
Garlic cloves, minced	2	2
(or 1/2 tsp., 2 mL, powder)		
Salt	1/4 tsp.	1 mL
Pepper	1/2 tsp.	2 mL
Large egg, fork-beaten	1	1
Chopped fresh spinach leaves, lightly packed	3 cups	750 mL
2% cottage cheese	1 cup	250 mL
Cooked whole wheat lasagna noodles	9	9
Grated Italian cheese blend	3/4 cup	175 mL

Heat canola oil in large frying pan on medium. Add beef. Scramble-fry for about 5 minutes until no longer pink. Drain.

Add mushrooms and onion. Cook for about 8 minutes, stirring often, until onion is softened.

Add next 7 ingredients. Heat and stir until boiling.

Combine next 3 ingredients in small bowl.

Layer ingredients in greased 5 to 7 quart (5 to 7 L) slow cooker as follows:

1. 1/3 beef mixture

2. 3 noodles

3. Half spinach mixture

4. 1/3 beef mixture

5. 3 noodles

(continued on next page)

6. Remaining spinach mixture

7. Remaining noodles

8. Remaining beef mixture

Sprinkle with Italian cheese blend. Cook, covered, on Low for 4 to 5 hours or on High for 2 to 2 1/2 hours. Let stand, uncovered, for 10 minutes. Serves 6.

1 serving: 247 Calories; 5.8 g Total Fat (1.7 g Mono, 0.7 g Poly, 1.8 g Sat); 61 mg Cholesterol; 30 g Carbohydrate; 4 g Fibre; 23 g Protein; 410 mg Sodium

Pictured on page 90.

Beef Creole

This hearty tomato dish is loaded with veggies and a hint of cayenne spice. Best enjoyed over brown rice or whole wheat pasta. Store leftovers in an airtight container in the freezer for up to three months.

Chopped onion	1 1/2 cups	375 mL
Chopped celery	1 1/2 cups	375 mL
Chopped green pepper	1 1/2 cups	375 mL
Boneless beef blade steak, trimmed of fat, cut into 1 inch (2.5 cm) pieces	2 lbs.	900 g
Can of diced tomatoes (with juice) (14 oz., 398 mL)	1	1
Prepared beef broth	1 cup	250 mL
Sliced fresh white mushrooms	1 cup	250 mL
Can of tomato paste (5 1/2 oz., 156 mL)	1	1
Paprika	1 tsp.	5 mL
Dried basil	1/2 tsp.	2 mL
Dried oregano	1/2 tsp.	2 mL
Garlic powder	1/2 tsp.	2 mL
Granulated sugar	1/2 tsp.	2 mL
Cayenne pepper	1/4 tsp.	1 mL
Salt	1/8 tsp.	0.5 mL

Layer first 4 ingredients, in order given, in 4 to 5 quart (4 to 5 L) slow cooker.

Combine remaining 11 ingredients in medium bowl. Pour over top. Do not stir. Cook, covered, on Low for 8 to 9 hours or on High for 4 to 4 1/2 hours. Skim and discard fat. Stir. Makes about 9 cups (2.25 L).

1 cup (250 mL): 278 Calories; 17.1 g Total Fat (7.3 g Mono, 0.7 g Poly, 6.8 g Sat); 68 mg Cholesterol; 10 g Carbohydrate; 2 g Fibre; 20 g Protein; 310 mg Sodium

Meat Sauce for Many

When you make a meat sauce in the slow cooker, all that's left to do is cook up some noodles and toss a salad. Freeze in portions to save for pasta nights.

Lean ground beef	2 lbs.	900 g
Hot Italian sausage, casing removed	1 lb.	454 g
Sliced fresh white mushrooms	4 cups	1 L
Tomato pasta sauce	10 cups	2.5 L
Italian seasoning	2 tbsp.	30 mL

Scramble-fry ground beef and sausage in large greased frying pan on medium-high for about 10 minutes until no longer pink. Drain. Transfer to 4 to 5 quart (4 to 5 L) slow cooker.

Add mushrooms to same greased frying pan. Cook on medium-high for about 5 minutes until softened. Add to slow cooker.

Add pasta sauce and Italian seasoning. Stir well. Cook, covered, on Low for 6 to 8 hours or on High for 3 to 4 hours. Makes about 13 cups (3.25 L).

1/2 cup (125 mL): 136 Calories; 6.7 g Total Fat (1.3 g Mono, 0.4 g Poly, 2.3 g Sat); 28 mg Cholesterol; 10 g Carbohydrate; trace Fibre; 10 g Protein; 377 mg Sodium

Mushroom Beef Sauce

Use a combination of your favourite mushrooms in this succulent beef and red wine sauce. The results are delicious and versatile—serve over potatoes, rice or pasta for a complete meal, and garnish with chopped fresh parsley.

Stewing beef, trimmed of fat, cut into 1 inch (2.5 cm) cubes	2 lbs.	900 g
Envelope of mushroom pasta sauce mix (1 1/4 oz., 38 g)	1	1
Butter (or hard margarine)	1 tbsp.	15 mL
Sliced fresh mixed mushrooms	4 cups	1 L
Dry (or alcohol-free) red wine	3/4 cup	175 mL
Water	3/4 cup	175 mL

Combine beef and sauce mix in 4 to 5 quart (4 to 5 L) slow cooker.

Melt butter in large frying pan on medium. Add mushrooms. Cook for about 8 minutes, stirring often, until browned. Transfer to slow cooker.

Add wine and water. Cook, covered, on Low for 8 to 9 hours or on High for 4 to 4 1/2 hours. Skim and discard fat. Makes about 5 1/2 cups (1.4 L).

1/2 cup (125 mL): 194 Calories; 11.8 g Total Fat (4.8 g Mono, 0.4 g Poly, 4.7 g Sat); 53 mg Cholesterol; 3 g Carbohydrate; trace Fibre; 15 g Protein; 203 mg Sodium

Classic Shepherd's Pie

A traditional dish with comforting, familiar flavours. Everyone will love this smarter version of the family favourite.

Canola oil	1 tsp.	5 mL
Lean ground beef	1 1/2 lbs.	680 g
Chopped onion	1 cup	250 mL
Chopped celery	1/2 cup	125 mL
All-purpose flour	3 tbsp.	45 mL
Dried oregano	1 tsp.	5 mL
Dried thyme	1/2 tsp.	2 mL
Pepper	1/2 tsp.	2 mL
Prepared beef broth	2 cups	500 mL
Frozen mixed vegetables	3 cups	750 mL
Tomato paste (see Tip, page 83)	2 tbsp.	30 mL
Warm mashed potatoes	4 1/2 cups	1.1 L
(about 2 lbs., 900 g, uncooked)		
Salt	1/4 tsp.	1 mL
Pepper	1/4 tsp.	1 mL
Paprika	1/4 tsp.	1 mL

Heat canola oil in large frying pan on medium-high. Add next 3 ingredients. Scramble-fry for about 10 minutes until beef is no longer pink. Drain.

Add next 4 ingredients. Heat and stir for 1 minute. Slowly add broth, stirring constantly until boiling and thickened.

Add mixed vegetables and tomato paste. Stir. Transfer to greased 3 1/2 to 4 quart (3.5 to 4 L) slow cooker.

Combine next 3 ingredients in medium bowl. Spread evenly over beef mixture. Do not stir. Place double layer of tea towels over slow cooker liner. Cover with lid. Cook on Low for 5 to 6 hours or on High for 2 1/2 to 3 hours.

Sprinkle with paprika. Serves 8.

1 serving: 236 Calories; 4.0 g Total Fat (1.9 g Mono, 0.6 g Poly, 1.2 g Sat); 45 mg Cholesterol; 31 g Carbohydrate; 5 g Fibre; 23 g Protein; 402 mg Sodium

Texas Chili

Forget ground beef—diced beef roast cooks up tender in the slow cooker for a real Texas-style chili, with lots of beans and tomatoes too. Increase the chili powder if you like a stronger-flavoured chili.

Boneless beef blade (or chuck) roast, cut into 1/2 inch (12 mm) pieces	3 lbs.	1.4 kg
Salt, sprinkle		
Pepper, sprinkle		
Chopped onion	2 1/2 cups	625 mL
Cans of stewed tomatoes (14 oz., 398 mL, each)	3	3
Cans of red kidney beans (14 oz., 398 mL, each), rinsed and drained	3	3
Chili powder	2 tbsp.	30 mL

Heat large well-greased frying pan on medium-high. Cook beef, in 3 batches, for about 5 minutes, stirring occasionally, until browned. Transfer to 4 to 5 quart (4 to 5 L) slow cooker. Sprinkle with salt and pepper.

Add onion to same greased frying pan. Cook for about 5 minutes, stirring often, until softened. Add to slow cooker.

Process 2 cans of stewed tomatoes in blender or food processor until smooth. Add to slow cooker. Stir. Add remaining can of tomatoes, kidney beans and chili powder. Stir well. Cook, covered, on Low for 9 to 10 hours or on High for 4 1/2 to 5 hours. Makes about 12 cups (3 L).

1 cup (250 mL): 424 Calories; 21.1 g Total Fat (9.1 g Mono, 1.1 g Poly, 7.7 g Sat); 77 mg Cholesterol; 30 g Carbohydrate; 9 g Fibre; 28 g Protein; 371 mg Sodium

Pictured on page 89.

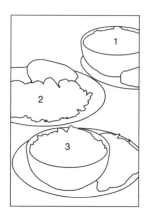

1. Texas Chili, above
2. Steak and Veggie Dinner, page 101
3. Tender Beef with Lemon Parsley, page 105

Falafel Meatloaf Pie

This meatloaf has had a Mediterranean makeover, served with tangy purchased tzatziki.
Use leftovers for delicious gyro sandwiches or wraps.

Lean ground beef	1 1/2 lbs.	680 g
Large egg, fork-beaten	1	1
Box of falafel mix (10 oz., 285 g)	1	1
Chili paste (sambal oelek)	2 tsp.	10 mL
Tzatziki	1/2 cups	125 mL
Water	3/4 cup	175 mL
Boiling water	2 cups	500 mL
Tzatziki	1 cup	250 mL

Scramble-fry ground beef in large greased frying pan on medium-high for about 5 minutes until no longer pink. Transfer to large bowl.

Add next 5 ingredients. Mix well. Press evenly into greased 8 inch (20 cm) springform pan.

Put an even layer (2 to 3 inches, 5 to 7.5 cm, thick) of crumpled foil into bottom of 5 to 7 quart (5 to 7 L) slow cooker (see Tip, page 195). Pour boiling water into slow cooker. Place pan over foil, pushing down gently to settle evenly. Cook, covered, on Low for 5 to 6 hours or on High for 2 1/2 to 3 hours until centre is firm. Remove pan from slow cooker. Let stand on wire rack for 10 minutes. Serve with second amount of tzatziki. Cuts into 8 wedges.

1 wedge with 2 tbsp. (30 mL) tzatziki: 328 Calories; 15.5 g Total Fat (0.3 g Mono, 0.2 g Poly, 5.2 g Sat); 82 mg Cholesterol; 24 g Carbohydrate; 2 g Fibre; 24 g Protein; 626 mg Sodium

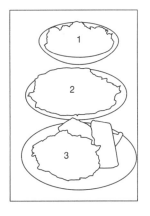

1. Ginger Beef and Broccoli, page 92
2. Rainbow Rouladen, page 99
3. Beef Mushroom Lasagna, page 84

Ginger Beef and Broccoli

A slow cooker version of a takeout favourite! Savoury beef and tender vegetables with garlic and ginger are great for spooning over egg noodles or brown rice.

Canola oil	2 tsp.	10 mL
Lean ground beef	1 1/2 lbs.	680 g
Prepared beef broth	1 cup	250 mL
Water	1/2 cup	125 mL
Minute tapioca	3 tbsp.	45 mL
Finely grated ginger root	1 tbsp.	15 mL
(or 3/4 tsp., 4 mL, ground ginger)		
Soy sauce	1 tbsp.	15 mL
Dried crushed chilies	1/2 tsp.	2 mL
Garlic cloves, minced	2	2
(or 1/2 tsp., 2 mL, powder)		
Sliced onion	2 cups	500 mL
Broccoli florets	3 cups	750 mL
Sliced red pepper	2 cups	500 mL
Water	1 tbsp.	15 mL
Thin teriyaki basting sauce	1 tbsp.	15 mL
Roasted sesame seeds	1 tsp.	5 mL
Sesame oil (for flavour)	1 tsp.	5 mL

Heat canola oil in large frying pan on medium-high. Add beef. Scramble-fry for about 8 minutes until no longer pink. Drain. Transfer to 3 1/2 to 4 quart (3.5 to 4 L) slow cooker.

Combine next 7 ingredients in small bowl. Pour over beef.

Add onion. Stir. Cook, covered, on Low for 4 to 5 hours or on High for 2 to 2 1/2 hours. Skim and discard fat.

Put next 3 ingredients in large microwave-safe bowl. Microwave, covered, on high for about 5 minutes until tender-crisp (see Tip, page 128). Drain. Add to slow cooker.

Add remaining 3 ingredients. Stir. Makes about 6 cups (1.5 L).

1 cup (250 mL): 219 Calories; 7.4 g Total Fat (2.9 g Mono, 1.1 g Poly, 1.8 g Sat); 60 mg Cholesterol; 14 g Carbohydrate; 2 g Fibre; 25 g Protein; 516 mg Sodium

Pictured on page 90.

Lazy Cabbage Roll Casserole

Finally, a healthier version of this homestyle favourite—even with the bacon. It's got all the classic flavours without the fussy rolling.

Coarsely chopped cabbage	3 cups	750 mL
Bacon slices, chopped	4	4
Chopped onion	2 cups	500 mL
Lean ground beef	1 lb.	454 g
Garlic cloves, minced (or 1/2 tsp., 2 mL, powder)	2	2
Celery seed	1/2 tsp.	2 mL
Pepper	1/2 tsp.	2 mL
Long-grain brown rice	1 1/2 cups	375 mL
Coarsely chopped cabbage	3 cups	750 mL
Can of diced tomatoes (with juice) (28 oz., 796 mL)	1	1
Prepared vegetable broth	2 cups	500 mL
Hot pepper sauce	1/2 tsp.	2 mL

Place first amount of cabbage in greased 4 to 5 quart (4 to 5 L) slow cooker.

Cook bacon in large frying pan on medium until crisp. Transfer with slotted spoon to plate lined with paper towel to drain. Drain and discard all but 1 tsp. (5 mL) drippings. Increase heat to medium-high.

Add next 5 ingredients to same frying pan. Scramble-fry for about 10 minutes until beef is no longer pink. Drain. Layer over cabbage in slow cooker.

Scatter rice and bacon over top.

Layer second amount of cabbage over bacon.

Combine remaining 3 ingredients in medium bowl. Pour over top. Do not stir. Cook, covered, on Low for 9 to 10 hours or on High for 4 1/2 to 5 hours. Stir. Makes about 12 cups (3 L).

1 cup (250 mL): 223 Calories; 7.8 g Total Fat (0.8 g Mono, 0.4 g Poly, 2.8 g Sat); 28 mg Cholesterol; 26 g Carbohydrate; 3 g Fibre; 11 g Protein; 324 mg Sodium

Prairie Fire Chili

Curl up with a piping hot serving of this hearty chili, loaded with beans, corn and tomatoes.
Store in an airtight container in the freezer for up to three months.

Canola oil	2 tsp.	10 mL
Lean ground beef	1 lb.	454 g
Halved fresh white mushrooms	3 cups	750 mL
Prepared beef broth	2 cups	500 mL
Chopped carrot	1 1/2 cups	375 mL
Chopped onion	1 1/2 cups	375 mL
Chopped celery	1 cup	250 mL
Dried black beans, soaked in water overnight, rinsed and drained	1 cup	250 mL
Water	1 cup	250 mL
Chili powder	2 tbsp.	30 mL
Brown sugar, packed	1 tsp.	5 mL
Dried oregano	1 tsp.	5 mL
Ground cumin	1 tsp.	5 mL
Cayenne pepper	1/2 tsp.	2 mL
Garlic cloves, minced	2	2
Salt	1/8 tsp.	0.5 mL
Pepper	1/2 tsp.	2 mL
Can of tomato sauce (14 oz., 398 mL)		
Chopped seeded tomato	3/4 cup	175 mL
Fresh (or frozen, thawed) kernel corn	3/4 cup	175 mL
Lime juice	2 tbsp.	30 mL
Finely chopped fresh jalapeño pepper (see Tip, page 167)	2 tsp.	10 mL

Sour cream, for garnish
Sliced fresh jalapeño pepper, for garnish

Heat canola oil in large frying pan on medium. Add beef. Scramble-fry for about 10 minutes until no longer pink. Drain. Transfer to 4 to 5 quart (4 to 5 L) slow cooker.

Add next 15 ingredients. Stir. Cook, covered, on High for 5 to 6 hours until beans are tender.

Add next 5 ingredients. Stir. Cook on High for about 20 minutes until heated through.

Garnish individual servings with sour cream and jalapeño pepper. Makes about 9 3/4 cups (2.4 L).

1 cup (250 mL): 186 Calories; 3.2 g Total Fat (1.4 g Mono, 0.6 g Poly, 0.7 g Sat); 25 mg Cholesterol; 24 g Carbohydrate; 4 g Fibre; 15 g Protein; 485 mg Sodium

Pictured on page 108.

Beef

Beefy Mac and Cheese

This easy, family-friendly pasta dish has lots of cheesy flavour. Sprinkle with Parmesan cheese or chili flakes and serve with garlic bread.

Lean ground beef	1 lb.	454 g
Chopped onion	1 cup	250 mL
Salt, sprinkle		
Pepper, sprinkle		
Cooked elbow macaroni (about 1 3/4 cups, 425 mL, uncooked)	4 cups	1 L
Tomato basil pasta sauce	3 cups	750 mL
Grated Cheddar cheese	2 cups	500 mL
Water	1/2 cup	125 mL

Scramble-fry ground beef and onion in large greased frying pan on medium for about 10 minutes until beef is no longer pink. Sprinkle with salt and pepper. Transfer to greased 3 1/2 to 4 quart (3.5 to 4 L) slow cooker. Add remaining 4 ingredients. Stir. Cook, covered, on Low for 3 to 4 hours or on High for 1 1/2 to 2 hours until heated through and cheese is melted. Makes about 8 cups (2 L).

1 cup (250 mL): 381 Calories; 18.0 g Total Fat (3.0 g Mono, 0.4 g Poly, 8.3 g Sat); 67 mg Cholesterol; 29 g Carbohydrate; 1 g Fibre; 24 g Protein; 639 mg Sodium

Luau Meatballs

These sweet and sour meatballs are smothered in a tasty pineapple and green pepper sauce.

Box of frozen cooked meatballs, thawed (2 lbs., 900 g)	1	1
Cans of crushed pineapple (with juice), 14 oz., 398 mL, each	2	2
Thick teriyaki basting sauce	2/3 cup	150 mL
Water	1/3 cup	75 mL
Pepper, sprinkle		
Cornstarch	3 tbsp.	45 mL
Diced green pepper	1 1/2 cups	375 mL

Put meatballs into 4 to 5 quart (4 to 5 L) slow cooker.

Combine pineapple, teriyaki sauce, water and a sprinkle of pepper in medium bowl. Pour over meatballs. Cook, covered, on Low for 6 to 8 hours or on High for 3 to 4 hours.

Stir second amount of water into cornstarch in small bowl until smooth. Pour over meatballs. Add green pepper. Stir well. Cook, covered, on High for about 20 minutes until boiling and thickened. Makes about 9 cups (2.25 L).

1 cup (250 mL): 418 Calories; 23.8 g Total Fat (trace Mono, 0.1 g Poly, 10.0 g Sat); 47 mg Cholesterol; 33 g Carbohydrate; 4 g Fibre; 6 g Protein; 1370 mg Sodium

Beef

Unsloppy Joe Filling

This favourite bun filling has a sweet, mellow tomato flavour, and oats hold the meaty mixture together for minimal mess—ideal for kids! Easy to freeze in smaller portions for a hot lunch or supper in a hurry.

Lean ground beef	3 lbs.	1.4 kg
Finely chopped onion	1 cup	250 mL
Cans of condensed tomato soup (10 oz., 284 mL, each)	2	2
Ketchup	2 1/2 cups	625 mL
Quick-cooking rolled oats	1 cup	250 mL

Scramble-fry ground beef and onion in large greased frying pan on medium-high for about 10 minutes until no longer pink. Transfer to 3 1/2 to 4 quart (3.5 to 4 L) slow cooker.

Add soup and ketchup. Stir. Cook, covered, on Low for 5 to 6 hours or on High for 2 1/2 to 3 hours.

Add oats. Stir well. Cook, covered, on High for about 20 minutes until thickened. Makes about 9 cups (2.25 L).

1/2 cup (125 mL): 236 Calories; 8.2 g Total Fat (0.2 g Mono, 0.1 g Poly, 3.1 g Sat); 49 mg Cholesterol; 25 g Carbohydrate; 1 g Fibre; 16 g Protein; 478 mg Sodium

Pictured on page 107.

Sandwich Brisket

Once this fork-tender beef brisket has cooled, slice it up for weekday sandwiches or freeze for later use. Heat the cooking liquid for dipping, or make gravy for hot beef sandwiches. Cooled brisket can also be julienned for stir-fries or salads.

Boneless beef brisket roast	4 lbs.	1.8 kg
Chopped onion	1 cup	250 mL
Garlic cloves, minced (or 3/4 tsp., 4 mL, powder)	3	3
Salt	1/4 tsp.	1 mL
Pepper	1/4 tsp.	1 mL
Prepared beef broth	1 cup	250 mL
Red wine vinegar	1/4 cup	60 mL

Place brisket in 5 to 7 quart (5 to 7 L) slow cooker.

Heat medium greased frying pan on medium. Add onion and garlic. Cook, stirring often, for about 10 minutes, until starting to brown. Sprinkle with salt and pepper.

(continued on next page)

Add broth and vinegar to onion mixture. Bring to a boil. Pour over brisket. Cook, covered, on High for 4 1/2 to 5 hours until brisket is very tender. Remove brisket from slow cooker. Cool completely. Wrap in plastic wrap. Let stand in refrigerator for 6 hours or overnight. Chill cooking liquid. Remove and discard fat from brisket and cooking liquid. Makes about 1 1/4 cups (250 mL) cooking liquid. Slice brisket thinly. Serve brisket with cooking liquid. Makes about 2.2 lbs (1 kg) brisket.

3 oz. (85 g) portion with 1/4 cup (60 mL) cooking liquid: 203 Calories; 7.0 g Total Fat (3.0 g Mono, 0.4 g Poly, 2.5 g Sat); 64 mg Cholesterol; 2 g Carbohydrate; trace Fibre; 31 g Protein; 261 mg Sodium

Corned Beef and Winter Vegetables

This tender and flavourful corned beef brisket is slow cooked in apple cider with winter vegetables—perfect for a cozy autumn supper. Serve alongside boiled or mashed potatoes to complete the meal.

Corned beef brisket, rinsed and drained	2 1/2 lbs.	1.1 kg
Baby carrots	3 cups	750 mL
Chopped, peeled yellow turnip (rutabaga), 1 1/2 inch (3.8 cm) pieces	3 cups	750 mL
Sweet apple cider	3 cups	750 mL
Fresh (or frozen, thawed) Brussels sprouts, cut in half	3 cups	750 mL

Place brisket in 5 to 7 quart (5 to 7 L) slow cooker. Add carrots and turnip. Pour apple cider over top. Cook, covered, on High for 4 to 5 hours.

Add Brussels sprouts. Cook, covered, on High for about 30 minutes until Brussels sprouts are tender. Transfer brisket to cutting board. Cover with foil. Let stand for 10 minutes. Slice brisket across the grain. Transfer to large serving platter. Transfer vegetables with slotted spoon to serving bowl. Skim and discard fat from cooking liquid. Serve with vegetables and cooking liquid. Serves 8.

1 serving with 1/2 cup (125 mL) cooking liquid: 374 Calories; 21.3 g Total Fat (10.2 g Mono, 0.8 g Poly, 6.7 g Sat); 77 mg Cholesterol; 22 g Carbohydrate; 3 g Fibre; 23 g Protein; 1798 mg Sodium

Peppered Beef Dip

Beef au jus is a great change from the usual lunchtime fare, and you'll get a hands-on meal out of this classic diner favourite! Add onions, peppers and cheese for a Philly cheese steak.

Boneless beef blade (or chuck) roast	3 lbs.	1.4 kg
Pepper	1 tbsp.	15 mL
Can of condensed beef broth (10 oz., 284 mL)	1	1
Can of condensed onion soup (10 oz., 284 mL)	1	1
Panini buns, split	6	6

Sprinkle roast with pepper. Heat large greased frying pan on medium-high. Add roast. Cook for about 8 minutes, turning occasionally, until browned on all sides. Transfer to 4 to 5 quart (4 to 5 L) slow cooker.

Add broth and soup to same frying pan. Heat and stir, scraping any brown bits from bottom of pan, until boiling. Pour over roast. Cook, covered, on Low for 8 to 9 hours or on High for 4 to 4 1/2 hours. Transfer roast to cutting board. Cover with foil. Let stand for 10 minutes. Skim and discard fat from cooking liquid. Carefully process in blender until smooth (see Safety Tip, page 9). Makes about 2 1/2 cups (625 mL) cooking liquid. Cut roast into thin slices.

Fill buns with beef. Cut each bun in half. Serve with small bowl of cooking liquid for dipping. Makes 12 sandwiches.

1 sandwich with 3 tbsp (45 mL) cooking liquid: 395 Calories; 21.3 g Total Fat (8.6 g Mono, 0.9 g Poly, 7.6 g Sat); 77 mg Cholesterol; 24 g Carbohydrate; 2 g Fibre; 26 g Protein; 653 mg Sodium

Onion Pepper Swiss Steak

For a weekend supper for the family, serve with garlic mashed potatoes or your favourite pasta.

Boneless beef blade steaks, trimmed of fat, cut into 4 pieces	1 1/2 lbs.	680 g
Salt, sprinkle		
Pepper, sprinkle		
All-purpose flour	3 tbsp.	45 mL
Thinly sliced onion	2 cups	500 mL
Thinly sliced green pepper	1 3/4 cups	425 mL
Can of diced tomatoes (with juice) (14 oz., 398 mL)	1	1
Salt, sprinkle		
Pepper, sprinkle		

(continued on next page)

Sprinkle steaks with salt and pepper. Press into flour in small shallow dish until coated on all sides. Heat large greased frying pan on medium-high. Add steaks. Cook for about 2 minutes per side until browned. Transfer to 3 1/2 to 4 quart (3.5 to 4 L) slow cooker.

Add next 5 ingredients. Cook, covered, on Low for 6 to 7 hours or on High for 3 to 3 1/2 hours. Transfer to serving platter. Serves 4.

1 serving: 378 Calories; 19.2 g Total Fat (7.7 g Mono, 1.2 g Poly, 6.8 g Sat); 112 mg Cholesterol; 16 g Carbohydrate; 2 g Fibre; 35 g Protein; 690 mg Sodium

Rainbow Rouladen

A lighter take on the traditional roast beef dinner! Beef rolls are filled with colourful veggies and pickles, and there's lots of gravy to spoon over the accompanying potatoes.

Prepared horseradish	3 tbsp.	45 mL
Dry mustard	1 tsp.	5 mL
Pepper	1/4 tsp.	1 mL
Beef rouladen steaks, 1/4 inch (6 mm) thick	8	8
Carrot sticks, 1/4 x 4 inch, (6 mm x 10 cm) pieces	8	8
Thick red pepper strips	8	8
Thick yellow pepper strips	8	8
Large dill pickles, quartered lengthwise	2	2
Low-sodium prepared beef broth	3 1/2 cups	875 mL
Minute tapioca	3 tbsp.	45 mL
Dry mustard	2 tsp.	10 mL

Combine first 3 ingredients in small bowl.

Arrange steaks on work surface. Spread horseradish mixture over steaks.

Arrange next 4 ingredients on 1 short end of each steak. Starting at same short end, roll up to enclose filling. Arrange rolls, seam-side down, in single layer in 5 to 7 quart (5 to 7 L) slow cooker.

Combine remaining 3 ingredients in medium bowl. Pour over top. Do not stir. Cook, covered, on Low for 6 to 7 hours or on High for 3 to 3 1/2 hours. Transfer rolls with slotted spoon to serving plate. Cover to keep warm. Skim and discard fat from cooking liquid. Carefully process in blender in batches until smooth (see Safety Tip, page 9). Pour sauce over rolls. Serves 8.

1 roll with 1/4 cup (60 mL) sauce: 270 Calories; 14.1 g Total Fat (6.0 g Mono, 0.6 g Poly, 5.5 g Sat); 81 mg Cholesterol; 6 g Carbohydrate; 1 g Fibre; 28 g Protein; 728 mg Sodium

Pictured on page 90.

Beef

Beer-braised Flank Steak

Tender, melt-in-your-mouth steak with a rich, beer-infused sauce—no one will peg this as a lower-sodium offering. Serve with egg noodles or mashed potatoes and steamed vegetables.

All-purpose flour	1/4 cup	60 mL
Dried marjoram	1/2 tsp.	2 mL
Dried thyme	1/2 tsp.	2 mL
Pepper	1/2 tsp.	2 mL
Flank steak, trimmed of fat	1 1/2 lbs.	680 g
Canola oil	1 tsp.	5 mL
Chopped onion	2 cups	500 mL
Garlic clove, minced	1	1
(or 1/4 tsp., 1 mL, powder)		
Dark beer	1 1/4 cups	300 mL
Prepared beef broth	1 cup	250 mL
Dijon mustard	1 tbsp.	15 mL
Steak sauce	1 tbsp.	15 mL
Tomato paste (see Tip, page 83)	1 tbsp.	15 mL
Sour cream	1/4 cup	60 mL

Combine first 4 ingredients in small bowl. Reserve 3 tbsp. (45 mL) in small cup. Rub remaining flour mixture over both sides of steak. Place steak in 4 to 5 quart (4 to 5 L) slow cooker.

Heat canola oil in large frying pan on medium. Add onion and garlic. Cook for about 8 minutes, stirring often, until softened. Add reserved flour mixture. Heat and stir for 1 minute.

Add next 5 ingredients. Stir. Pour over steak. Cook, covered, on Low for 7 to 8 hours or on High for 3 1/2 to 4 hours. Transfer steak to cutting board. Cover with foil. Let stand for 10 minutes. Skim and discard fat from cooking liquid.

Add sour cream. Stir. Slice steak across the grain and arrange on large serving plate. Pour sauce over top. Serves 6.

1 serving: 265 Calories; 10.4 g Total Fat (3.6 g Mono, 0.6 g Poly, 4.5 g Sat); 50 mg Cholesterol; 12 g Carbohydrate; 1 g Fibre; 26 g Protein; 275 mg Sodium

Steak and Veggie Dinner

On busy autumn days, make this all-in-one comfort dish in the slow cooker. A little salt and pepper is all you need to season this flavourful, family-friendly meal. Serve with crusty bread to mop up the sauce.

Unpeeled red potatoes, cut into 2 inch (5 cm) pieces	2 1/2 lbs.	1.1 kg
Sliced carrot (1 1/2 inch, 3.8 cm, thick)	2 1/2 cups	625 mL
Boneless beef blade steak, cut into 6 pieces	2 lbs.	900 g
Chopped onion	2 cups	500 mL
Salt	1/4 tsp.	1 mL
Pepper	1/4 tsp.	1 mL
Can of Italian-style stewed tomatoes (19 oz., 540 mL), cut up	1	1

Combine potatoes and carrot in 5 to 7 quart (5 to 7 L) slow cooker.

Heat large well-greased frying pan on medium-high. Add beef. Cook for about 2 minutes per side until browned. Transfer to slow cooker.

Add onion to same greased frying pan. Cook for about 5 minutes, stirring often, until softened. Add to beef. Sprinkle with salt and pepper.

Pour tomatoes over top. Cook, covered, on Low for 9 to 10 hours or on High for 4 1/2 to 5 hours. Serves 6.

1 serving: 495 Calories; 19.4 g Total Fat (8.1 g Mono, 1.8 g Poly, 6.3 g Sat); 100 mg Cholesterol; 45 g Carbohydrate; 7 g Fibre; 34 g Protein; 664 mg Sodium

Pictured on page 89.

Tomato Paprikash

Tender, bite-sized beef pairs well with tomatoes and paprika in this rich, saucy dish.
It can be served with boiled potatoes or spooned over egg noodles.

Chopped onion	1 1/2 cups	375 mL
Boneless beef blade steak, trimmed of fat, cut into 1 inch (2.5 cm) cubes	3 lbs.	1.4 kg
Salt	1/4 tsp.	1 mL
Pepper	1/4 tsp.	1 mL
Can of diced tomatoes (with juice) (14 oz., 398 mL)	1	1
Can of tomato paste (5 1/2 oz., 156 mL)	1	1
Paprika	2 tbsp.	30 mL
Water		
Salt	1/4 tsp.	1 mL
Pepper	1/4 tsp.	1 mL

Put onion into 4 to 5 quart (4 to 5 L) slow cooker. Arrange beef over top. Sprinkle with salt and pepper.

Combine remaining 6 ingredients in medium bowl. Pour over beef. Cook, covered, on Low for 8 to 10 hours or on High for 4 to 5 hours. Makes about 8 cups (2 L).

3/4 cup (175 mL): 262 Calories; 13.8 g Total Fat (5.4 g Mono, 0.7 g Poly, 5.1 g Sat); 86 mg Cholesterol; 8 g Carbohydrate; 2 g Fibre; 26 g Protein; 433 mg Sodium

Stuffed Peppers

These colourful peppers are stuffed with savoury beef and rice—a pretty dish to serve for company. Spoon extra tomato sauce over the servings.

Large red peppers	4	4
Lean ground beef	1 lb.	454 g
Finely chopped onion	1/4 cup	60 mL
Salt, sprinkle		
Pepper, sprinkle		
Cooked long-grain white rice (about 1/2 cup, 125 mL, uncooked)	1 1/2 cups	375 mL
Tomato and herb pasta sauce	3 cups	750 mL

Cut 1/2 inch (12 mm) from top of each pepper. Remove seeds and ribs. Trim bottom of each pepper so it will sit flat, being careful not to cut into cavity. Set aside. Discard stems from tops, dicing remaining pepper surrounding stem.

(continued on next page)

Beef

Scramble-fry beef, onion and diced pepper in large greased frying pan on medium for about 10 minutes until beef is no longer pink. Sprinkle with salt and pepper. Transfer to large bowl.

Add rice and 3/4 cup (175 mL) pasta sauce to beef mixture. Stir. Spoon into prepared peppers. Arrange stuffed peppers in 5 to 7 quart (5 to 7 L) slow cooker. Pour remaining pasta sauce over and around peppers. Cook, covered, on Low for 4 to 5 hours or on High for 2 to 2 1/2 hours. Serve sauce with peppers. Makes about 1 cup (250 mL) sauce and 4 peppers.

1 pepper with 1/4 cup (60 mL) sauce: 454 Calories; 18.4 g Total Fat (0.7 g Mono, 0.6 g Poly, 5.6 g Sat); 74 mg Cholesterol; 41 g Carbohydrate; 4 g Fibre; 29 g Protein; 1079 mg Sodium

Pot Roast with Onion Gravy

The dark onion gravy paired with this tender beef is perfect with mashed potatoes. Use the leftovers to make a hot beef sandwich on whole wheat the next day.

Boneless beef cross-rib roast, trimmed of fat	3 lbs.	1.4 kg
Salt	1/4 tsp.	1 mL
Pepper	1/4 tsp.	1 mL
Canola oil	2 tsp.	10 mL
Sliced onion	3 cups	750 mL
Dried oregano	1 tsp.	5 mL
Dried thyme	1 tsp.	5 mL
Garlic cloves, minced (or 1/2 tsp., 2 mL, powder)	2	2
Prepared beef broth	1 cup	250 mL
Tomato paste (see Tip, page 83)	1 tbsp.	15 mL
Balsamic vinegar	1 tbsp.	15 mL

Sprinkle roast with salt and pepper. Heat canola oil in large frying pan on medium-high. Add roast. Cook for about 8 minutes, turning occasionally, until browned on all sides. Transfer to 4 to 5 quart (4 to 5 L) slow cooker. Reduce heat to medium.

Add onion to same frying pan. Cook for about 5 minutes, stirring often, until onion starts to soften.

Add next 3 ingredients. Heat and stir for about 1 minute until fragrant.

Add broth and tomato paste. Heat and stir, scraping any brown bits from bottom of pan, until boiling. Pour over roast. Cook, covered, on Low for 8 to 9 hours or on High for 4 to 4 1/2 hours. Transfer roast to cutting board. Cover with foil. Let stand for 10 minutes. Skim and discard fat from cooking liquid.

Add vinegar to cooking liquid. Carefully process in blender until smooth (see Safety Tip, page 9). Slice roast and arrange on large serving plate. Serve with sauce. Serves 10.

1 serving: 279 Calories; 16.6 g Total Fat (7.3 g Mono, 0.9 g Poly, 6.2 g Sat); 77 mg Cholesterol; 4 g Carbohydrate; 1 g Fibre; 27 g Protein; 182 mg Sodium

Peppered Roast

For even better flavour, prepare this pot roast the day before.

Sliced onion	4 cups	1 L
Boneless beef blade (or cross-rib) roast	3 lbs.	1.4 kg
Pepper	1/4 tsp.	1 mL
Can of tomato paste (5 1/2 oz., 156 mL)	1	1
Soy sauce	1/4 cup	60 mL
Envelope of green peppercorn sauce mix (1 1/4 oz., 38 g)	1	1
Water	2 cups	500 mL

Put onion into 4 to 5 quart (4 to 5 L) slow cooker. Place roast over onion. Sprinkle generously with pepper.

Combine next 4 ingredients in medium bowl. Pour over roast. Cook, covered, on High for 4 1/2 to 5 hours. Transfer roast to cutting board. Cover with foil. Let stand for 10 minutes. Skim and discard fat from sauce. Slice roast and arrange on large serving plate (see Note, below). Pour sauce over top. Serves 10.

1 serving: 523 Calories; 35.5 g Total Fat (15.2 g Mono, 1.3 g Poly, 14.0 g Sat); 142 mg Cholesterol; 11 g Carbohydrate; 2 g Fibre; 39 g Protein; 852 mg Sodium

Note: The cold roast slices very neatly, so chill the leftovers overnight before cutting. Pour some of the sauce into a casserole dish, arrange sliced beef over top and cover with remaining sauce. Reheat, covered, in 350°F (175°C) oven for about 45 minutes until hot.

Sweet Mustard Roast Beef

Nothing beats a hearty roast beef and veggie dinner—and when you use the slow cooker, this comfort meal is easy too! Add a tossed salad and dinner is ready.

Sliced onion	2 cups	500 mL
Chopped carrot	2 cups	500 mL
Water	1/2 cup	125 mL
Boneless beef blade (or chuck) roast	3 lbs.	1.4 kg
Dijon mustard	1/3 cup	75 mL
Fancy (mild) molasses	3 tbsp.	45 mL

Put onion into greased 5 to 7 quart (5 to 7 L) slow cooker. Scatter carrot over onion. Pour water over top.

(continued on next page)

Beef

Sprinkle roast with salt and pepper. Heat large greased frying pan on medium-high. Add roast. Cook for about 8 minutes, turning occasionally, until browned on all sides.

Combine mustard and molasses in small bowl. Brush over roast. Place roast over carrots. Cook, covered, on Low for 8 to 10 hours or on High for 4 to 5 hours. Transfer roast to work surface. Cover with foil. Let stand for 10 minutes. Cut into slices. Transfer vegetables with slotted spoon to serving bowl. Skim and discard fat from cooking liquid. Makes 4 cups (1 L) cooking liquid. Serve with beef and vegetables. Serves 10.

1 serving with 6 tbsp (90 mL) cooking liquid: 350 Calories; 23.4 g Total Fat (10.2 g Mono, 1.0 g Poly, 9.1 g Sat); 92 mg Cholesterol; 9 g Carbohydrate; 1 g Fibre; 24 g Protein; 240 mg Sodium

Tender Beef with Lemon Parsley

Our simplified version of traditional gremolata—a fresh parsley and lemon mixture—adds freshness to melt-in-your-mouth beef stew, which is excellent over rice or noodles.

Medium lemons	2	2
Chopped fresh parsley	1/2 cup	125 mL
Sliced onion	2 cups	500 mL
Salt	1/4 tsp.	1 mL
Pepper	1/4 tsp.	1 mL
Boneless beef blade (or cross-rib) roast, cut into 1 1/2 inch (3.8 cm) pieces	2 1/2 lbs.	1.1 kg
Roasted garlic tomato pasta sauce	3 cups	750 mL
Water	1/2 cup	125 mL

Grate 1 tbsp. (15 mL) lemon zest into small bowl. Add parsley. Stir. Chill, covered.

Put onion into 3 1/2 to 4 quart (3.5 to 4 L) slow cooker. Sprinkle with salt and pepper.

Heat large well-greased frying pan on medium-high. Cook beef, in 2 batches, for about 5 minutes, stirring occasionally, until browned. Transfer to slow cooker.

Squeeze 1/3 cup (75 mL) lemon juice into medium bowl. Add pasta sauce and 1/2 cup (125 mL) water. Stir. Pour over beef. Stir well. Cook, covered, on Low for 8 to 10 hours or on High for 4 to 5 hours. Skim and discard fat. Stir. Sprinkle with parsley mixture. Makes about 7 1/2 cups (1.9 L).

3/4 cup (175 mL): 315 Calories; 21.1 g Total Fat (9.4 g Mono, 1.2 g Poly, 7.8 g Sat); 77 mg Cholesterol; 9 g Carbohydrate; 2 g Fibre; 21 g Protein; 382 mg Sodium

Pictured on page 89.

Beer-braised Pot Roast

This roast is tender and flavourful, and the sauce has molasses sweetness and a hint of horseradish. Serve slices over egg noodles with a side of mixed veggies.

Boneless beef cross-rib roast	4 lbs.	1.8 kg
Salt	1/4 tsp.	1 mL
Pepper	1/4 tsp.	1 mL
Stout beer	1 1/4 cups	300 mL
Fancy (mild) molasses	1/4 cup	60 mL
Envelope of vegetable soup mix (1 1/4 oz., 40 g)	1	1
Creamed horseradish	1 tbsp.	15 mL

Sprinkle roast generously with salt and pepper. Place in 4 to 5 quart (4 to 5 L) slow cooker.

Combine next 3 ingredients in small bowl. Pour over roast. Cook, covered, on High for 5 to 6 hours. Transfer roast to cutting board. Cover with foil. Let stand for 10 minutes. Skim and discard fat from cooking liquid. Carefully process in blender in batches (see Safety Tip, page 9). Transfer to medium bowl.

Add horseradish. Stir. Cut roast into thin slices. Transfer to large serving platter. Pour sauce over top. Serves 12.

1 serving: 383 Calories; 25.7 g Total Fat (11.0 g Mono, 0.9 g Poly, 10.2 g Sat); 102 mg Cholesterol; 8 g Carbohydrate; trace Fibre; 27 g Protein; 226 mg Sodium

1. Barbecued Pulled Pork, page 142
2. Pulled Chicken Fajitas, page 173
3. Unsloppy Joe Filling, page 96

Cherry Beef Roast

This roast is a melt-in-your-mouth main course
with a sweet and smoky sauce to drizzle over top.

Seasoned salt	1 tsp.	5 mL
Boneless beef cross-rib roast	3 1/2 lbs.	1.6 kg
Hickory barbecue sauce	1 cup	250 mL
Cherry jam	1/2 cup	125 mL
Prepared beef broth	1/2 cup	125 mL

Rub seasoned salt over roast. Heat large greased frying pan on medium-high. Add roast. Cook for about 8 minutes, turning occasionally, until browned on all sides. Transfer to 4 to 5 quart (4 to 5 L) slow cooker.

Stir remaining 3 ingredients in small bowl until smooth. Pour over roast. Cook, covered, on Low for 8 to 10 hours or on High for 4 to 5 hours. Transfer roast to cutting board. Cover with foil. Let stand for 10 minutes. Skim and discard fat from cooking liquid. Carefully process with hand blender or in blender in batches until smooth (see Safety Tip, page 9). Makes about 3 1/2 cups (875 mL) sauce. Slice roast and arrange on large serving plate. Serve with sauce. Serves 10.

1 serving with 5 1/2 tbsp (82 mL) sauce: 616 Calories; 42.0 g Total Fat (18.2 g Mono, 1.8 g Poly, 16.4 g Sat);
165 mg Cholesterol; 14 g Carbohydrate; trace Fibre; 43 g Protein; 515 mg Sodium

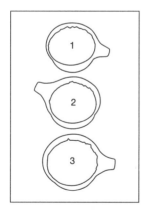

1. Prairie Fire Chili, page 94
2. Chili Lime Pork Ragout, page 138
3. Wheat Chicken Chili, page 174

Props: Stokes

Creamy Seafood Stew

This thick and comforting stew, packed with hearty basa and shrimp, is seasoned with tarragon and bay leaf.

Butter	2 tbsp.	30 mL
Chopped onion	1 cup	250 mL
Chopped carrot	1/2 cup	125 mL
Chopped celery	1/2 cup	125 mL
All-purpose flour	3 tbsp.	45 mL
Low-sodium prepared chicken broth	1 cup	250 mL
Chopped peeled potato	3 cups	750 mL
Low-sodium prepared chicken broth	1 1/2 cups	375 mL
Diced butternut squash	1 cup	250 mL
Dried tarragon	1 tsp.	5 mL
Bay leaf	1	1
Salt	1/8 tsp.	0.5 mL
Pepper	1/4 tsp.	1 mL
Basa fillets, any small bones removed, cut into 1 inch (2.5 cm) pieces	1 lb.	454 g
Uncooked medium shrimp (peeled and deveined)	1 lb.	454 g
Warm milk	1/2 cup	125 mL

Melt butter in large frying pan on medium. Add next 3 ingredients. Cook for about 5 minutes, stirring often, until celery starts to soften.

Add flour. Heat and stir for 1 minute. Slowly add first amount of broth, stirring constantly until boiling and thickened. Transfer to 4 to 5 quart (4 to 5 L) slow cooker.

Add next 7 ingredients. Stir. Cook, covered, on Low for 6 to 8 hours or on High for 3 to 4 hours. Remove and discard bay leaf. Mash several times with potato masher to break up potato.

Add remaining 3 ingredients. Stir. Cook, covered, on High for about 40 minutes until fish flakes easily when tested with fork. Makes about 8 cups (2 L).

1 cup (250 mL): 223 Calories; 4.5 g Total Fat (1.0 g Mono, 0.7 g Poly, 2.2 g Sat); 121 mg Cholesterol; 20 g Carbohydrate; 3 g Fibre; 25 g Protein; 384 mg Sodium

Fennel Clam Pasta Sauce

This satisfying clam and tomato sauce includes chilies for just a touch of lingering heat—wonderful spooned over whole wheat linguine or rotini.

Chopped fennel bulb (white part only)	2 cups	500 mL
Can of diced tomatoes (with juice) (14 oz., 398 mL)	1	1
Chopped green pepper	1 cup	250 mL
Chopped leek (white part only)	1 cup	250 mL
Water	1 cup	250 mL
Can of tomato paste (5 1/2 oz., 156 mL)	1	1
Reserved liquid from clams	2/3 cup	150 mL
Garlic cloves, minced (or 1/2 tsp., 2 mL, powder)	2	2
Granulated sugar	2 tsp.	10 mL
Bay leaves	2	2
Fennel seed, crushed (see Tip, below)	1 tsp.	5 mL
Dried crushed chilies	1/4 tsp.	1 mL
Can of whole baby clams (5 oz., 142 g), drained and liquid reserved (see Tip, page 59)	1	1
Grape tomatoes, halved	16	16

Combine first 12 ingredients in 3 1/2 to 4 quart (3.5 to 4 L) slow cooker. Chill clams. Cook, covered, on Low for 8 to 9 hours or on High for 4 to 4 1/2 hours.

Add clams and tomato. Stir. Cook, covered, on High for about 10 minutes until heated through. Remove and discard bay leaves. Makes about 6 cups (1.5 L).

1 cup (250 mL): 98 Calories; 1.0 g Total Fat (0.1 g Mono, 0.1 g Poly, 0.3 g Sat); 19 mg Cholesterol; 16 g Carbohydrate; 4 g Fibre; 7 g Protein; 315 mg Sodium

 To crush fennel seed, place it in a large resealable freezer bag. Seal the bag and gently hit the seed with a rolling pin or the flat side of meat mallet.

Fish Burritos

Fish finger food, but not in stick form! These tasty burritos will be a hit with your family.

Can of black beans (19 oz., 540 mL), rinsed and drained	1	1
Sliced onion	1 1/2 cups	375 mL
Fresh (or frozen, thawed) kernel corn	1 cup	250 mL
Lime juice	1 tbsp.	15 mL
Chopped pickled pepper rings	2 tsp.	10 mL
Chili powder	1 tsp.	5 mL
Ground cumin	1/2 tsp.	2 mL
Garlic clove, minced (or 1/4 tsp., 1 mL, powder)	1	1
Salt	1/8 tsp.	0.5 mL
Pepper	1/4 tsp.	1 mL
Thinly sliced red pepper	1 cup	250 mL
Thinly sliced yellow pepper	1 cup	250 mL
Tilapia fillets, any small bones removed	3/4 lb.	340 g
Whole wheat flour tortillas (10 inch, 25 cm, diameter)	8	8
Shredded romaine lettuce, lightly packed	1 cup	250 mL
Chopped seeded tomato	1/2 cup	125 mL
Grated jalapeño Monterey Jack cheese	1/2 cup	125 mL
Finely chopped green onion	2 tbsp.	30 mL

Combine first 10 ingredients in 3 1/2 to 4 quart (3.5 to 4 L) slow cooker. Cook, covered, on Low for 4 to 5 hours or on High for 2 to 2 1/2 hours.

Add red and yellow pepper. Stir.

Arrange fillets over top. Cook, covered, on High for about 25 minutes until fish flakes easily when tested with fork. Transfer fillets with slotted spoon to large plate. Break into small pieces with fork.

Using slotted spoon, arrange black bean mixture down centre of each tortilla. Top with fish and remaining 4 ingredients. Fold sides over filling. Roll up from bottom to enclose filling. Makes 8 burritos.

1 burrito: 307 Calories; 4.7 g Total Fat (0.3 g Mono, 1.1 g Poly, 1.7 g Sat); 28 mg Cholesterol; 58 g Carbohydrate; 9 g Fibre; 21 g Protein; 656 mg Sodium

Pictured on page 270.

Herbed Seafood Risotto

A colourful, delicately textured risotto with rich herb flavour, a hint of citrus and perfectly tender seafood. Full-flavour impact in a light main course.

Canola oil	1 tsp.	5 mL
Chopped fennel bulb (white part only)	1 cup	250 mL
Chopped onion	1 cup	250 mL
Garlic cloves, minced	2	2
(or 1/2 tsp., 2 mL, powder)		
Prepared vegetable broth	2 cups	500 mL
Diced red pepper	1 1/2 cups	375 mL
Diced yellow pepper	1 1/2 cups	375 mL
Arborio rice	1 cup	250 mL
Diced zucchini (with peel)	1 cup	250 mL
Dried basil	1 tsp.	5 mL
Dried dillweed	1 tsp.	5 mL
Small bay scallops	1/2 lb.	225 g
Haddock fillet, any small bones removed	1/2 lb.	225 g
Chopped fresh parsley	3 tbsp.	45 mL
(or 1 1/2 tsp., 7 mL, flakes)		
Grated Parmesan cheese	3 tbsp.	45 mL
Lemon juice	2 tbsp.	30 mL
Grated lemon zest (see Tip, page 278)	1 tsp.	5 mL
Pepper	1/2 tsp.	2 mL

Heat canola oil in large frying pan on medium. Add next 3 ingredients. Cook for about 8 minutes, stirring often, until fennel is softened. Transfer to 4 to 5 quart (4 to 5 L) slow cooker.

Add next 7 ingredients. Stir. Cook, covered, on Low for 5 hours or on High for 2 1/2 hours.

Pour water into medium saucepan until about 1 inch (2.5 cm) deep. Bring to a boil. Add scallops. Cook, uncovered, for about 1 minute until scallops turn opaque. Transfer with slotted spoon to rice mixture.

Add fillet to same pot. Cook, uncovered, for about 2 minutes until fish flakes easily when tested with fork. Transfer with slotted spoon to large plate. Break into small pieces with fork. Add to rice mixture.

Add remaining 5 ingredients. Stir gently. Makes about 6 1/2 cups (1.6 L).

1 cup (250 mL): 180 Calories; 2.6 g Total Fat (0.5 g Mono, 0.5 g Poly, 0.6 g Sat); 34 mg Cholesterol; 23 g Carbohydrate; 3 g Fibre; 17 g Protein; 292 mg Sodium

Pictured on page 162.

Fish & Seafood

Indian Fish Curry

Enjoy this vibrant coconut curry filled with halibut, cauliflower and a gentle heat. Served with brown rice, it makes for a satisfying meal.

Butter	1 tbsp.	15 mL
Chopped onion	2 cups	500 mL
Curry powder	2 tbsp.	30 mL
Finely grated ginger root	2 tsp.	10 mL
(or 1/2 tsp., 2 mL, ground ginger)		
Garlic cloves, minced	2	2
(or 1/2 tsp., 2 mL, powder)		
Cauliflower florets, halved	1 1/2 cups	375 mL
Diced unpeeled potato	1 1/2 cups	375 mL
Coconut milk	1 cup	250 mL
Prepared vegetable broth	1 cup	250 mL
Unsweetened applesauce	1 cup	250 mL
Brown sugar, packed	2 tsp.	10 mL
Cayenne pepper	1/4 tsp.	1 mL
Salt	1/4 tsp.	1 mL
Halibut fillets, any small bones removed,	1 lb.	454 g
cut into 1 inch (2.5 cm) pieces		
Chopped fresh spinach leaves,	1 cup	250 mL
lightly packed		
Chopped tomato	1 cup	250 mL
Frozen peas, thawed	1 cup	250 mL

Melt butter in large frying pan on medium. Add onion. Cook for about 10 minutes, stirring often, until softened.

Add next 3 ingredients. Heat and stir for about 1 minute until fragrant. Transfer to 3 1/2 to 4 quart (3.5 to 4 L) slow cooker.

Add next 8 ingredients. Stir. Cook, covered, on Low for 5 to 6 hours or on High for 2 1/2 to 3 hours.

Add remaining 4 ingredients. Cook, covered, on High for about 30 minutes until fish flakes easily when tested with fork. Makes about 8 cups (2 L).

1 cup (250 mL): 224 Calories; 9.3 g Total Fat (1.2 g Mono, 0.7 g Poly, 6.5 g Sat); 22 mg Cholesterol; 21 g Carbohydrate; 5 g Fibre; 16 g Protein; 220 mg Sodium

Jamaican Shrimp and Rice

A satisfying Caribbean-inspired rice and bean mix, packed with coconut brown rice, kidney beans, shrimp and a mild chili heat.

Brown sugar, packed	2 tsp.	10 mL
Dried thyme	1/2 tsp.	2 mL
Garlic powder	1/2 tsp.	2 mL
Ground allspice	1/2 tsp.	2 mL
Ground ginger	1/2 tsp.	2 mL
Dried crushed chilies	1/4 tsp.	1 mL
Ground cinnamon	1/4 tsp.	1 mL
Salt	1/4 tsp.	1 mL
Pepper	1/4 tsp.	1 mL
Canola oil	1 tsp.	5 mL
Chopped onion	1 1/2 cups	375 mL
Water	2 cups	500 mL
Cans of red kidney beans (14 oz., 398 mL, each), rinsed and drained	2	2
Long-grain brown rice	2 cups	500 mL
Can of coconut milk (14 oz., 398 mL)	1	1
Uncooked large shrimp (peeled and deveined)	3/4 lb.	340 g

Combine first 9 ingredients in small bowl. Reserve 1 tsp. (5 mL) in small cup.

Heat canola oil in large frying pan on medium. Add onion. Cook for about 7 minutes, stirring often, until softened. Add brown sugar mixture. Heat and stir for about 1 minute until fragrant. Add water. Heat and stir until boiling. Transfer to 4 to 5 quart (4 to 5 L) slow cooker.

Add next 3 ingredients. Stir. Cook, covered, on Low for 5 to 6 hours or on High for 2 1/2 to 3 hours.

Arrange shrimp over rice mixture. Sprinkle with reserved brown sugar mixture. Cook, covered, on High for about 15 minutes until shrimp turn pink. Stir. Makes about 11 cups (2.75 L).

1 cup (250 mL): 302 Calories; 9.7 g Total Fat (1.0 g Mono, 0.8 g Poly, 7.2 g Sat); 47 mg Cholesterol; 41 g Carbohydrate; 6 g Fibre; 14 g Protein; 188 mg Sodium

Salmon Loaf

This loaf has moist, rich flavour and is great option for lunch or a light dinner.

Large eggs, fork-beaten	2	2
Mashed waxy potatoes	2 cups	500 mL
(about 3/4 lb., 340 g, uncooked)		
Quick-cooking rolled oats	1 3/4 cups	425 mL
Chopped green onion	1/2 cup	125 mL
Chopped fresh dill	1 tbsp.	15 mL
(or 3/4 tsp., 4 mL, dried)		
Lemon juice	1 tbsp.	15 mL
Grated lemon zest (see Tip, page 278)	1 tsp.	5 mL
Salt	1/2 tsp.	2 mL
Pepper	1/4 tsp.	1 mL
Cans of red salmon, drained, skin	2	2
and round bones removed		
(7 1/2 oz., 213 g, each)		
Boiling water	2 cups	500 mL

Combine first 9 ingredients in large bowl.

Add salmon. Mix well. Press evenly in greased 8 inch (20 cm) springform pan. Put an even layer (2 to 3 inches, 5 to 7.5 cm, thick) of crumpled foil into bottom of 5 to 7 quart (5 to 7 L) slow cooker (see Tip, page 195). Pour boiling water into slow cooker. Place pan on foil, pushing down gently to settle evenly. Place double layer of tea towels over slow cooker liner. Cover with lid. Cook on High for 2 to 2 1/2 hours until centre is firm. Transfer pan to wire rack. Let stand for 10 minutes. Cuts into 8 wedges.

1 wedge: 215 Calories; 8.5 g Total Fat (0.5 g Mono, 0.2 g Poly, 1.7 g Sat); 87 mg Cholesterol; 21 g Carbohydrate; 3 g Fibre; 16 g Protein; 391 mg Sodium

South Asian Steamed Salmon

Enjoy tender salmon slowly steamed on a bed of spicy, flavourful barley and tender veggies.

Prepared vegetable broth	2 cups	500 mL
Chopped onion	1 cup	250 mL
Diced carrot	1 cup	250 mL
Pot barley	1 cup	250 mL
Water	1 cup	250 mL
Chopped pickled pepper rings	3 tbsp.	45 mL
Sesame oil (for flavour)	1 tsp.	5 mL
Garlic clove, minced	1	1
(or 1/4 tsp., 1 mL, powder)		
Halved sugar snap peas, trimmed	1 1/2 cups	375 mL
Salmon fillets, skin and any small bones removed	1 lb.	454 g
Rice vinegar	1/4 cup	60 mL
Granulated sugar	2 tbsp.	30 mL
Roasted sesame seeds	1 tbsp.	15 mL

Combine first 8 ingredients in greased 4 to 5 quart (4 to 5 L) slow cooker. Cook, covered, on Low for 4 to 5 hours or on High for 2 to 2 1/2 hours.

Add peas. Stir. Arrange fillets over barley mixture.

Stir vinegar and sugar in small bowl until sugar is dissolved. Drizzle over fillets. Cook, covered, on High for about 20 minutes until fish flakes easily when tested with fork.

Sprinkle with sesame seeds. Serves 4.

1 serving: 450 Calories; 10.8 g Total Fat (2.4 g Mono, 2.9 g Poly, 1.3 g Sat); 62 mg Cholesterol; 58 g Carbohydrate; 11 g Fibre; 30 g Protein; 313 mg Sodium

Pictured on page 198.

Wild Rice Fennel Salmon

A dish with the delicate flavours and fantastic textures of wild rice, barley and hearty chunks of salmon. Chives add a burst of bright colour and freshness.

Chopped fennel bulb (white part only)	3 cups	750 mL
Sliced leek (white part only)	2 cups	500 mL
Prepared vegetable (or chicken) broth	1 1/2 cups	375 mL
Dry (or alcohol-free) white wine	1/2 cup	125 mL
Pot barley	1/2 cup	125 mL
Wild rice	1/2 cup	125 mL
Pepper	1/4 tsp.	1 mL
Salmon fillets, skin and any small bones removed, cut into 1 1/2 inch (3.8 cm) pieces	1 1/2 lbs.	680 g
Salt, sprinkle		
Pepper, sprinkle		
Chopped fresh chives (or green onion)	2 tbsp.	30 mL

Combine first 7 ingredients in greased 4 to 5 quart (4 to 5 L) slow cooker. Cook, covered, on Low for 6 hours or on High for 3 hours. Stir.

Sprinkle fish with salt and second amount of pepper. Arrange over fennel mixture. Cook, covered, on High for about 20 minutes until fish flakes easily when tested with fork.

Add chives. Stir gently. Makes about 8 cups (2 L).

1 cup (250 mL): 248 Calories; 6.0 g Total Fat (1.8 g Mono, 2.3 g Poly, 0.9 g Sat); 47 mg Cholesterol; 25 g Carbohydrate; 4 g Fibre; 21 g Protein; 148 mg Sodium

Pictured on page 162.

Salmon Patties

Smother these crusty coated patties with your favourite condiments.

Large eggs, fork-beaten	2	2
Canned salmon, drained, skin and round bones removed (7.5 oz., 213 g, each)	2	2
Water	1/2 cup	125 mL
Soda cracker crumbs	1 cup	250 mL
Celery salt	1/2 tsp.	2 mL
Onion powder	1/2 tsp.	2 mL
Salt	1/4 tsp.	1 mL

(continued on next page)

Fish & Seafood

Dill weed	1/4 tsp.	1 mL
Pepper	1/8 tsp.	0.5 mL
Corn flake crumbs	1/2 cup	125 mL

Combine first 9 ingredients in bowl. Mix well. Shape into 8 patties.

Coat with corn flake crumbs. Place 4 patties in bottom of 3 1/2 quart (3.5 L) or 5 quart (5 L) slow cooker. Place remaining patties on top. Cover. Cook on Low for 4 to 5 hours or on High for 2 to 2 1/2 hours. Makes 4 patties.

1 pattie: 210 Calories; 10 g Total Fat (2 g Mono, 0 g Poly, 2.5 g Sat); 105 mg Cholesterol; 15 g Carbohydrate; <1 g Fibre; 16 g Protein; 810 mg Sodium

Satay Fish and Shrimp

Rich, creamy and spicy stew with tender chunks of potato, fish, shrimp and peanut butter for a delicious satay flavour. A comforting dish to serve with brown rice.

Can of chickpeas (garbanzo beans) (19 oz., 540 mL), rinsed and drained	1	1
Prepared chicken broth	1 cup	250 mL
Peanut butter	1/3 cup	75 mL
Apple cider vinegar	3 tbsp.	45 mL
Liquid honey	3 tbsp.	45 mL
Soy sauce	2 tbsp.	30 mL
Chili paste (sambal oelek)	1 tbsp.	15 mL
Chopped ginger root (or 3/4 tsp., 4 mL, ground ginger)	1 tbsp.	15 mL
Garlic cloves, chopped (or 1/2 tsp., 2 mL, powder)	2	2
Diced unpeeled potato	4 cups	1 L
Chopped onion	2 cups	500 mL
Chopped red pepper	1 cup	250 mL
Sliced celery	1 cup	250 mL
Sole fillets, any small bones removed, cut into 1 inch (2.5 cm) pieces	1 lb.	454 g
Uncooked small shrimp (peeled and deveined)	1/2 lb.	225 g

Process first 9 ingredients in food processor until smooth. Transfer to 3 1/2 to 4 quart (3.5 to 4 L) slow cooker.

Add next 4 ingredients. Stir. Cook, covered, on Low for 6 to 7 hours or on High for 3 to 3 1/2 hours.

Add fish and shrimp. Stir gently. Cook, covered, on High for about 20 minutes until fish flakes easily when tested with fork. Makes about 8 cups (2 L).

1 cup (250 mL): 318 Calories; 7.9 g Total Fat (3.1 g Mono, 2.5 g Poly, 1.5 g Sat); 70 mg Cholesterol; 38 g Carbohydrate; 6 g Fibre; 25 g Protein; 694 mg Sodium

Seafood Quinoa Jambalaya

A nicely textured jambalaya with nutritious quinoa and sweet, tender seafood. The heat is very mild, but you can add more cayenne pepper if you like things hotter.

Canola oil	2 tsp.	10 mL
Chopped onion	1 1/2 cups	375 mL
Chopped celery	1 cup	250 mL
Tomato paste (see Tip, page 83)	2 tbsp.	30 mL
Chili powder	2 tsp.	10 mL
Garlic cloves, minced	2	2
(or 1/2 tsp., 2 mL, powder)		
Dried oregano	1 tsp.	5 mL
Dried thyme	1 tsp.	5 mL
Salt	1/8 tsp.	0.5 mL
Pepper	1/2 tsp.	2 mL
Cayenne pepper	1/4 tsp.	1 mL
Low-sodium prepared chicken broth	3 cups	750 mL
Quinoa, rinsed and drained	1 1/2 cups	375 mL
Small bay scallops	1/2 lb.	225 g
Uncooked medium shrimp	1/2 lb.	225 g
(peeled and deveined)		
Chopped green pepper	3/4 cup	175 mL
Chopped seeded tomato	3/4 cup	175 mL
Chopped yellow pepper	3/4 cup	175 mL

Heat canola oil in large frying pan on medium. Add onion and celery. Cook for about 10 minutes, stirring often, until softened.

Add next 8 ingredients. Heat and stir for about 1 minute until fragrant.

Add 1 cup (250 mL) broth. Heat and stir until boiling. Transfer to 3 1/2 to 4 quart (3.5 to 4 L) slow cooker. Add quinoa and remaining broth. Stir. Cook, covered, on Low for 4 to 5 hours or on High for 2 to 2 1/2 hours.

Add remaining 5 ingredients. Stir. Cook, covered, on High for about 20 minutes until peppers are tender-crisp and shrimp turn pink. Makes about 8 cups (2 L).

1 cup (250 mL): 221 Calories; 3.9 g Total Fat (1.3 g Mono, 1.5 g Poly, 0.4 g Sat); 54 mg Cholesterol; 30 g Carbohydrate; 3 g Fibre; 17 g Protein; 373 mg Sodium

Slow Cooker Bouillabaisse

This healthy take on a seafood favourite boasts a savoury broth rich with veggies, shrimp, fish and clams. Pairs perfectly with whole grain bread.

Canola oil	2 tsp.	10 mL
Chopped onion	2 cups	500 mL
Chopped celery	1 cup	250 mL
Garlic cloves, minced (or 1/2 tsp., 2 mL, powder)	2	2
Can of diced tomatoes (with juice) (28 oz., 796 mL)	1	1
Chopped zucchini (with peel)	3 cups	750 mL
Prepared vegetable broth	1 cup	250 mL
Water	1 cup	250 mL
Dry (or alcohol-free) white wine	1/2 cup	125 mL
Tomato paste (see Tip, page 83)	1/4 cup	60 mL
Italian seasoning	2 tsp.	10 mL
Brown sugar, packed	1/2 tsp.	2 mL
Chili paste (sambal oelek)	1/2 tsp.	2 mL
Bay leaves	2	2
Haddock fillets, any small bones removed, cut into 1 inch (2.5 cm) pieces	1 lb.	454 g
Uncooked medium shrimp (peeled and deveined)	3/4 lb.	340 g
Can of whole baby clams (with liquid) (5 oz., 142 g)	1	1

Fresh basil leaves, for garnish

Heat canola oil in large frying pan on medium. Add next 3 ingredients. Cook for about 10 minutes, stirring often, until celery is softened. Transfer to 4 to 5 quart (4 to 5 L) slow cooker.

Add next 10 ingredients. Stir. Cook, covered, on Low for 8 to 9 hours or on High for 4 to 4 1/2 hours. Remove and discard bay leaves.

Add next 3 ingredients to slow cooker. Stir. Cook, covered, on High for about 30 minutes until fish flakes easily when tested with fork.

Garnish with fresh basil. Makes about 12 1/2 cups (3.1 L).

1 cup (250 mL): 124 Calories; 2.0 g Total Fat (0.6 g Mono, 0.5 g Poly, 0.3 g Sat); 71 mg Cholesterol; 9 g Carbohydrate; 2 g Fibre; 16 g Protein; 329 mg Sodium

Pictured on page 162.

Spanish Fisherman's Stew

Serve this appealing, tomato-based snapper stew with crusty whole wheat bread.

Canola oil	2 tsp.	10 mL
Finely chopped onion	1 cup	250 mL
Garlic cloves, minced	2	2
(or 1/2 tsp., 2 mL, powder)		
Can of diced tomatoes (with juice)	1	1
(14 oz., 398 mL)		
Dry (or alcohol-free) white wine	1/2 cup	125 mL
Prepared chicken broth	1/2 cup	125 mL
Smoked (sweet) paprika	1 tsp.	5 mL
Dried crushed chilies	1/4 tsp.	1 mL
Red baby potatoes, quartered	1 lb.	454 g
Bay leaves	2	2
Sprig of fresh rosemary	1	1
Sprig of fresh thyme	1	1
Snapper fillets, any small bones removed,	1 lb.	454 g
cut into 1 inch (2.5 cm) pieces		
Chopped orange pepper	1 cup	250 mL
Chopped yellow pepper	1 cup	250 mL
Chopped fresh parsley (or 1 tsp.,	2 tbsp.	30 mL
5 mL, flakes)		

Heat canola oil in medium frying pan on medium. Add onion and garlic. Cook for about 8 minutes, stirring often, until softened.

Add next 5 ingredients. Stir. Bring to a boil. Transfer to 3 1/2 to 4 quart (3.5 to 4 L) slow cooker.

Add next 4 ingredients. Stir. Cook, covered, on Low for 4 to 5 hours or on High for 2 to 2 1/2 hours. Remove and discard bay leaves and herb sprigs.

Add next 3 ingredients. Stir. Cook, covered, on High for about 15 minutes until fish flakes easily when tested with fork.

Sprinkle with parsley. Makes about 7 cups (1.75 L).

1 cup (250 mL): 182 Calories; 2.5 g Total Fat (1.0 g Mono, 0.8 g Poly, 0.3 g Sat); 24 mg Cholesterol; 19 g Carbohydrate; 2 g Fibre; 16 g Protein; 237 mg Sodium

Pictured on page 72.

Tuna Vegetable Casserole

A lower-sodium version with all the flavour of the original. No canned soup here—just chunky tuna, pasta and creamy sauce.

Water	8 cups	2 L
Salt	1 tsp.	5 mL
Whole wheat elbow macaroni	2 cups	500 mL
Herb and garlic cream cheese	3/4 cup	175 mL
Pepper	1/4 tsp.	1 mL
Frozen mixed vegetables, thawed	2 cups	500 mL
Sliced fresh white mushrooms	2 cups	500 mL
Cans of solid white tuna in water (6 oz., 170 g, each), drained, broken up	2	2
Grated Parmesan cheese	2 tbsp.	30 mL

Combine water and salt in large saucepan. Bring to a boil. Add pasta. Boil, uncovered, for 8 to 10 minutes, stirring occasionally, until tender but firm. Drain, reserving 1 1/2 cups (375 mL) cooking liquid in pot. Transfer pasta to greased 3 1/2 to 4 quart (3.5 to 4 L) slow cooker.

Add cream cheese and pepper to cooking liquid. Heat and stir on medium until smooth. Transfer to slow cooker.

Add remaining 4 ingredients. Stir. Cook, covered, on Low for 4 to 5 hours or on High for 2 to 2 1/2 hours. Let stand, uncovered, for 10 minutes. Stir. Makes about 8 cups (2 L).

1 cup (250 mL): 228 Calories; 7.4 g Total Fat (0.4 g Mono, 0.6 g Poly, 4.0 g Sat); 42 mg Cholesterol; 25 g Carbohydrate; 3 g Fibre; 17 g Protein; 325 mg Sodium

Shrimp Marinara

Delicious shrimp in an Italian spiced sauce. Serve over rice or pasta.

Canned tomatoes, with juice, broken up (14 oz., 398 mL)	1	1
Finely chopped onion	1 cup	250 mL
Garlic cloves, minced (or 1/2 tsp., 2 mL, garlic powder)	2	2
Dried whole oregano	3/4 tsp.	4 mL
Salt	1 tsp.	5 mL
Pepper	1/4 tsp.	1 mL
Parsley flakes	1/2 tsp.	2 mL
Granulated sugar	1/2 tsp.	2 mL
Cooked fresh (or cooked frozen, thawed) shelled shrimp	1 lb.	454 g
Grated Parmesan cheese, sprinkle		

Combine first 8 ingredients in 3 1/2 quart (3.5 L) slow cooker. Cover. Cook on Low for 6 to 7 hours or on High for 3 to 3 1/2 hours until onion is cooked.

Add shrimp. Stir. Cook on High for about 15 minutes until heated through.

Serve over rice or pasta. Sprinkle with cheese. Makes 3 1/3 cups (825 mL).

3/4 cup (175 mL): 130 Calories; 1.5 g Fat (0 g Mono, 0 g Poly, 0 g Sat); 80 g Cholesterol; 7 g Carbohydrate; 1 g Fibre; 21 g Protein; 820 mg Sodium

1. Red-peppered Chorizo, page 26
2. Smokin' Smokies, page 28
3. Pork and Guacamole Tostadas, page 26

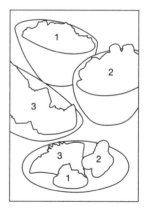

Ale-sauced Pork Roast

You're sure to enjoy this tender pork roast and gravy, deeply flavoured with dark beer and Dijon. The gravy goes great with baked potatoes.

Canola oil	1 tsp.	5 mL
Boneless pork loin roast, trimmed of fat	3 lbs.	1.4 kg
Pepper, sprinkle		
Dark beer	1 1/2 cups	375 mL
Can of condensed onion soup	1	1
(10 oz., 284 mL)		
Dijon mustard	2 tbsp.	30 mL
Water	1 tbsp.	15 mL
Cornstarch	2 tsp.	10 mL

Heat canola oil in large frying pan on medium-high. Sprinkle roast with pepper. Add to frying pan. Cook for about 8 minutes, turning occasionally, until browned on all sides. Transfer roast to 4 to 5 quart (4 to 5 L) slow cooker. Drain and discard drippings from pan.

Add next 3 ingredients to same frying pan. Heat and stir, scraping any brown bits from bottom of pan, until boiling. Pour over roast. Cook, covered, on Low for 7 to 8 hours or on High for 3 1/2 to 4 hours. Transfer roast to cutting board. Cover with foil. Let stand for 10 minutes. Skim and discard fat from cooking liquid.

Stir water into cornstarch in small cup until smooth. Add to cooking liquid. Stir. Cook, covered, on High for about 10 minutes until boiling and thickened. Thinly slice roast and arrange on large serving plate. Serve with sauce. Serves 8.

1 serving: 291 Calories; 12.5 g Total Fat (5.7 g Mono, 1.3 g Poly, 4.3 g Sat); 96 mg Cholesterol; 5 g Carbohydrate; trace Fibre; 35 g Protein; 427 mg Sodium

Pictured on page 216.

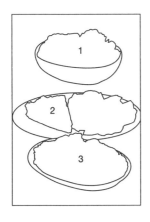

1. Chicken Cacciatore, page 164
2. Moroccan Chicken Couscous Pie, page 166
3. Apricot Chicken, page 160

Chili Rhubarb Pork

This lean and moist pork roast has a sweet fruity sauce with a hint of spicy heat—just the thing to jazz up your next Sunday dinner.

Boneless pork loin roast	3 lbs.	1.4 kg
Salt, sprinkle		
Pepper, sprinkle		
Frozen rhubarb, thawed	1 cup	250 mL
Ketchup	1/2 cup	125 mL
Brown sugar, packed	1/4 cup	60 mL
Chili paste (sambal oelek)	2 tsp.	10 mL
Water	1 cup	250 mL

Sprinkle roast with salt and pepper. Cook in large greased frying pan on medium-high for about 8 minutes, turning occasionally, until browned on all sides. Transfer to 4 to 5 quart (4 to 5 L) slow cooker.

Process remaining 5 ingredients in blender or food processor until smooth. Pour over roast. Cook, covered, on Low for 8 to 9 hours or on High for 4 to 4 1/2 hours. Transfer roast to cutting board. Cover with foil. Let stand for 10 minutes. Skim and discard fat from cooking liquid. Carefully process liquid in blender until smooth (see Safety Tip, page 9). Makes about 2 1/2 cups (625 mL) sauce. Cut roast into thin slices. Serve with sauce. Serves 10.

1 serving with 1/4 cup (60 mL) sauce: 332 Calories; 13.6 g Total Fat (6.2 g Mono, 1.2 g Poly, 4.8 g Sat); 110 mg Cholesterol; 12 g Carbohydrate; trace Fibre; 39 g Protein; 249 mg Sodium

 The microwaves used in our test kitchen are 900 watts, but microwaves are sold in many different powers. You should be able to find the wattage of yours by opening the door and looking for the mandatory label. If your microwave is more than 900 watts, you may need to reduce the cooking time. If it's less than 900 watts, you'll probably need to increase the cooking time.

Jamaican Pork and Couscous

Mildly spiced chops and a sweet couscous blend. Both components are made separately in the slow cooker—the couscous cooks up quickly and dinner is ready!

Brown sugar, packed	1 tsp.	5 mL
Dried thyme	1/2 tsp.	2 mL
Ground allspice	1/2 tsp.	2 mL
Ground ginger	1/2 tsp.	2 mL
Cayenne pepper	1/4 tsp.	1 mL
Ground cinnamon	1/4 tsp.	1 mL
Salt	1/4 tsp.	1 mL
Pepper	1/4 tsp.	1 mL
Bone-in pork chops, trimmed of fat	8	8
Canola oil	2 tsp.	10 mL
Chopped onion	1 1/2 cups	375 mL
Chopped peeled orange-fleshed sweet potato	1 1/2 cups	375 mL
Unsweetened applesauce	1 cup	250 mL
Prepared chicken broth	3/4 cup	175 mL
Frozen peas, thawed	1 cup	250 mL
Whole wheat couscous	1 cup	250 mL
Lime juice	1 tbsp.	15 mL

Combine first 8 ingredients in small cup. Rub over both sides of pork chops.

Heat canola oil in large frying pan on medium-high. Cook pork chops, in 2 batches, for about 1 minute per side, until browned. Transfer to large plate.

Combine next 4 ingredients in 5 to 7 quart (5 to 7 L) slow cooker. Arrange pork chops over top. Do not stir. Place double layer of tea towels over slow cooker liner. Cover with lid. Cook on Low for 5 to 6 hours or on High for 2 1/2 to 3 hours. Transfer pork chops to large serving plate. Cover to keep warm. Skim and discard fat from cooking liquid.

Add remaining 3 ingredients to slow cooker. Stir. Cook, covered, on High for about 10 minutes until liquid is absorbed and couscous is tender. Serve with pork chops. Serves 8.

1 serving: 402 Calories; 17.5 g Total Fat (7.6 g Mono, 1.7 g Poly, 5.9 g Sat); 95 mg Cholesterol; 27 g Carbohydrate; 5 g Fibre; 33 g Protein; 283 mg Sodium

Pictured on page 180.

Sweet and Sour Pork Chops

Pork and pineapple pair up in a sweet, tangy and lemony sauce—another great dish to serve alongside lots of fluffy rice.

Boneless pork shoulder butt steaks, trimmed of fat, cut in half	3 lbs.	1.4 kg
Salt	1/4 tsp.	1 mL
Pepper	1/4 tsp.	1 mL
Can of crushed pineapple (with juice) (14 oz., 398 mL)	1	1
Lemon pie filling powder (not instant), stir before measuring	9 tbsp.	135 mL
Ketchup	1/2 cup	125 mL
Medium lemon	1	1

Heat large well-greased frying pan on medium-high. Add half of pork. Sprinkle with salt and pepper. Cook pork for 2 to 3 minutes per side until browned. Repeat with remaining pork. Transfer to 4 to 5 quart (4 to 5 L) slow cooker.

Combine next 3 ingredients in medium bowl.

Grate 1/2 tsp. (2 mL) lemon zest into small bowl. Set aside. Squeeze 2 tbsp. (30 mL) lemon juice into pineapple mixture. Stir. Pour over pork. Cook, covered, on Low for 6 to 7 hours or on High for 3 to 3 1/2 hours. Add lemon zest. Stir. Serves 8.

1 serving: 390 Calories; 16.9 g Total Fat (7.5 g Mono, 1.5 g Poly, 6.2 g Sat); 101 mg Cholesterol; 29 g Carbohydrate; trace Fibre; 31 g Protein; 306 mg Sodium

Sweet and Sour Pork Ribs

The classic flavours of sweet and sour are infused into these delicious pork ribs. Serve with white rice for a crowd-pleasing meal.

Pork side ribs, trimmed of fat and cut into 3-bone portions	3 lbs.	1.4 kg
Salt, sprinkle		
Pepper, sprinkle		
Rice vinegar	2 tbsp.	30 mL
Garlic cloves, minced (or 1/2 tsp., 2 mL, powder)	2	2
Grated ginger root (or 1/2 tsp., 2 mL, powder)	2 tsp.	10 mL
Sweet and sour sauce	2 cups	500 mL
Sweet and sour sauce	1 cup	250 mL

(continued on next page)

Heat large greased frying pan on medium-high. Add ribs. Sprinkle with salt and pepper. Cook for about 2 minutes per side until browned. Transfer to 3 1/2 to 4 quart (3.5 to 4 L) slow cooker.

Combine next 4 ingredients in medium bowl. Pour over ribs. Cook, covered, on Low for 8 to 9 hours or on High for 4 to 4 1/2 hours. Transfer ribs to large shallow bowl. Cover to keep warm.

Skim and discard fat from cooking liquid. Add second amount of sweet and sour sauce. Stir. Pour over ribs. Makes 10 portions.

1 portion: 605 Calories; 43.1 g Total Fat (18.6·g Mono, 3.3 g Poly, 15.0 g Sat); 161 mg Cholesterol; 20 g Carbohydrate; trace Fibre; 33 g Protein; 472 mg Sodium

Braised Pork Steaks

These fork-tender pork steaks coated with a thick, tasty sauce are a Southern-style treat! Serve with mashed potatoes and a side of warm biscuits.

All-purpose flour	1/2 cup	125 mL
Montreal steak spice	1 tbsp.	15 mL
Boneless pork shoulder blade steaks, cut in half	1 1/2 lbs.	680 g
Prepared chicken broth	1 cup	250 mL
Water	1 1/2 cups	375 mL
Dijon mustard	2 tbsp.	30 mL

Combine flour and steak spice in large resealable freezer bag. Add pork. Turn to coat. Heat large well-greased frying pan on medium-high. Add pork. Reserve remaining flour mixture. Cook for 2 to 3 minutes per side until browned. Transfer to 4 to 5 quart (4 to 5 L) slow cooker.

Add reserved flour mixture to same frying pan. Heat and stir for 1 minute. Gradually add broth and water, whisking constantly until smooth. Heat and stir for 1 to 2 minutes until starting to thicken. Pour over pork. Cook, covered, on Low for 6 to 7 hours or on High for 3 to 3 1/2 hours. Transfer pork with slotted spoon to serving platter.

Add mustard to sauce. Stir. Makes about 1 1/2 cups (375 mL) sauce. Serve with pork. Serves 6.

1 serving with 1/4 cup (60 mL) sauce: 240 Calories; 13.8 g Total Fat (6.4 g Mono, 1.8 g Poly, 4.3 g Sat); 67 mg Cholesterol; 8 g Carbohydrate; trace Fibre; 20 g Protein; 682 mg Sodium

Country Ribs and Sauerkraut

This simple dish adds tomatoes to the classic combination of pork ribs, onion and sauerkraut— the result is a blend of savoury, sweet and sour flavours, and a dish that feeds a crowd!

Can of diced tomatoes (19 oz., 540 mL), drained	1	1
Can of wine sauerkraut (14 oz., 398 mL), rinsed and drained	1	1
Chopped onion	1 cup	250 mL
Brown sugar, packed	1/2 cup	125 mL
Boneless country-style pork ribs	3 lbs.	1.4 kg

Combine first 4 ingredients in large bowl. Transfer half of sauerkraut mixture to 3 1/2 to 4 quart (3.5 to 4 L) slow cooker.

Add ribs. Spoon remaining sauerkraut mixture over ribs. Cook, covered, on Low for 8 to 9 hours or on High for 4 to 4 1/2 hours. Makes about 8 cups (2 L).

1 cup (250 mL): 457 Calories; 27.4 g Total Fat (11.8 g Mono, 2.5 g Poly, 10.2 g Sat); 111 mg Cholesterol; 20 g Carbohydrate; 2 g Fibre; 31 g Protein; 563 mg Sodium

Hoisin Honey Ribs

These sweet, saucy and very tender pork ribs have an Asian flavour that goes well with basmati rice and stir-fry vegetables.

Hoisin sauce	1/2 cup	125 mL
Liquid honey	1/2 cup	125 mL
Soy sauce	1/3 cup	75 mL
Garlic cloves, minced (or 1/2 tsp., 2 mL, powder)	2	2
Pork side ribs, trimmed of fat and cut into 3-bone portions	3 lbs.	1.4 kg

Combine first 4 ingredients in large bowl. Reserve 1/3 cup (75 mL).

Add ribs. Stir until coated. Transfer to 3 1/2 to 4 quart (3.5 to 4 L) slow cooker. Cook, covered, on Low for 8 to 9 hours or on High for 4 to 4 1/2 hours. Transfer ribs to serving platter. Brush with reserved hoisin mixture. Makes 10 portions.

1 portion: 558 Calories; 40.3 g Total Fat (18.3 Mono, 3.2 g Poly, 15.0 g Sat); 161 mg Cholesterol; 22 g Carbohydrate; trace Fibre; 34 g Protein; 1270 mg Sodium

Peachy Ribs

Enjoy the flavours of tender, barbecue-flavoured pork ribs with a touch of summery peach sweetness. Drizzle the smooth, tasty sauce over the ribs for even more flavour.

Pork side ribs, trimmed of fat and cut into 3-bone portions	3 lbs.	1.4 kg
Salt, sprinkle		
Pepper, sprinkle		
All-purpose flour	1/4 cup	60 mL
Can of sliced peaches (14 oz., 398 mL), drained and juice reserved, chopped	1	1
Barbecue sauce	1/4 cup	60 mL
Peach jam	1/4 cup	60 mL

Sprinkle ribs with salt and pepper. Put into large resealable freezer bag. Add flour. Seal bag. Turn until coated. Put ribs into 3 1/2 to 4 quart (3.5 to 4 L) slow cooker.

Spoon peaches over top. Combine barbecue sauce, jam and reserved peach juice in small bowl. Pour over peaches. Cook, covered, on Low for 8 to 10 hours or on High for 4 to 5 hours. Transfer ribs to large serving platter. Cover to keep warm. Skim and discard fat from cooking liquid. Carefully process in blender until smooth (see Safety Tip, page 9). Pour sauce over ribs. Makes 10 portions.

1 portion: 558 Calories; 40.4 g Total Fat (18.4 g Mono, 3.2 g Poly, 15.0 g Sat); 161 mg Cholesterol; 13 g Carbohydrate; 1 g Fibre; 33 g Protein; 250 mg Sodium

Mango Chutney Pork

Tender pork medallions and a sweet, tangy chutney sauce look lovely dished up over a bowl of fluffy rice.

Mango chutney	3/4 cup	175 mL
Hot curry paste	2 tbsp.	30 mL
Water	2/3 cup	150 mL
Thinly sliced onion	2 cups	500 mL
Pork tenderloin, trimmed of fat and cut into 1/2 inch (12 mm) slices	2 lbs.	900 g
Salt, sprinkle		
Pepper, sprinkle		
Chopped red pepper	1 1/2 cups	375 mL

Process chutney, curry paste and water in blender or food processor until smooth.

Heat large greased frying pan on medium. Add onion. Cook for about 10 minutes, stirring often, until softened. Transfer to 3 1/2 to 4 quart (3.5 to 4 L) slow cooker.

Increase heat to medium-high. Add half of pork to same greased frying pan. Sprinkle with salt and pepper. Cook for about 2 minutes per side until browned. Arrange over onion. Repeat with remaining pork.

Scatter red pepper over pork. Pour curry mixture over top. Do not stir. Cook, covered, on Low for 6 to 8 hours or on High for 3 to 4 hours. Makes about 4 cups (1 L).

1/2 cup (125 mL): 236 Calories; 8.2 g Total Fat (2.4 g Mono, 0.8 g Poly, 1.7 g Sat); 74 mg Cholesterol; 16 g Carbohydrate; 1 g Fibre; 24 g Protein; 493 mg Sodium

Pictured on page 197.

Fennel Pork and Beans

Not your usual pork and beans—this uptown version has delicious tenderloin and green beans paired with delicately flavoured fennel. Perfect for serving with brown rice or whole wheat couscous.

Pork tenderloin, trimmed of fat, cut into 1/2 inch (12 mm) slices	2 1/2 lbs.	1.1 kg
Salt	1/2 tsp.	2 mL
Pepper	1/4 tsp.	1 mL
Canola oil	2 tsp.	10 mL
Canola oil	1 tsp.	5 mL
Sliced fennel bulb (white part only)	3 cups	750 mL
Sliced onion	2 cups	500 mL
Fennel seed, crushed (see Tip, page 111)	1/2 tsp.	2 mL
Garlic cloves, minced (or 1/2 tsp., 2 mL, powder)	2	2
Prepared chicken broth	1/2 cup	125 mL
White wine vinegar	1 tbsp.	15 mL
Granulated sugar	1 tsp.	5 mL
Halved fresh (or frozen, thawed) green beans	3 cups	750 mL
Water	1 tbsp.	15 mL
Chopped fresh oregano (or 1/2 tsp., 2 mL, dried)	2 tsp.	10 mL

Sprinkle both sides of pork with salt and pepper. Heat first amount of canola oil in large frying pan on medium-high. Cook pork, in 2 batches, for about 2 minutes per side, until browned. Transfer to large plate. Reduce heat to medium.

Heat second amount of canola oil in same frying pan on medium. Add fennel bulb and onion. Cook for about 10 minutes, stirring often, until fennel bulb is softened. Add fennel seed and garlic. Heat and stir for about 1 minute until fragrant. Transfer to 3 1/2 to 4 quart (3.5 to 4 L) slow cooker. Add pork.

Combine next 3 ingredients in small bowl. Pour over pork. Do not stir. Cook, covered, on Low for 4 to 5 hours or on High for 2 to 2 1/2 hours.

Put green beans into medium microwave-safe bowl. Sprinkle with water. Microwave, covered, on high (100%) for about 5 minutes until tender-crisp (see Tip, page 128). Drain. Add to pork mixture.

Add oregano. Stir. Makes about 9 cups (2.25 L).

1 cup (250 mL): 198 Calories; 6.0 g Total Fat (2.9 g Mono, 1.0 g Poly, 1.6 g Sat); 82 mg Cholesterol; 7 g Carbohydrate; 2 g Fibre; 28 g Protein; 281 mg Sodium

Hot and Sour Pork Hot Pot

Vitamin-rich red pepper and carrot add lively colour to this Asian-inspired dish. Serve with rice or Asian noodles.

Prepared vegetable broth	1 cup	250 mL
Water	1 cup	250 mL
Dried shiitake mushrooms	8	8
Canola oil	2 tsp.	10 mL
Pork tenderloin, trimmed of fat, cut into 1/4 inch (6 mm) slices	1 lb.	454 g
Can of cut baby corn (14 oz., 398 mL), drained	1	1
Can of shoestring-style bamboo shoots (8 oz., 227 mL), drained	1	1
Soy sauce	2 tsp.	10 mL
Finely grated ginger root	1 tsp.	5 mL
Sesame oil (for flavour)	1 tsp.	5 mL
Star anise	1	1
Dried crushed chilies	1/2 tsp.	2 mL
Garlic clove, minced	1	1
Rice vinegar	4 tsp.	20 mL
Water	1 tbsp.	15 mL
Cornstarch	2 tbsp.	30 mL
Chopped bok choy	2 cups	500 mL
Thinly sliced carrot	1 cup	250 mL
Thinly sliced red pepper	1 cup	250 mL
Sliced green onion	2 tbsp.	30 mL

Combine broth and water in small saucepan. Bring to a boil. Add mushrooms. Remove from heat. Let stand, covered, for about 20 minutes until softened. Transfer with slotted spoon to cutting board. Remove and discard stems. Slice thinly. Strain broth mixture through fine sieve into 3 1/2 to 4 quart (3.5 to 4 L) slow cooker. Add mushrooms.

Heat canola oil in large frying pan on medium-high. Cook pork, in 2 batches, for about 2 minutes per side, until browned. Add to slow cooker.

Add next 8 ingredients. Stir. Cook, covered, on Low for 3 to 4 hours or on High for 1 1/2 to 2 hours. Remove and discard anise.

Stir next 3 ingredients in small bowl until smooth. Add to slow cooker.

Add remaining 4 ingredients. Stir. Cook, covered, on High for about 10 minutes until boiling and thickened. Makes about 8 cups (2 L).

1 cup (250 mL): 153 Calories; 4.3 g Total Fat (1.7 g Mono, 0.8 g Poly, 0.9 g Sat); 37 mg Cholesterol; 16 g Carbohydrate; 3 g Fibre; 14 g Protein; 225 mg Sodium

Coconut Curry Pork

A mild, flavourful curry with a bit of sweetness from coconut, fresh notes of lime and plenty of well-textured veggies. Store in an airtight container in the freezer for up to three months.

Chopped onion	2 cups	500 mL
Sliced carrot	2 cups	500 mL
Water	1 cup	250 mL
Thai red curry paste	2 tbsp.	30 mL
Salt	3/4 tsp.	4 mL
Pepper	1/4 tsp.	1 mL
Boneless pork shoulder blade steak, trimmed of fat, cut into 3/4 inch (2 cm) pieces	2 lbs.	900 g
Peeled orange-fleshed sweet potatoes, cut into 1 inch (2.5 cm) cubes	2 lbs.	900 g
Lime juice	2 tbsp.	30 mL
Cornstarch	2 tbsp.	30 mL
Sugar snap peas, trimmed	2 cups	500 mL
Can of coconut milk (14 oz., 398 mL)	1	1
Sliced yellow pepper	1 cup	250 mL
Grated lime zest (see Tip, page 278)	1 tsp.	5 mL

Combine onion and carrot in 4 to 5 quart (4 to 5 L) slow cooker.

Whisk next 4 ingredients in medium bowl until smooth. Add pork and sweet potato. Stir. Add to slow cooker. Cook, covered, on Low for 7 to 8 hours or on High for 3 1/2 to 4 hours.

Stir lime juice into cornstarch in small bowl until smooth. Add to slow cooker.

Add remaining 4 ingredients. Stir. Cook, covered, on High for about 40 minutes until boiling and thickened and peas are tender-crisp. Makes about 10 1/2 cups (2.6 L).

1 cup (250 mL): 318 Calories; 14.0 g Total Fat (2.8 g Mono, 0.7 g Poly, 9.0 g Sat); 56 mg Cholesterol; 29 g Carbohydrate; 5 g Fibre; 20 g Protein; 472 mg Sodium

Pictured on page 56.

Chili Lime Pork Ragout

This ragout is loaded with nutritious spinach and has plenty of sweet sauce flavoured with lime and cilantro—great for serving over couscous, rice or barley.

Cubed peeled orange-fleshed sweet potato	5 cups	1.25 L
All-purpose flour	1/4 cup	60 mL
Chili powder	2 tsp.	10 mL
Garlic powder	1/2 tsp.	2 mL
Salt	1/2 tsp.	2 mL
Cayenne pepper	1/4 tsp.	1 mL
Boneless pork shoulder blade steaks, trimmed of fat, cut into 1 inch (2.5 cm) cubes	2 lbs.	900 g
Canola oil	1 tbsp.	15 mL
Chopped onion	1 1/2 cups	375 mL
Prepared chicken broth	1/2 cup	125 mL
Water	1/2 cup	125 mL
Chopped fresh spinach leaves, lightly packed	2 cups	500 mL
Chopped fresh cilantro (or parsley)	1 tbsp.	15 mL
Lime juice	1 tbsp.	15 mL
Liquid honey	2 tsp.	10 mL
Grated lime zest (see Tip, page 278)	1 tsp.	5 mL

Put sweet potato into 3 1/2 to 4 quart (3.5 to 4 L) slow cooker.

Combine next 5 ingredients in large resealable freezer bag. Add half of pork. Seal bag. Toss until coated. Remove pork. Repeat with remaining pork. Reserve remaining flour mixture.

Heat canola oil in large frying pan on medium. Cook pork, in 2 batches, for about 5 minutes, stirring occasionally, until browned. Transfer with slotted spoon to slow cooker.

Add onion to same frying pan. Cook for about 5 minutes, stirring often, until onion starts to soften. Add reserved flour mixture. Heat and stir for 1 minute. Add broth and water. Heat and stir, scraping any brown bits from bottom of pan, until boiling. Pour over pork. Cook, covered, on Low for 7 to 8 hours or on High for 3 1/2 to 4 hours.

Add remaining 5 ingredients. Stir. Makes about 7 1/2 cups (1.9 L).

1 cup (250 mL): 301 Calories; 9.5 g Total Fat (4.5 g Mono, 1.4 g Poly, 2.8 g Sat); 79 mg Cholesterol; 26 g Carbohydrate; 3 g Fibre; 27 g Protein; 362 mg Sodium

Pictured on page 108.

Smoky Pulled Pork Wraps

Wraps filled with pulled pork and coleslaw are inspired by Southern-style barbecue. Make the coleslaw ahead of time so it can chill while the pork is in the slow cooker.

Boneless pork shoulder blade roast, trimmed of fat	3 lbs.	1.4 kg
Salsa	1 cup	250 mL
Can of tomato paste (5 1/2 oz., 156 mL)	1	1
Chopped chipotle peppers in adobo sauce (see Tip, page 56)	2 tsp.	10 mL
Pepper	1/2 tsp.	2 mL
Salsa	1 cup	250 mL
White vinegar	1/4 cup	60 mL
Brown sugar, packed	2 tbsp.	30 mL
Canola oil	2 tsp.	10 mL
Dry mustard	1 tsp.	5 mL
Celery seed	1/2 tsp.	2 mL
Pepper	1/4 tsp.	1 mL
Coleslaw mix	6 cups	1.5 L
Whole wheat flour tortillas (10 inch, 25 cm, diameter)	12	12

Place roast in 3 1/2 to 4 quart (3.5 to 4 L) slow cooker.

Combine next 4 ingredients in medium bowl. Spoon over roast. Cook, covered, on High for 4 1/2 to 5 hours. Transfer roast to large plate. Skim and discard fat from sauce. Shred pork using 2 forks. Remove and discard any fat. Return pork to slow cooker.

Add second amount of salsa. Stir. Cook, covered, on High for about 20 minutes until heated through.

Combine next 6 ingredients in large bowl. Add coleslaw mix. Toss. Chill, covered, for 2 hours, stirring occasionally.

To serve, arrange pork mixture down centre of each tortilla. Spoon coleslaw mixture over top. Fold bottom ends of tortillas over filling. Fold in sides, slightly overlapping, leaving top ends open. Makes 12 wraps.

1 wrap: 384 Calories; 13.1 g Total Fat (5.6 g Mono, 1.7 g Poly, 4.3 g Sat); 67 mg Cholesterol; 50 g Carbohydrate; 5 g Fibre; 29 g Protein; 592 mg Sodium

Cabbage Pork Dinner

This delicious, all-in-one dinner is ready to eat when you walk in the door. Garnish with fresh dill for a fabulous finish to this easy meal.

Baby potatoes, larger ones cut in half	1 1/2 lbs.	680 g
Coleslaw mix, lightly packed	7 cups	1.75 L
Salt, sprinkle		
Pepper, sprinkle		
Boneless pork shoulder blade steak, cut into 1 inch (2.5 cm) pieces	1 1/2 lbs.	680 g
Pepper, sprinkle		
Chopped onion	1 cup	250 mL
Tomato cream pasta sauce	2 2/3 cups	650 mL

Put potatoes into greased 4 to 5 quart (4 to 5 L) slow cooker. Spread coleslaw mix evenly over top. Sprinkle with salt and pepper.

Heat large greased frying pan on medium-high. Add pork. Sprinkle with pepper. Cook for about 5 minutes, stirring occasionally, until browned. Arrange over cabbage.

Add onion to same greased frying pan. Reduce heat to medium. Cook for about 5 minutes, stirring often, until softened. Spread evenly over pork.

Pour pasta sauce over onion. Do not stir. Cook, covered, on Low for 5 to 6 hours or on High for 2 1/2 to 3 hours. Makes about 8 cups (2 L).

1 cup (250 mL): 270 Calories; 10.4 g Total Fat (4.4 g Mono, 1.1 g Poly, 3.2 g Sat); 50 mg Cholesterol; 26 g Carbohydrate; 3 g Fibre; 19 g Protein; 358 mg Sodium

Apple Chops

Baked potatoes are the perfect accompaniment for moist and tangy pork chops paired with a sweet barbecue sauce.

Bone-in pork chops, trimmed of fat	8	8
Chopped onion	1 cup	250 mL
Barbecue sauce	3/4 cup	175 mL
Can of kernel corn (7 oz., 199 mL)	1	1
Thinly sliced peeled tart apple (such as Granny Smith)	1 1/2 cups	375 mL
Barbecue sauce	1/4 cup	60 mL

Heat large well-greased frying pan on medium-high. Cook pork chops, in 2 batches, for about 2 minutes per side until browned. Transfer to 5 to 7 quart (5 to 7 L) slow cooker.

(continued on next page)

Add onion to same greased frying pan. Reduce heat to medium. Cook for about 5 minutes, stirring often, until softened. Spread evenly over pork chops.

Drizzle first amount of barbecue sauce over onion. Layer corn and apple over top, in order given. Drizzle with second amount of barbecue sauce. Do not stir. Cook, covered, on Low for 6 to 7 hours or on High for 3 to 3 1/2 hours. Transfer pork chops to large serving platter. Makes about 2 1/3 cups (575 mL) sauce. Serve with pork chops.

1 serving with 1/3 cup (75 mL) sauce: 254 Calories; 13.0 g Total Fat (6.0 g Mono, 1.7 g Poly, 3.9 g Sat); 61 mg Cholesterol; 13 g Carbohydrate; 2 g Fibre; 20 g Protein; 388 mg Sodium

Mushroom Pork Marsala

Tender meat infused with the deep, earthy flavours of mushroom and wine. This rich and decadent dish tastes best spooned over egg noodles or potatoes.

Boneless pork shoulder butt steak, trimmed of fat, cut into 3/4 inch (2 cm) pieces	2 lbs.	900 g
Fresh brown (or white) mushrooms, quartered	2 cups	500 mL
Marsala wine	1 cup	250 mL
Can of condensed cream of wild mushroom soup (10 oz., 284 mL)	1	1
Package of wild mushroom roast gravy sauce mix (1 oz., 30 g)	1	1
Water	1/2 cup	125 mL

Heat large greased frying pan on medium-high. Cook pork, in 2 batches, for about 5 minutes, stirring occasionally, until browned. Transfer to 3 1/2 to 4 quart (3.5 to 4 L) slow cooker.

Add mushrooms and Marsala to same frying pan. Heat and stir, scraping any brown bits from bottom of pan, until boiling. Add to slow cooker.

Add soup, gravy mix and water to slow cooker. Stir. Cook, covered, on Low for 8 to 10 hours or on High for 4 to 5 hours. Makes about 4 cups (1 L).

1/2 cup (125 mL): 280 Calories; 14.2 g Total Fat (5.4 g Mono, 1.2 g Poly, 4.6 g Sat); 69 mg Cholesterol; 9 g Carbohydrate; trace Fibre; 21 g Protein; 503 mg Sodium

Pictured on page 197.

Barbecued Pulled Pork

If you've got a crowd to feed, serve up a batch of this tangy pulled pork with split hamburger or Kaiser buns. Try serving this Memphis-style, with a few spoonfuls of well-drained coleslaw right in your bun.

Boneless pork shoulder butt roasts (about 2 3/4 lbs., 1.25 kg, each)	2	2
Hickory barbecue sauce	2 cups	500 mL
Apple cider vinegar	3 tbsp.	45 mL
Garlic cloves, minced (or 1 tsp., 5 mL, powder)	4	4
Worcestershire sauce	2 tsp.	10 mL
Water	1/2 cup	125 mL
Hickory barbecue sauce	1 cup	250 mL

Put roasts into 5 to 7 quart (5 to 7 L) slow cooker.

Combine next 5 ingredients in medium bowl. Pour over roasts. Cook, covered, on High for 4 to 5 hours until tender. Transfer roasts to large plate. Shred pork using 2 forks. Remove and discard any visible fat. Skim and discard fat from sauce. Return pork to sauce.

Add second amount of barbecue sauce. Stir. Cook, covered, on High for 30 minutes until heated through. Makes about 10 cups (2.5 L).

1/2 cup (125 mL): 375 Calories; 17.9 g Total Fat (7.9 g Mono, 1.6 g Poly, 6.5 g Sat); 106 mg Cholesterol; 21 g Carbohydrate; trace Fibre; 30 g Protein; 417 mg Sodium

Pictured on page 107.

1. Chicken Stew, page 186
2. Cajun Turkey Stew, page 199
3. Pineapple Chicken, page 189

West Indies Rice Casserole

Salty ham bites are nicely balanced with sweet potato and spicy jerk seasoning in this tasty rice dish. Stir the ham in at the end of cooking to distribute it and the sweet potato evenly.

Prepared chicken broth	2 cups	500 mL
Jerk seasoning paste	1 tbsp.	15 mL
Cubed fresh peeled orange-fleshed sweet potato	2 cups	500 mL
Long grain white rice	2 cups	500 mL
Water	1 cup	250 mL
Salt, sprinkle		
Pepper, sprinkle		
Ham steak (about 1 lb., 454 g), cut into quarters	1	1

Whisk broth and jerk paste in 4 to 5 quart (4 to 5 L) slow cooker until smooth. Add sweet potato, rice, water and salt and pepper. Stir.

Heat large greased frying pan on medium-high. Add ham. Cook for about 1 minute per side until starting to brown. Place over rice mixture. Cook, covered, on Low for 5 to 6 hours or on High for 2 1/2 to 3 hours. Transfer ham to work surface. Dice. Return to slow cooker. Stir gently. Makes about 7 cups (1.75 L).

1 cup (250 mL): 336 Calories; 4.2 g Total Fat (1.9 g Mono, 0.7 g Poly, 1.2 g Sat); 29 mg Cholesterol;
54 g Carbohydrate; 2 g Fibre; 18 g Protein; 1472 mg Sodium

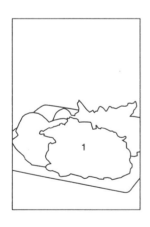

1. Apple Cabbage Chicken, page 157

Red Beans and Rice

A colourful, spicy combination with creamy rice, satisfying beans and hot sausage throughout. Serve this fibre-rich meal as you would chili, in hearty bowlfuls.

Hot Italian sausage, casing removed	3/4 lb.	340 g
Chopped onion	1 cup	250 mL
Chopped celery	1/2 cup	125 mL
Finely chopped carrot	1/2 cup	125 mL
Dried thyme	1/2 tsp.	2 mL
Cayenne pepper	1/4 tsp.	1 mL
Garlic clove, minced	1	1
(or 1/4 tsp., 1 mL, powder)		
Low-sodium prepared chicken broth	2 1/2 cups	625 mL
Can of red kidney beans	1	1
(19 oz., 540 mL), rinsed and drained		
Long-grain brown rice	1 cup	250 mL
Chopped seeded tomato	2 cups	500 mL
Chopped green pepper	1 cup	250 mL
Chopped red pepper	1 cup	250 mL

Scramble-fry sausage in large frying pan on medium for about 8 minutes until no longer pink. Drain. Transfer to greased 3 1/2 to 4 quart (3.5 to 4 L) slow cooker.

Add next 3 ingredients to same frying pan. Cook for about 8 minutes, stirring often, until onion is softened.

Add next 3 ingredients. Heat and stir for about 1 minute until fragrant. Add broth. Heat and stir until boiling. Transfer to slow cooker.

Add beans and rice. Stir. Cook, covered, on Low for 5 to 6 hours or on High for 2 1/2 to 3 hours.

Add remaining 3 ingredients. Stir. Cook, covered, on High for about 30 minutes until peppers are tender-crisp. Makes about 8 cups (2 L).

1 cup (250 mL): 335 Calories; 13.1 g Total Fat (5.4 g Mono, 1.8 g Poly, 4.3 g Sat); 26 mg Cholesterol; 38 g Carbohydrate; 7 g Fibre; 16 g Protein; 855 mg Sodium

Bratwurst Stew

Sausage makes a unique substitute for beef in this filling and hearty stew.

Baby potatoes, larger ones cut in half	2 lbs.	900 g
Baby carrots	3 cups	750 mL
Uncooked bratwurst sausage, cut into 2 inch (5 cm) pieces	2 lbs.	900 g
Pepper	1/4 tsp.	1 mL
Can of condensed onion soup (10 oz., 284 mL)	1	1
Sour cream	1/4 cup	60 mL

Layer first 3 ingredients, in order given, in 4 to 5 quart (4 to 5 L) slow cooker. Sprinkle with pepper.

Pour soup over top. Cook, covered, on Low for 8 to 10 hours or on High for 4 to 5 hours. Transfer sausage, potato and carrot with slotted spoon to large serving platter. Cover to keep warm. Skim and discard fat from cooking liquid.

Add sour cream. Stir until combined. Pour sauce over sausage and vegetables. Serves 8.

1 serving: 482 Calories; 31.6 g Total Fat (9.3 g Mono, 2.0 g Poly, 7.8 g Sat); 93 mg Cholesterol; 29 g Carbohydrate; 3 g Fibre; 18 g Protein; 1443 mg Sodium

Sausage Cabbage Stew

This hearty stew's peppery kick will keep you cozy on a cold winter's day.

Hot Italian sausage, casing removed	1 1/2 lbs.	680 g
Chopped onion	1 1/2 cups	375 mL
Diced peeled potato	3 cups	750 mL
Cans of stewed tomatoes (14 oz., 398 mL, each)	2	2
Water	1 cup	250 mL
Pepper, sprinkle		
Shredded cabbage	4 cups	1 L

Scramble-fry sausage and onion in large greased frying pan on medium-high until sausage is no longer pink. Drain. Transfer to 3 1/2 to 4 quart (3.5 to 4 L) slow cooker.

Add potato, tomatoes, water and pepper. Stir. Cook, covered, on Low for 6 to 7 hours or on High for 3 to 3 1/2 hours.

Add cabbage. Stir. Cook, covered, on High for about 1 hour until cabbage is tender. Makes about 8 3/4 cups (2.2 L).

1 cup (250 mL): 379 Calories; 21.9 g Total Fat (9.6 g Mono, 2.8 g Poly, 7.5 g Sat); 44 mg Cholesterol; 28 g Carbohydrate; 3 g Fibre; 18 g Protein; 1404 mg Sodium

Sausage, Kale and Bean Stew

A hearty, warming mixture full of flavour, fibre and texture with sausage, beans, rice and kale—you'll want to dig right in! Store in an airtight container in the freezer for up to three months.

Water	4 cups	1 L
Chopped carrot	2 cups	500 mL
Chopped kale leaves, lightly packed (see Tip, 223)	2 cups	500 mL
Chopped onion	2 cups	500 mL
Brown basmati rice	1 cup	250 mL
Dried romano beans, soaked in water overnight, rinsed and drained	1 cup	250 mL
Dried oregano	1 1/2 tsp.	7 mL
Dried rosemary, crushed	3/4 tsp.	4 mL
Dried thyme	3/4 tsp.	4 mL
Garlic cloves, minced (or 1/4 tsp., 1 mL, powder)	4	4
Pepper	1/4 tsp.	1 mL
Kielbasa (or other spiced cooked lean sausage), halved lengthwise and sliced crosswise	3/4 lb.	340 g
Finely chopped pickled jalapeño peppers (see Tip, page 167)	2 tsp.	10 mL

Combine first 11 ingredients in 5 to 7 quart (5 to 7 L) slow cooker. Cook, covered, on High for 4 to 4 1/2 hours until beans are tender.

Add kielbasa and jalapeño peppers. Stir. Cook, covered, on High for about 30 minutes until heated through. Makes about 11 1/2 cups (2.9 L).

1 cup (250 mL): 150 Calories; 3.3 g Total Fat (1.1 g Mono, 1.0 g Poly, 0.9 g Sat); 19 mg Cholesterol; 24 g Carbohydrate; 3 g Fibre; 8 g Protein; 293 mg Sodium

Pictured on page 180.

Pork Tamale Pie

Turn on the slow cooker in the morning and your meal is almost ready when you arrive home!
Just add the biscuit topping and cook for half an hour.

Chopped onion	1 cup	250 mL
Chopped celery	1 cup	250 mL
Sliced carrot	1 cup	250 mL
Stewing pork, trimmed of fat	1 1/2 lbs.	680 g
Can of cream-style corn (10 oz., 284 mL)	1	1
Medium salsa	1 cup	250 mL
Frozen kernel corn, thawed	3/4 cup	175 mL
Can of sliced black olives (4 1/2 oz., 125 mL), drained	1	1
Chili powder	1 tsp.	5 mL
Dried crushed chilies	1/2 tsp.	2 mL
Pepper	1/2 tsp.	2 mL
All-purpose flour	3/4 cup	175 mL
Yellow cornmeal	1/4 cup	60 mL
Grated Parmesan cheese	2 tbsp.	30 mL
Baking powder	1 1/2 tsp.	7 mL
Baking soda	1/4 tsp.	1 mL
Cold butter, cut up	1 1/2 tbsp.	25 mL
Buttermilk (or soured milk, see Tip, page 254)	1/3 cup	75 mL
Frozen kernel corn, thawed	2 tbsp.	30 mL

Layer first 4 ingredients, in order given, in 4 to 5 quart (4 to 5 L) slow cooker.

Combine next 7 ingredients in medium bowl. Pour over pork. Do not stir. Cook, covered, on Low for 8 to 10 hours or on High for 4 to 5 hours.

For topping, combine next 5 ingredients in large bowl. Cut in butter until mixture resembles coarse crumbs. Make a well in centre.

Add buttermilk and corn to well. Stir until just moistened. Turn out onto lightly floured surface. Gently press and shape dough to fit slow cooker. Place dough over pork mixture. Cook, covered, on High for about 30 minutes until wooden pick inserted in centre of biscuit comes out clean. Serves 6.

1 serving: 476 Calories; 23 g Total Fat (10.0 g Mono, 2.2 g Poly, 8.5 g Sat); 78 mg Cholesterol; 39 g Carbohydrate; 3 g Fibre; 27 g Protein; 841 mg Sodium

Italiano Pasta Sauce

Serve this sweet tomato sauce over your favourite pasta for a delicious meal anytime! Sausage, onion and artichoke add richness and hearty textures.

Cans of Italian-style stewed tomatoes (19 oz., 540 g, each), cut up	2	2
Hot Italian sausage, casing removed	1 lb.	454 g
Chopped onion	1 cup	250 mL
Cans of artichoke hearts (14 oz., 398 mL, each), drained, quartered	2	2
Tomato basil pasta sauce	4 cups	1 L

Put tomatoes into 4 to 5 quart (4 to 5 L) slow cooker.

Scramble-fry sausage and onion in large greased frying pan on medium-high for about 8 minutes until sausage is no longer pink. Drain. Add to slow cooker.

Add artichoke and pasta sauce. Stir. Cook, covered, on Low for 6 to 8 hours or on High for 3 to 4 hours. Makes about 12 cups (3 L).

3/4 cup (175 mL): 182 Calories; 9.3 g Total Fat (3.6 g Mono, 1.0 g Poly, 2.7 g Sat); 16 mg Cholesterol; 14 g Carbohydrate; 1 g Fibre; 9 g Protein; 849 mg Sodium

Pictured on page 179.

Pork & Lamb

Rosemary Lamb Roast

Take a vacation from your usual Sunday roast beef and try lamb instead! This roast is accompanied by a lovely rosemary sauce.

Canola oil	2 tsp.	10 mL
Boneless leg of lamb roast, trimmed of fat	3 1/2 lbs.	1.6 kg
Salt	3/4 tsp.	4 mL
Pepper	1/2 tsp.	2 mL
Sliced onion	2 cups	500 mL
Dried rosemary, crushed	1 tsp.	5 mL
Garlic cloves, minced (or 1/2 tsp., 2 mL, powder)	2	2
Dry (or alcohol-free) red wine	1/2 cup	125 mL
Prepared beef broth	1/2 cup	125 mL
Bay leaves	2	2

Heat canola oil in large frying pan on medium-high. Sprinkle roast with salt and pepper. Add to frying pan. Cook for about 8 minutes, turning occasionally, until browned on all sides. Transfer to 5 to 7 quart (5 to 7 L) slow cooker. Reduce heat to medium.

Add onion to same frying pan. Cook for about 8 minutes, stirring often, until starting to brown. Add rosemary and garlic. Heat and stir for about 1 minute until fragrant.

Add remaining 3 ingredients. Heat and stir, scraping any brown bits from bottom of pan, until boiling. Pour over roast. Cook, covered, on Low for 7 to 8 hours or on High for 3 1/2 to 4 hours. Transfer roast to cutting board. Cover with foil. Let stand for 10 minutes. Skim and discard fat from cooking liquid. Remove and discard bay leaves. Carefully process in blender until smooth (see Safety Tip, page 9). Slice roast and arrange on large serving plate. Serve with sauce. Serves 10.

1 serving: 223 Calories; 8.1 g Total Fat (3.7 g Mono, 0.8 g Poly, 2.6 g Sat); 93 mg Cholesterol; 3 g Carbohydrate; trace Fibre; 31 g Protein; 292 mg Sodium

Savoury Lamb Shanks

Appetizing, fall-off-the-bone lamb and a pumpkin-coloured sauce with notes of balsamic and herbs—this combination exemplifies the "bountiful harvest"! Make it a meal with baked potatoes.

Chopped carrot	1 1/2 cups	375 mL
Chopped onion	1 1/2 cups	375 mL
Chopped celery	1 cup	250 mL
Prepared beef broth	1 cup	250 mL
Port wine	1/2 cup	125 mL
Bay leaves	2	2
Dried marjoram	1 tsp.	5 mL
Dried rosemary, crushed	1/2 tsp.	2 mL
Garlic cloves, minced (or 1/2 tsp., 2 mL, powder)	2	2
Canola oil	1 tbsp.	15 mL
Lamb shanks (about 3 lbs., 1.4 kg), trimmed of fat (see Note, below)	6	6
Salt	1/2 tsp.	2 mL
Pepper	1/2 tsp.	2 mL
Balsamic vinegar	1 tbsp.	15 mL

Combine first 9 ingredients in 5 to 7 quart (5 to 7 L) slow cooker.

Heat canola oil in large frying pan on medium-high. Sprinkle lamb shanks with salt and pepper. Add to pan. Cook for about 8 minutes, turning occasionally, until browned on all sides. Transfer with slotted spoon to slow cooker. Drain. Cook, covered, on Low for 8 to 9 hours or on High for 4 to 4 1/2 hours. Remove and discard bay leaves. Transfer lamb shanks to large serving plate. Cover with foil. Let stand for 10 minutes. Skim and discard fat from cooking liquid. Carefully process in blender until smooth (see Safety Tip, page 9).

Add vinegar. Stir. Serve with lamb shanks. Serves 6.

1 serving: 500 Calories; 17.6 g Total Fat (8.0 g Mono, 1.8 g Poly, 5.6 g Sat); 197 mg Cholesterol; 11 g Carbohydrate; 2 g Fibre; 65 g Protein; 539 mg Sodium

Note: Lamb shanks are commonly found in frozen bulk packages. If using frozen shanks, remember to thaw them before using.

Curried Lamb Shanks

*Rustic lamb shanks are the perfect cut to slow cook with fragrant curry and sweet potato—
and there's plenty of rich sauce to spoon over rice or cooked veggies.*

Lamb shanks (about 3 lbs., 1.4 kg), see Note, page 152	6	6
Hot curry paste	2 tbsp.	30 mL
Pepper	1/4 tsp.	1 mL
Envelope of onion soup mix (1 1/4 oz., 38 g)	1	1
Water	2 cups	500 mL
Fresh peeled orange-fleshed sweet potato, cut into 1 inch (2.5 cm) pieces	2 lbs.	900 g
Hot curry paste	1 tbsp.	15 mL
Ketchup	1 tbsp.	15 mL

Rub lamb shanks with first amount of curry paste. Sprinkle with pepper. Heat large well-greased frying pan on medium-high. Add lamb shanks. Cook for about 8 minutes, turning occasionally, until browned on all sides. Transfer to 5 to 7 quart (5 to 7 L) slow cooker.

Combine soup mix and water in small bowl. Add to slow cooker. Stir. Cook, covered, on Low for 6 hours or on High for 3 hours.

Add sweet potato. Cook, covered, on High for 1 1/2 to 2 hours until lamb shanks and sweet potato are tender. Transfer lamb shanks to serving bowl. Cover to keep warm. Transfer all but 1/2 cup (125 mL) sweet potato with slotted spoon to separate serving bowl. Cover to keep warm. Skim and discard fat from cooking liquid.

Transfer remaining liquid and sweet potato to blender. Add second amount of curry paste and ketchup. Carefully process in batches until smooth (see Safety Tip, page 9). Pour over lamb. Serves 6.

1 serving: 375 Calories; 14.3 g Total Fat (5.8 g Mono, 1.4 g Poly, 5.0 g Sat); 80 mg Cholesterol; 36 g Carbohydrate; 5 g Fibre; 24 g Protein; 956 mg Sodium

French Lamb Casserole

This rich, comforting dish was inspired by the classic French cassoulet (ka-soo-LAY). Make it a meal with a baguette, steamed green beans and a bottle of wine.

Lamb shank, trimmed of fat, meat cut into 3/4 inch (2 cm) pieces, bone reserved (see Note, page 152)	1 lb.	454 g
Can of diced tomatoes (with juice) (28 oz., 796 mL)	1	1
Cans of black-eyed peas (19 oz., 540 mL each), rinsed and drained	2	2
Smoked ham sausage, cut into 1/4 inch (6 mm) slices	4 oz.	113 g
Onion soup mix, stir before measuring	3 tbsp.	45 mL

Heat medium greased frying pan on medium-high. Add lamb. Cook for about 8 minutes, stirring occasionally, until browned. Transfer to 4 to 5 quart (4 to 5 L) slow cooker.

Add remaining 4 ingredients and reserved bone. Stir. Cook, covered, on Low for 8 to 10 hours or on High for 4 to 5 hours. Remove and discard bone. Makes about 6 cups (1.5 L).

1 cup (250 mL): 276 Calories; 10.1 g Total Fat (2.1 g Mono, 0.5 g Poly, 3.5 g Sat); 39 mg Cholesterol; 32 g Carbohydrate; 6 g Fibre; 20 g Protein; 2017 mg Sodium

Pictured on page 215.

Variation: Lamb shoulder may be substituted, but the lamb bone does provide extra richness.

Irish Stew

There's an extra touch of "Irish" brewed into this simple lamb and vegetable stew—dark stout beer, such as Ireland's famous Guinness, is simmered in the broth.

Baby potatoes, larger ones cut in half	1 lb.	454 g
Baby carrots	2 cups	500 mL
Boneless lamb shoulder, trimmed of fat and cut into 1 1/2 inch (3.8 cm) pieces	3 lbs.	1.4 kg
Salt, sprinkle		
Pepper, sprinkle		
Stout beer	1 3/4 cups	425 mL
Can of condensed onion soup (10 oz., 284 mL)	1	1

(continued on next page)

Combine potatoes and carrot in 5 to 7 quart (5 to 7 L) slow cooker.

Sprinkle lamb with salt and pepper. Heat large well-greased frying pan on medium-high. Cook lamb, in 2 batches, for about 5 minutes, stirring occasionally, until browned. Add to slow cooker.

Add beer and soup to same frying pan. Heat and stir, scraping any brown bits from bottom of pan, until boiling. Add to slow cooker. Stir. Cook, covered, on Low for 8 to 10 hours or on High for 4 to 5 hours. Makes about 9 cups (2.25 L).

1 cup (250 mL): 417 Calories; 23.3 g Total Fat (9.3 g Mono, 2.1 g Poly, 9.2 g Sat); 111 mg Cholesterol; 16 g Carbohydrate; 1 g Fibre; 30 g Protein; 397 mg Sodium

Pictured on page 197.

Variation: You can substitute a honey brown or a lager beer if you want a lighter-tasting broth.

Greek Pasta Bake

This filling dish features tomato-saucy pasta with lots of lemony ground lamb for a Greek flair. Round it out with a Greek salad and garlic toast.

Lean ground lamb	1 1/2 lbs.	680 g
Greek seasoning	1 tbsp.	15 mL
Grated lemon zest	1 tsp.	5 mL
Salt, sprinkle		
Pepper, sprinkle		
Four-cheese tomato pasta sauce	4 cups	1 L
Cooked rigatoni pasta (about 3 cups, 750 mL, uncooked)	5 cups	1.25 L

Scramble-fry lamb in large greased frying pan on medium-high for about 10 minutes until no longer pink.

Add Greek seasoning, lemon zest, salt and pepper. Stir.

To assemble, layer ingredients in greased 5 to 7 quart (5 to 7 L) slow cooker as follows:

1. 3/4 cup (175 mL) pasta sauce

2. 1/3 of pasta

3. 1 cup (250 mL) lamb mixture

Repeat steps 1 to 3 to make 2 more layers. Top with remaining pasta sauce.

Cook, covered, on Low for 3 to 4 hours or on High for 1 1/2 to 2 hours until heated through. Serves 8.

1 serving: 450 Calories; 20.7 g Total Fat (7.4 g Mono, 1.4 g Poly, 7.0 g Sat); 83 mg Cholesterol; 37 g Carbohydrate; 3 g Fibre; 27 g Protein; 792 mg Sodium

Tangiers Tagine

Rich and saucy tagine with moist, tender lamb, chickpeas and veggies—a sweet and nicely seasoned dish to serve over whole wheat couscous. Store in an airtight container in the freezer for up to three months.

Boneless lamb shoulder, trimmed of fat, cut into 1 inch (2.5 cm) pieces	2 lbs.	900 g
Can of chickpeas (garbanzo beans) (19 oz., 540 mL), rinsed and drained	1	1
Cauliflower florets	2 cups	500 mL
Sliced carrot (3/4 inch, 2 cm, pieces)	2 cups	500 mL
Coarsely chopped onion	1 cup	250 mL
Pitted prunes, halved	1 cup	250 mL
Prepared beef broth	2 cups	500 mL
Can of crushed tomatoes (14 oz., 398 mL)	1	1
Ground cumin	2 tsp.	10 mL
Curry powder	1 tsp.	5 mL
Garlic cloves, minced (or 1/2 tsp., 2 mL, powder)	2	2
Ground cinnamon	1/2 tsp.	2 mL
Dried crushed chilies	1/4 tsp.	1 mL
Salt	1/4 tsp.	1 mL
Pepper	1/4 tsp.	1 mL
Chopped fresh mint	1/4 cup	60 mL

Combine first 6 ingredients in 5 to 7 quart (5 to 7 L) slow cooker.

Combine next 9 ingredients in medium bowl. Pour over lamb mixture. Stir. Cook, covered, on Low for 9 to 10 hours or on High for 4 1/2 to 5 hours.

Add mint. Stir. Makes about 12 cups (3 L).

1 cup (250 mL): 244 Calories; 9.2 g Total Fat (3.6 g Mono, 0.8 g Poly, 3.9 g Sat); 52 mg Cholesterol; 22 g Carbohydrate; 5 g Fibre; 18 g Protein; 369 mg Sodium

Apple Cabbage Chicken

Tender chicken in a rich, savoury sauce with lovely apple notes—the perfect pairing for the traditional-tasting combination of bacon and cabbage. Serve this dish with steamed baby potatoes.

Shredded green cabbage, lightly packed	3 cups	750 mL
Bacon slices, chopped	4	4
Boneless, skinless chicken thighs, trimmed of fat, halved	2 lbs.	900 g
Salt	1/4 tsp.	1 mL
Pepper	1/4 tsp.	1 mL
Sliced onion	1 cup	250 mL
Garlic cloves, minced (or 1/2 tsp., 2 mL, powder)	2	2
Apple cider	1 cup	250 mL
Apple cider vinegar	2 tbsp.	30 mL
Dijon mustard (with whole seeds)	1 tbsp.	15 mL
Dried dillweed	2 tsp.	10 mL
Dried thyme	1/2 tsp.	2 mL
Salt	1/4 tsp.	1 mL
Pepper	1/4 tsp.	1 mL
Frozen peas, thawed	1 cup	250 mL
Grated peeled tart apple (such as Granny Smith)	1 cup	250 mL

Put cabbage into 3 1/2 to 4 quart (3.5 to 4 L) slow cooker.

Cook bacon in large frying pan on medium until crisp. Transfer with slotted spoon to paper towel-lined plate to drain. Drain and discard all but 1 tsp. (5 mL) drippings.

Sprinkle chicken with salt and pepper. Add to same frying pan. Cook chicken, in 2 batches, for about 2 minutes per side, until browned. Transfer with slotted spoon to slow cooker. Reduce heat to medium.

Add onion and garlic to same frying pan. Cook for about 5 minutes, stirring often, until onion is softened.

Combine next 7 ingredients in small bowl. Add to onion mixture. Heat and stir, scraping any brown bits from bottom of pan, until boiling. Pour over chicken. Scatter bacon over top. Cook, covered, on Low for 5 to 6 hours or on High for 2 1/2 to 3 hours.

Add peas and apple. Stir gently. Cook, covered, on High for about 15 minutes until heated through. Makes about 6 cups (1.5 L).

1 cup (250 mL): 330 Calories; 14.3 g Total Fat (5.5 g Mono, 2.9 g Poly, 4.1 g Sat); 104 mg Cholesterol; 18 g Carbohydrate; 4 g Fibre; 32 g Protein; 492 mg Sodium

Pictured on page 144.

Chicken Biryani

This colourful and high-fibre blend of rice, lentils and veggies goes great with naan bread. The warm curry flavours are balanced with a sprinkle of fresh cilantro. Store any leftovers in an airtight container in the freezer for up to three months.

Canola oil	1/2 tsp.	2 mL
Boneless, skinless chicken thighs, trimmed of fat, cut into 1 inch (2.5 cm) pieces	1 1/2 lbs.	680 g
Chopped onion	1 cup	250 mL
Long-grain brown rice	1 1/2 cups	375 mL
Curry powder	1 tbsp.	15 mL
Finely grated ginger root (or 3/4 tsp., 4 mL, ground ginger)	1 tbsp.	15 mL
Garlic cloves, minced (or 1/2 tsp., 2 mL, powder)	2	2
Granulated sugar	1/2 tsp.	2 mL
Dried crushed chilies	1/4 tsp.	1 mL
Ground cinnamon	1/4 tsp.	1 mL
Prepared chicken broth	3 cups	750 mL
Can of lentils (19 oz., 540 mL), rinsed and drained	1	1
Cauliflower florets	2 cups	500 mL
Chopped carrot	2 cups	500 mL
Chopped tomato	2 cups	500 mL
Frozen tiny peas, thawed	1 cup	250 mL
Chopped fresh cilantro (or parsley)	2 tbsp.	30 mL

Heat canola oil in large frying pan on medium-high. Cook chicken, in 2 batches, for about 5 minutes, stirring occasionally, until browned. Transfer with slotted spoon to greased 4 to 5 quart (4 to 5 L) slow cooker. Reduce heat to medium.

Add onion to same frying pan. Cook for about 5 minutes, stirring often, until onion starts to brown.

Add next 7 ingredients. Heat and stir for 1 minute. Add broth. Heat and stir, scraping any brown bits from bottom of pan, until boiling. Add to slow cooker.

Add next 3 ingredients. Stir. Cook, covered, on Low for 7 to 8 hours or on High for 3 1/2 to 4 hours.

Add tomato and peas. Stir. Cook, covered, on High for about 5 minutes until heated through.

Sprinkle with cilantro. Makes about 11 cups (2.75 L).

1 cup (250 mL): 276 Calories; 5.9 g Total Fat (2.2 g Mono, 1.5 g Poly, 1.5 g Sat); 42 mg Cholesterol; 36 g Carbohydrate; 8 g Fibre; 20 g Protein; 358 mg Sodium

Chicken Barley Risotto

A thick, filling barley risotto with bites of chicken, sweet cranberries and a good dose of vegetables. Store in an airtight container in the freezer for up to three months.

Canola oil	2 tsp.	10 mL
Boneless, skinless chicken thighs, trimmed of fat, cut into 1 inch (2.5 cm) pieces	2 lbs.	900 g
Canola oil	1 tsp.	5 mL
Chopped fresh brown (or white) mushrooms	2 cups	500 mL
Chopped celery	1 cup	250 mL
Chopped onion	1 cup	250 mL
Apple juice	1 cup	250 mL
Prepared chicken broth	3 cups	750 mL
Pearl barley	1 cup	250 mL
Dried cranberries	3/4 cup	175 mL
Worcestershire sauce	2 tsp.	10 mL
Poultry seasoning	1 tsp.	5 mL
Pepper	1/4 tsp.	1 mL
Frozen peas, thawed	1 cup	250 mL
Apple cider vinegar	2 tbsp.	30 mL

Heat first amount of canola oil in large frying pan on medium-high. Cook chicken, in 2 batches, for about 4 minutes, stirring occasionally, until browned. Transfer with slotted spoon to 4 to 5 quart (4 to 5 L) slow cooker. Reduce heat to medium.

Heat second amount of canola oil in same frying pan. Add next 3 ingredients. Cook for about 5 minutes, stirring often, until onion starts to soften. Add apple juice. Heat and stir, scraping any brown bits from bottom of pan, until boiling. Pour over chicken.

Add next 6 ingredients. Stir. Cook, covered, on Low for 7 to 8 hours or on High for 3 1/2 to 4 hours.

Add peas and vinegar. Stir. Cook, covered, on High for about 10 minutes until heated through. Makes about 9 1/2 cups (2.4 L).

1 cup (250 mL): 308 Calories; 9.0 g Total Fat (3.5 g Mono, 2.1 g Poly, 2.0 g Sat); 64 mg Cholesterol; 34 g Carbohydrate; 5 g Fibre; 23 g Protein; 359 mg Sodium

Apricot Chicken

A family-friendly and not-too-spicy curry. Serve over brown rice and garnish individual servings with chopped fresh chives.

Sliced onion	1 1/2 cups	375 mL
Boneless, skinless chicken breast halves, halved	2 lbs.	900 g
Prepared chicken broth	1 cup	250 mL
Apricot jam, warmed	1/2 cup	125 mL
Chopped dried apricot	1/2 cup	125 mL
Dijon mustard	1 tbsp.	15 mL
Curry powder	2 tsp.	10 mL
Finely grated ginger root (or 1/4 tsp., 1 mL, ground ginger)	1 tsp.	5 mL
Garlic clove, minced (or 1/4 tsp., 1 mL, powder)	1	1
Pepper	1/8 tsp.	0.5 mL
Plain yogurt	1/4 cup	60 mL

Put onion into 3 1/2 to 4 quart (3.5 to 4 L) slow cooker. Arrange chicken over top.

Combine next 8 ingredients in medium bowl. Pour over chicken. Cook, covered, on Low for 6 to 7 hours or on High for 3 to 3 1/2 hours. Transfer chicken to serving bowl. Cover to keep warm.

Add yogurt to slow cooker. Stir. Pour over chicken. Serves 8.

1 serving: 211 Calories; 2.9 g Total Fat (1.0 g Mono, 0.6 g Poly, 0.8 g Sat); 63 mg Cholesterol; 22 g Carbohydrate; 1 g Fibre; 25 g Protein; 198 mg Sodium

Pictured on page 126.

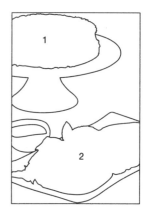

1. Toffee Pudding Cake, page 264
2. Tri-Colour Turkey Roll, page 195

Pineapple Chicken and Beans

Serve this sweet and smoky combination of chicken and beans with coleslaw and whole grain buns—or spoon it over whole wheat toast! It's hearty and satisfying with fruity pineapple bites.

Canola oil	1 tsp.	5 mL
Lean ground chicken	1 lb.	454 g
Chopped onion	1 1/2 cups	375 mL
Cans of white kidney beans (19 oz., 540 mL, each), rinsed and drained	2	2
Can of crushed pineapple (14 oz., 398 mL), drained	1	1
Can of tomato sauce (7 1/2 oz., 213 mL)	1	1
Barbecue sauce	1/2 cup	125 mL
Dijon mustard	2 tbsp.	30 mL
Finely grated ginger root (or 1/2 tsp., 2 mL, ground ginger)	2 tsp.	10 mL
Garlic clove, minced (or 1/4 tsp., 1 mL, powder)	1	1

Heat canola oil in large frying pan on medium-high. Add chicken and onion. Scramble-fry for about 8 minutes until chicken is no longer pink. Transfer to 3 1/2 to 4 quart (3.5 to 4 L) slow cooker.

Add remaining 7 ingredients. Stir. Cook, covered, on Low for 6 to 8 hours or on High for 3 to 4 hours. Makes about 6 1/2 cups (1.6 L).

1 cup (250 mL): 304 Calories; 6.8 g Total Fat (0.6 g Mono, 0.4 g Poly, 1.7 g Sat); 46 mg Cholesterol; 41 g Carbohydrate; 8 g Fibre; 21 g Protein; 608 mg Sodium

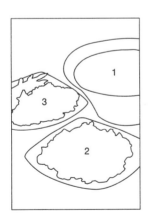

1. Slow Cooker Bouillabaisse, page 121
2. Herbed Seafood Risotto, page 113
3. Wild Rice Fennel Salmon, page 118

Chicken Cacciatore

Serve this delightful dish of chicken and veggies over broad whole wheat noodles or brown rice. Fresh basil adds a nice finishing touch. Store in an airtight container in the freezer for up to three months.

Chopped onion	2 cups	500 mL
Chopped fennel bulb (white part only)	2 cups	500 mL
Chopped green pepper	2 cups	500 mL
Small whole fresh white mushrooms	2 cups	500 mL
Boneless, skinless chicken breast halves (4 oz., 113 g, each), halved crosswise	4	4
Boneless, skinless chicken thighs (about 3 oz., 85 g, each), trimmed of fat	8	8
Can of diced tomatoes (with juice) (28 oz., 796 mL)	1	1
Can of tomato paste (5 1/2 oz., 156 mL)	1	1
Dry (or alcohol-free) white wine	1/2 cup	125 mL
Granulated sugar	2 tsp.	10 mL
Italian seasoning	1 tsp.	5 mL
Bay leaf	1	1
Salt	1/4 tsp.	1 mL
Pepper	1/2 tsp.	2 mL
Chopped fresh basil	3 tbsp.	45 mL

Layer first 6 ingredients, in order given, in 5 to 7 quart (5 to 7 L) slow cooker.

Combine next 8 ingredients in medium bowl. Pour over chicken. Do not stir. Cook, covered, on Low for 8 to 10 hours or on High for 4 to 5 hours. Remove and discard bay leaf. Skim and discard fat.

Add basil. Stir. Serves 12.

1 serving: 183 Calories; 4.9 g Total Fat (1.7 g Mono, 1.1 g Poly, 1.3 g Sat); 59 mg Cholesterol; 11 g Carbohydrate; 2 g Fibre; 21 g Protein; 281 mg Sodium

Pictured on page 126.

Ginger Chicken and Quinoa

A satisfying blend of quinoa, a high-protein grain, and tender chicken. Gentle ginger and colourful vegetables help to brighten it up.

Cooking oil	2 tsp.	10 mL
Boneless, skinless chicken thighs, trimmed of fat, halved	2 lbs.	900 g
Sliced carrot (about 1/2 inch, 12 mm, pieces)	1 1/2 cups	375 mL
Sliced leek (white part only), about 1/2 inch (12 mm) pieces	1 1/2 cups	375 mL
Sliced celery	1 cup	250 mL
Dry (or alcohol-free) white wine	1/2 cup	125 mL
Prepared chicken broth	1 1/2 cups	375 mL
Quinoa, rinsed and drained	1 cup	250 mL
Finely grated ginger root (or 3/4 tsp., 4 mL, ground ginger)	1 tbsp.	15 mL
Garlic clove, minced (or 1/4 tsp., 1 mL, powder)	1	1
Granulated sugar	1/4 tsp.	1 mL
Salt	1/8 tsp.	0.5 mL
Pepper	1/4 tsp.	1 mL
Thinly sliced bok choy	1 cup	250 mL
Grated orange zest	1/4 tsp.	1 mL

Heat cooking oil in large frying pan on medium-high. Add chicken. Cook for about 8 minutes, stirring occasionally, until browned. Transfer with slotted spoon to 3 1/2 to 4 quart (3.5 to 4 L) slow cooker. Reduce heat to medium.

Add next 3 ingredients to same frying pan. Cook for about 5 minutes, stirring often, until leek starts to soften. Add wine. Heat and stir, scraping any brown bits from bottom of pan, until boiling. Add to slow cooker.

Add next 7 ingredients. Stir. Cook, covered, on Low for 3 to 4 hours or on High for 1 1/2 to 2 hours.

Add bok choy and orange zest. Stir. Makes about 9 1/2 cups (2.4 L).

1 cup (250 mL): 251 Calories; 9.5 g Total Fat (3.7 g Mono, 2.5 g Poly, 2.3 g Sat); 63 mg Cholesterol; 18 g Carbohydrate; 2 g Fibre; 21 g Protein; 262 mg Sodium

Moroccan Chicken Couscous Pie

These wedges of spiced chicken and couscous have a mild heat that builds—an entirely unexpected dish from your slow cooker!

Canola oil	2 tsp.	10 mL
Lean ground chicken	1 lb.	454 g
Chopped onion	3/4 cup	175 mL
Finely chopped carrot	1/4 cup	60 mL
Finely chopped red pepper	1/4 cup	60 mL
Brown sugar, packed	1 tsp.	5 mL
Ground cumin	1/2 tsp.	2 mL
Salt	1/2 tsp.	2 mL
Pepper	1/2 tsp.	2 mL
Garlic clove, minced	1	1
(or 1/4 tsp., 1 mL, powder)		
Cayenne pepper	1/4 tsp.	1 mL
Ground cinnamon	1/4 tsp.	1 mL
Ground coriander	1/4 tsp.	1 mL
Large egg, fork-beaten	1	1
Whole wheat couscous	3/4 cup	175 mL
Orange juice	1/2 cup	125 mL
Prepared chicken broth	1/2 cup	125 mL
Chopped sliced natural almonds, toasted	3 tbsp.	45 mL
(see Tip, page 267)		
Balsamic vinegar	1 tbsp.	15 mL
Boiling water	2 cups	500 mL

Heat canola oil in large frying pan on medium. Add chicken. Scramble-fry for about 8 minutes until no longer pink. Transfer to large bowl.

Add next 3 ingredients to same frying pan. Cook for about 5 minutes, stirring often, until onion is softened.

Add next 8 ingredients. Heat and stir for about 1 minute until fragrant. Add to chicken.

Add next 6 ingredients. Mix well. Press evenly in greased 8 inch (20 cm) springform pan. Put an even layer (2 to 3 inches, 5 to 7.5 cm, thick) of crumpled foil into bottom of 5 to 7 quart (5 to 7 L) slow cooker (see Tip, page 195). Pour boiling water into slow cooker. Place pan on foil, pushing down gently to settle evenly. Cook, covered, on Low for 5 to 6 hours or on High for 2 1/2 to 3 hours until centre is firm. Transfer pan to wire rack. Let stand for 10 minutes. Cuts into 8 wedges.

1 wedge: 170 Calories; 7.8 g Total Fat (1.7 g Mono, 0.8 g Poly, 1.7 g Sat); 64 mg Cholesterol; 14 g Carbohydrate; 2 g Fibre; 12 g Protein; 240 mg Sodium

Pictured on page 126.

Coconut Mango Chicken

Tender, moist chicken is slow-cooked with a sweet, tropical mango sauce and topped with fresh basil for a tasty, complex flavour combination. Serve alongside brown rice.

Bone-in chicken thighs (5 oz., 140 g, each), trimmed of fat, skin removed	3 lbs.	1.4 kg
Frozen mango pieces, thawed	1 cup	250 mL
Mango chutney	1/4 cup	60 mL
Lime juice	3 tbsp.	45 mL
Small jalapeño pepper, seeds and ribs removed (see Tip, below)	1	1
Garlic cloves, chopped (or 1/2 tsp., 2 mL, powder)	2	2
Salt	1/2 tsp.	2 mL
Pepper	1/4 tsp.	1 mL
Medium unsweetened coconut, toasted (see Tip, page 267)	3 tbsp.	45 mL
Chopped fresh basil	1 tbsp.	15 mL
Grated lime zest (see Tip, page 278)	1/4 tsp.	1 mL

Arrange chicken in greased 3 1/2 to 4 quart (3.5 to 4 L) slow cooker.

Process next 7 ingredients in blender or food processor until smooth. Pour over chicken. Cook, covered, on Low for 6 to 7 hours or on High for 3 to 3 1/2 hours. Transfer chicken with slotted spoon to serving plate. Cover to keep warm. Skim and discard fat from cooking liquid.

Add remaining 3 ingredients to slow cooker. Stir. Serve with chicken. Serves 6.

1 serving: 392 Calories; 19.7 g Total Fat (6.6 g Mono, 3.9 g Poly, 6.1 g Sat); 149 mg Cholesterol; 11 g Carbohydrate; 1 g Fibre; 41 g Protein; 436 mg Sodium

 Hot peppers contain capsaicin in the seeds and ribs. Removing the seeds and ribs will reduce the heat. Wear rubber gloves when handling hot peppers and avoid touching your eyes. Wash your hands well afterward.

Saucy Beans and Chicken

A can of beans, a few slices of bacon and some chicken thighs are all you need for this delicious, all-in-one meal—perfect for when you're hosting a crowd for the playoffs!

Chopped onion	1 cup	250 mL
Bacon slices, diced	3	3
Bone-in chicken thighs, skin removed	3 lbs.	1.4 kg
Salt, sprinkle		
Pepper, sprinkle		
Can of baked beans in tomato sauce (14 oz., 398 mL)	1	1
Grated Cheddar cheese	1/2 cup	125 mL

Heat large frying pan on medium-high. Add onion and bacon. Cook for about 5 minutes, stirring often, until onion is softened. Transfer with slotted spoon to 4 to 5 quart (4 to 5 L) slow cooker.

Add chicken to same frying pan. Sprinkle with salt and pepper. Cook on medium-high for about 3 minutes per side until browned. Transfer to slow cooker. Cook, covered, on Low for 6 to 7 hours or on High for 3 to 3 1/2 hours. Transfer chicken with slotted spoon to medium bowl. Skim and discard fat from cooking liquid.

Add beans and cheese. Stir. Return chicken to slow cooker. Cook, covered, on High for about 15 minutes until heated through. Serves 4.

1 serving: 579 Calories; 27.9 g Total Fat (10.4 g Mono, 5.2 g Poly, 9.2 g Sat); 192 mg Cholesterol; 23 g Carbohydrate; 5 g Fibre; 56 g Protein; 869 mg Sodium

Thai Green Curry Chicken

This saucy curry has melt-in-your-mouth chicken, crisp colourful vegetables and an authentic coconut flavour. Serve with fragrant jasmine or basmati rice.

Boneless, skinless chicken thighs, halved	2 lbs.	900 g
Salt, sprinkle		
Pepper, sprinkle		
Thai green curry paste	2 tbsp.	30 mL
Water	1 1/2 cups	385 mL
Can of coconut milk (14 oz., 398 mL)	1	1
Cornstarch	2 tbsp.	30 mL
Frozen Oriental mixed vegetables, thawed	4 1/2 cups	1.1 L

Heat large well-greased frying pan on medium-high. Cook chicken, in 2 batches, for about 3 minutes per side until browned. Transfer to 4 to 5 quart (4 to 5 L) slow cooker. Sprinkle with salt and pepper.

Add curry paste and water to same frying pan. Heat and stir, scraping any brown bits from bottom of pan, until boiling. Add to slow cooker. Cook, covered, on Low for 6 to 7 hours or on High for 3 to 3 1/2 hours.

Stir coconut milk into cornstarch in medium bowl until smooth. Add to chicken mixture. Stir. Add vegetables. Stir. Cook, covered, on High for about 45 minutes until bubbling. Makes about 7 1/2 cups (1.9 L).

1 cup (250 mL): 337 Calories; 23.1 g Total Fat (5.0 g Mono, 2.7 g Poly, 12.9 g Sat); 79 mg Cholesterol; 9 g Carbohydrate; 2 g Fibre; 24 g Protein; 326 mg Sodium

Sloppy Jennies

A flavourful low-fat version of a classic, perfect for serving over whole wheat Kaiser rolls or spooning over multi-grain toast. The sweetness is nicely balanced with savoury dill and vegetables.

Canola oil	1 tsp.	5 mL
Lean ground turkey thigh	1 1/2 lbs.	680 g
Salt	1/4 tsp.	1 mL
Pepper	1/2 tsp.	2 mL
Chopped onion	2 cups	500 mL
Can of diced tomatoes (with juice) (14 oz., 398 mL)	1	1
Thinly sliced celery	1 1/2 cups	375 mL
Tomato paste (see Tip, page 83)	1/4 cup	60 mL
Dried dillweed	1 tsp.	5 mL
Granulated sugar	1 tsp.	5 mL
Chopped fresh spinach leaves, lightly packed	3 cups	750 mL

Heat canola oil in large frying pan on medium-high. Add turkey. Sprinkle with salt and pepper. Scramble-fry for about 5 minutes until no longer pink. Transfer to 3 1/2 to 4 quart (3.5 to 4 L) slow cooker.

Add next 6 ingredients. Stir. Cook, covered, on Low for 8 to 9 hours or on High for 4 to 4 1/2 hours.

Add spinach. Stir. Cook, covered, on High for about 5 minutes until spinach is wilted. Makes about 5 1/2 cups (1.4 L).

1 cup (250 mL): 232 Calories; 8.7 g Total Fat (0.5 g Mono, 0.3 g Poly, 2.3 g Sat); 71 mg Cholesterol; 13 g Carbohydrate; 3 g Fibre; 27 g Protein; 410 mg Sodium

Spanish Chicken with Bulgur

A thick, and filling blend of bulgur, tender chicken and olives, all finished with a sprinkle of fresh cilantro.

Boneless, skinless chicken thighs, trimmed of fat, halved	2 lbs.	900 g
Prepared chicken broth	1 1/2 cups	375 mL
Water	1/2 cup	125 mL
Chopped pitted prunes	1/4 cup	60 mL
Sliced green olives	1/4 cup	60 mL
Brown sugar, packed	2 tbsp.	30 mL
White wine vinegar	2 tbsp.	30 mL
Dried oregano	2 tsp.	10 mL
Bay leaf	1	1
Garlic clove, minced (or 1/4 tsp., 1 mL, powder)	1	1
Paprika	1/2 tsp.	2 mL
Pepper	1/2 tsp.	2 mL
Chopped red pepper	1 1/2 cups	375 mL
Bulgur, coarse grind	1 cup	250 mL
Chopped fresh cilantro (or parsley)	1 tbsp.	15 mL

Combine first 12 ingredients in 3 1/2 to 4 quart (3.5 to 4 L) slow cooker. Cook, covered, on Low for 5 to 6 hours or on High for 2 1/2 to 3 hours. Skim and discard fat. Remove and discard bay leaf.

Add red pepper and bulgur. Stir. Cook, covered, on High for about 30 minutes until red pepper and bulgur are tender.

Add cilantro. Stir. Makes about 7 cups (1.75 L).

1 cup (250 mL): 312 Calories; 11.4 g Total Fat (4.6 g Mono, 2.6 g Poly, 3.0 g Sat); 85 mg Cholesterol; 25 g Carbohydrate; 5 g Fibre; 27 g Protein; 345 mg Sodium

Spinach Chicken Rolls

Inviting spirals of chicken stuffed with flavourful spinach—an elegant main course that won't leave you feeling like you've overindulged.

Canola oil	1/2 tsp.	2 mL
Chopped onion	1 cup	250 mL
Dried thyme	1/4 tsp.	1 mL
Salt, sprinkle		
Pepper	1/4 tsp.	1 mL
Dry (or alcohol-free) white wine	1/2 cup	125 mL
Box of frozen chopped spinach (10 oz., 300 g), thawed and squeezed dry	1	1
Finely chopped roasted red peppers	2 tbsp.	30 mL
Italian seasoning	1/2 tsp.	2 mL
Boneless, skinless chicken breast halves (4 oz., 113 g, each)	6	6
Dijon mustard	1 1/2 tsp.	7 mL
Prepared chicken broth	2 cups	500 mL
Minute tapioca	2 tbsp.	30 mL

Heat canola oil in large frying pan on medium. Add next 4 ingredients. Cook for about 10 minutes, stirring often, until onion is softened.

Add wine. Heat and stir, scraping any brown bits from bottom of pan, until boiling. Transfer to 3 1/2 to 4 quart (3.5 to 4 L) slow cooker.

Combine next 3 ingredients in small bowl.

Place 1 chicken breast between 2 sheets of plastic wrap. Pound with mallet or rolling pin to 1/2 inch (12 mm) thickness. Spread mustard over chicken. Spread spinach mixture over mustard. Roll up tightly, jelly roll-style, from short side. Secure with wooden pick. Repeat with remaining chicken, mustard and spinach mixture. Arrange chicken rolls over onion mixture.

Combine broth and tapioca in medium bowl. Pour over top. Cook, covered, on High for 2 to 2 1/2 hours until internal temperature of rolls reaches 170°F (77°C). Transfer rolls to cutting board. Remove wooden picks. Cover to keep warm. Skim and discard fat from cooking liquid. Carefully process in blender until smooth (see Safety Tip, page 9). Slice chicken rolls. Serve with sauce. Serves 6.

1 roll with 1/4 cup (60 mL) sauce: 171 Calories; 1.9 g Total Fat (0.6 g Mono, 0.4 g Poly, 0.5 g Sat); 66 mg Cholesterol; 6 g Carbohydrate; 1 g Fibre; 28 g Protein; 381 mg Sodium

Pulled Chicken Fajitas

Pulled chicken, salsa and tortilla wraps are delicious on their own, but can easily be made more elaborate—add shredded lettuce, sour cream, guacamole, cheese, sliced green onion or jalapeño.

Boneless, skinless chicken breast halves	1 1/2 lbs.	680 g
Taco seasoning mix, stir before measuring	2 tbsp.	30 mL
Chunky salsa	1 1/2 cups	375 mL
Thinly sliced mixed peppers	2 cups	500 mL
Chunky salsa	1/2 cup	125 mL
Flour tortillas (9 inch, 22 cm, diameter)	8	8

Put chicken into 3 1/2 to 4 quart (3.5 to 4 L) slow cooker. Sprinkle with seasoning mix. Pour first amount of salsa over top. Cook, covered, on Low for 6 to 7 hours or on High for 3 to 3 1/2 hours. Transfer chicken to large plate. Shred with 2 forks. Return to slow cooker.

Add peppers and second amount of salsa. Stir. Cook, covered, on High for about 30 minutes until peppers are tender-crisp.

Spoon about 3/4 cup (175 mL) chicken mixture down centre of each tortilla. Fold bottom end of tortilla over filling. Fold in sides, leaving top end open. Makes 8 fajitas.

1 fajita: 266 Calories; 6.7 g Total Fat (0.9 g Mono, 0.6 g Poly, 1.7 g Sat); 50 mg Cholesterol; 31 g Carbohydrate; 1 g Fibre; 22 g Protein; 926 mg Sodium

Pictured on page 107.

Wheat Chicken Chili

This tasty chili has the surprising addition of chewy wheat, giving it even more fibre! Store in an airtight container in the freezer for up to three months.

Hard red wheat	1 cup	250 mL
Chopped onion	1 cup	250 mL
Chopped carrot	1 1/2 cups	375 mL
Chopped red pepper	1 cup	250 mL
Boneless, skinless chicken thighs, trimmed of fat, cut into 3/4 inch (2 cm) pieces	1 lb.	454 g
Can of diced tomatoes (with juice) (28 oz., 796 mL)	1	1
Can of red kidney beans (14 oz., 398 mL), rinsed and drained	1	1
Prepared chicken broth	1 1/2 cups	375 mL
Granulated sugar	1 tbsp.	15 mL
Finely chopped chipotle peppers in adobo sauce (see Tip, page 56)	1 tsp.	5 mL
Chili powder	1/2 tsp.	2 mL
Garlic powder	1/2 tsp.	2 mL
Salt	1/2 tsp.	2 mL
Ground cumin	1/4 tsp.	1 mL

Layer first 5 ingredients, in order given, in 3 1/2 to 4 quart (3.5 to 4 L) slow cooker.

Combine remaining 9 ingredients in large bowl. Pour over chicken. Do not stir. Cook, covered, on Low for 8 to 10 hours or on High for 4 to 5 hours. Makes about 9 cups (2.25 L).

1 cup (250 mL): 236 Calories; 4.9 g Total Fat (1.6 g Mono, 1.1 g Poly, 1.2 g Sat); 33 mg Cholesterol; 31 g Carbohydrate; 7 g Fibre; 17 g Protein; 602 mg Sodium

Pictured on page 108.

174

Poultry

Chicken Pesto Lasagna

Serve this rich, cheesy lasagna with a green salad and toasty garlic bread. Customize the flavour by using your favourite pasta sauce!

Chopped cooked chicken	3 cups	750 mL
Basil pesto	1/4 cup	60 mL
Tomato pasta sauce	4 cups	1 L
Cooked lasagna noodles	9	9
Grated Italian cheese blend	4 cups	1 L

Combine chicken and pesto in medium bowl.

To assemble, layer ingredients in greased 5 to 7 quart (5 to 7 L) slow cooker as follows:

1. 1 cup (250 mL) pasta sauce

2. 3 lasagna noodles

3. 1 cup (250 mL) chicken mixture

4. 1 cup (250 mL) cheese

5. 1 cup (250 mL) pasta sauce

6. 3 lasagna noodles

7. 1 cup (250 mL) chicken mixture

8. 1 cup (250 mL) cheese

9. 1 cup (250 mL) pasta sauce

10. Remaining lasagna noodles

11. Remaining chicken mixture

12. Remaining pasta sauce

13. Remaining cheese

Cook, covered, on Low for 4 to 5 hours or on High for 2 to 2 1/2 hours until heated through. Let stand, uncovered, for 10 minutes. Serves 6.

1 serving: 648 Calories; 34.0 g Total Fat (2.3 g Mono, 1.5 g Poly, 13 g Sat); 122 mg Cholesterol; 36 g Carbohydrate; 1 g Fibre; 48 g Protein; 1312 mg Sodium

Chicken Seafood Paella

Mildly spiced with smoked paprika, this paella's (pie-AY-yuh) combination of rice, chicken and seafood is a great introduction to the wonderful world of Spanish cuisine.

Boneless, skinless chicken thighs, halved	1 lb.	454 g
Smoked sweet paprika	3/4 tsp.	4 mL
Salt, sprinkle		
Pepper, sprinkle		
Package of Spanish-style rice mix (14 oz., 397 g)	1	1
Water	3 1/2 cups	875 mL
Frozen seafood medley, thawed	1/2 lb.	340 g
Frozen peas, thawed	1 cup	250 mL

Heat large greased frying pan on medium-high. Add chicken. Sprinkle with paprika, salt and pepper. Cook for about 3 minutes per side until browned. Transfer to 3 1/2 to 4 quart (3.5 to 4 L) slow cooker.

Add rice mix and water to slow cooker. Stir. Cook, covered, on Low for 6 to 7 hours or on High for 3 to 3 1/2 hours.

Add seafood and peas. Stir gently. Cook, covered, on High for about 20 minutes until seafood is cooked. Makes about 8 1/2 cups (2.1 L).

1 cup (250 mL): 162 Calories; 5.6 g Total Fat (2.2 g Mono, 1.4 g Poly, 1.4 g Sat); 86 mg Cholesterol; 11 g Carbohydrate; 2 g Fibre; 17 g Protein; 274 mg Sodium

Chicken Siciliana

Olives and capers intensify the flavours of this sauce rich with chicken and eggplant. Sicily traditionally specializes in tube-shaped pasta, so serve with tubetti, macaroni or penne for an authentic touch.

Boneless, skinless chicken thighs, quartered	1 1/2 lbs.	680 g
Balsamic vinegar	2 tbsp.	30 mL
Chopped peeled eggplant (1/2 inch, 12 mm, pieces)	4 cups	1 L
Spicy tomato pasta sauce	3 cups	750 mL
Black olive tapenade	1/4 cup	60 mL

Heat large greased frying pan on medium-high. Add chicken. Cook for 3 minutes per side until browned. Add balsamic vinegar. Stir. Transfer to 3 1/2 to 4 quart (3.5 to 4 L) slow cooker.

(continued on next page)

Add eggplant and tomato sauce. Stir. Cook, covered, on Low for 8 to 10 hours or on High for 4 to 5 hours.

Add tapenade. Stir. Makes about 7 cups (1.75 L).

1 cup (250 mL): 212 Calories; 9.6 g Total Fat (3.2 g Mono, 1.9 g Poly, 2.2 g Sat); 64 mg Cholesterol; 11 g Carbohydrate; 2 g Fibre; 20 g Protein; 748 mg Sodium

Florentine Chicken Lasagna

This colourful, well-layered lasagna has healthy, delicious ingredients such as spinach and lean chicken paired with rich tomato and cheese flavour.

Lean ground chicken (or turkey)	1 lb.	454 g
Tomato cheese pasta sauce	4 cups	1 L
Water	1/2 cup	125 mL
Grated Italian cheese blend	2 cups	500 mL
Oven-ready lasagna noodles, broken in half	9	9
Boxes of frozen chopped spinach (10 oz., 300 g, each), thawed, squeezed dry	2	2

Scramble-fry chicken in large greased frying pan on medium-high for about 5 minutes until no longer pink.

Add pasta sauce and water. Stir.

To assemble, layer ingredients in greased 5 to 7 quart (5 to 7 L) slow cooker as follows:

1. 1 1/4 cups (300 mL) chicken mixture

2. 1/4 cup (60 mL) cheese

3. 6 lasagna noodle halves

4. 1/3 spinach

5. 1 1/4 cups (300 mL) chicken mixture

6. 1/4 cup (60 mL) cheese

Repeat steps 3, 4, 5 and 6 twice to make another 2 layers. Top with remaining cheese. Cook, covered, on Low for 4 to 5 hours or on High for 2 to 2 1/2 hours. Let stand, uncovered, for 10 minutes. Serves 6.

1 serving: 489 Calories; 20.9 g Total Fat (0.4 g Mono, 0.2 g Poly, 7.1 g Sat); 77 mg Cholesterol; 48 g Carbohydrate; 5 g Fibre; 31 g Protein; 1265 mg Sodium

Chicken Sausage Pasta Sauce

This thick and chunky pasta sauce is best served with bite-sized pastas. You can also use it in your favourite lasagna recipe.

Chicken (or turkey) sausage, casing removed	1 1/2 lbs.	680 g
Finely chopped onion	1/2 cup	125 mL
Tomato basil pasta sauce	3 cups	750 mL
Chopped fresh white mushrooms	1 cup	250 mL
Chopped zucchini (with peel)	1 cup	250 mL

Scramble-fry sausage and onion in large greased frying pan on medium-high for about 10 minutes, until sausage is no longer pink. Drain. Transfer to 4 to 5 quart (4 to 5 L) slow cooker.

Add remaining 3 ingredients. Stir. Cook, covered, on Low for 4 to 5 hours or on High for 2 to 2 1/2 hours. Makes about 6 cups (1.5 L).

1/2 cup (125 mL): 149 Calories; 7.5 g Total Fat (1.7 g Mono, 0.9 g Poly, 3.6 g Sat); 40 mg Cholesterol; 6 g Carbohydrate; trace Fibre; 13 g Protein; 277 mg Sodium

Pictured on page 179.

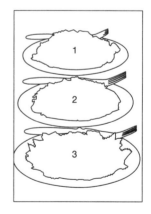

1. Italiano Pasta Sauce, page 150
2. Veggie Pasta Sauce, page 229
3. Chicken Sausage Pasta Sauce, above

Chicken in Mushroom Sauce

Creamy, smoky bacon and mushroom sauce coats well-seasoned chicken,
perfect to serve over a bed of noodles.

Bacon slices, diced	6	6
Boneless, skinless chicken thighs	2 lbs.	900 g
Pepper, sprinkle		
Can of condensed cream of mushroom	1	1
(10 oz., 284 mL)		
Prepared chicken broth	1 cup	250 mL
Dried thyme	3/4 tsp.	4 mL
Water	1 cup	250 mL

Cook bacon in large frying pan on medium until crisp. Transfer with slotted spoon to plate lined with paper towel to drain. Drain and discard all but 1 tbsp. (15 mL) drippings.

Cook chicken in same frying pan, in 2 batches, for about 5 minutes per side until browned. Transfer with slotted spoon to 3 1/2 to 4 quart (3.5 to 4 L) slow cooker. Drain and discard drippings. Scatter bacon over chicken. Sprinkle with pepper.

Add remaining 4 ingredients to same frying pan. Heat and stir, scraping any brown bits from bottom of pan, until boiling. Add to slow cooker. Cook, covered, on Low for 6 to 7 hours or on High for 3 to 3 1/2 hours. Serves 8.

1 serving: 236 Calories; 14.3 g Total Fat (4.9 g Mono, 2.4 g Poly, 4.1 g Sat); 83 mg Cholesterol; 3 g Carbohydrate; trace Fibre; 23 g Protein; 619 mg Sodium

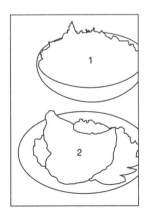

1. Sausage, Kale and Bean Stew, page 148
2. Jamaican Pork and Couscous, page 129

Props: KJ MacAlister

Cranberry Chicken Wings

These tasty wings are glazed with sweet and savoury sauce with a hint of cranberry tartness.

Split chicken wings, tips discarded	3 lbs.	1.4 kg
Can of jellied cranberry sauce (14 oz., 398 mL)	1	1
Barbecue sauce	1/2 cup	125 mL
Brown sugar, packed	1/4 cup	60 mL
Dijon mustard	2 tsp.	10 mL

Arrange chicken wings on greased baking sheet with sides. Broil on top rack in oven for about 6 minutes per side until browned. Transfer to 3 1/2 to 4 quart (3.5 to 4 L) slow cooker.

Whisk remaining 4 ingredients in medium bowl until smooth. Pour over chicken. Cook, covered, on Low for 4 to 5 hours or on High for 2 to 2 1/2 hours, stirring at halftime. Makes about 36 pieces.

1 wing: 109 Calories; 6.1 g Total Fat (trace Mono, trace Poly, 1.6 g Sat); 28 mg Cholesterol; 6 g Carbohydrate; trace Fibre; 7 g Protein; 63 mg Sodium

Orange Chicken and Rice

Vibrant citrus flavour infuses light and fluffy rice, served alongside tender, seasoned chicken.

Medium oranges	2	2
Long-grain white rice	2 cups	500 mL
Prepared chicken broth	2 cups	500 mL
Italian dressing	2 tbsp.	30 mL
Water	1 cup	250 mL
Salt	1/4 tsp.	1 mL
Pepper	1/4 tsp.	1 mL
Boneless, skinless chicken thighs	1 1/2 lbs.	680 g
Salt, sprinkle		
Italian dressing	3 tbsp.	45 mL

Grate 1 tsp. (5 mL) orange zest into 3 1/2 to 4 quart (3.5 to 4 L) slow cooker. Squeeze 1/2 cup (125 mL) orange juice and pour into slow cooker.

Add rice, broth, first amount of dressing, water, salt and pepper. Stir.

Put chicken into medium bowl. Sprinkle with salt. Pour second amount of dressing over top. Stir until coated. Heat large greased frying pan on medium-high. Add chicken. Discard any remaining dressing. Cook for about 3 minutes per side until browned. Arrange over rice mixture. Cook, covered, on Low for 4 to 5 hours or High for 2 to 2 1/2 hours. Serves 6.

1 serving: 466 Calories; 13.8 g Total Fat (4.0 g Mono, 2.4 g Poly, 3.1 g Sat); 74 mg Cholesterol; 56 g Carbohydrate; 1 g Fibre; 26 g Protein; 1012 mg Sodium

Lemonade Chicken

What says summer better than lemonade and barbecued chicken? Combine them in this flavourful chicken-and-potato meal and recreate the taste of summer all year.

All-purpose flour	1/3 cup	75 mL
Salt, sprinkle		
Pepper, sprinkle		
Bone-in chicken thighs, skin removed	3 lbs.	1.4 kg
Baby potatoes, larger ones cut in half	1 lb.	454 g
Frozen concentrated lemonade, thawed	3/4 cup	175 mL
Barbecue sauce	1/4 cup	60 mL

Combine flour, salt and pepper in large resealable freezer bag. Add chicken. Seal bag. Toss until coated. Remove chicken. Discard any remaining flour mixture.

Put potatoes into 3 1/2 to 4 quart (3.5 to 4 L) slow cooker. Arrange chicken over top.

Combine concentrated lemonade and barbecue sauce in small bowl. Pour over chicken. Cook, covered, on Low for 8 to 10 hours or on High for 4 to 5 hours. Serves 4.

1 serving: 607 Calories; 20.1 g Total Fat (7.6 g Mono, 4.6 g Poly, 5.5 g Sat); 172 mg Cholesterol; 53 g Carbohydrate; 2 g Fibre; 51 g Protein; 441 mg Sodium

Greek Lemon Drumettes

Savour the flavours of the Mediterranean with the fresh Parmesan, lemon and herb coating on these drumettes. Serve with fresh lemon wedges for an extra squeeze of citrus flavour.

Lemon yogurt	3/4 cup	175 mL
Chicken drumettes	3 lbs.	1.4 kg
Grated Parmesan cheese	1 1/2 cups	375 mL
Fine dry bread crumbs	1/2 cup	125 mL
Greek seasoning	2 tsp.	10 mL
Salt, sprinkle		
Pepper, sprinkle		

Measure yogurt into large bowl. Add drumettes. Stir until coated.

Combine remaining 5 ingredients in large resealable freezer bag. Add 1/3 of drumettes. Seal bag. Toss until coated. Repeat with remaining drumettes. Put drumettes into greased 3 1/2 to 4 quart (3.5 to 4 L) slow cooker. Cook, covered, on Low for 8 to 9 hours or High for 4 to 4 1/2 hours. Makes about 24 drumettes.

1 drumette: 173 Calories; 11.5 g Total Fat (trace Mono, trace Poly, 3.9 g Sat); 50 mg Cholesterol; 3 g Carbohydrate; trace Fibre; 14 g Protein; 217 mg Sodium

Chicken and Rice Casserole

When you're in need of comfort food, settle in with a bowl of this creamy rice casserole full of broccoli and tender chicken pieces.

Long-grain brown rice	1 1/2 cups	375 mL
Can of condensed cream of broccoli soup (10 oz., 284 mL)	1	1
Can of condensed cream of chicken soup (10 oz., 284 mL)	1	1
Water	1 1/2 cups	375 mL
Boneless, skinless chicken thighs	1 1/2 lbs.	680 g
Salt, sprinkle		
Pepper, sprinkle		
Frozen chopped broccoli, thawed	3 cups	750 mL

Combine first 4 ingredients in greased 3 1/2 to 4 quart (3.5 to 4 L) slow cooker.

Heat large greased frying pan on medium-high. Add chicken. Sprinkle with salt and pepper. Cook for about 3 minutes per side until browned. Arrange chicken over rice mixture in slow cooker. Cook, covered, on Low for 6 to 7 hours or on High for 3 to 3 1/2 hours.

Add broccoli. Stir. Cook, covered, on High for about 15 minutes until broccoli is tender. Makes about 7 1/2 cups (1.9 L).

1 cup (250 mL): 368 Calories; 12.3 g Total Fat (4.0 g Mono, 2.9 g Poly, 3.1 g Sat); 64 mg Cholesterol; 41 g Carbohydrate; 5 g Fibre; 24 g Protein; 687 mg Sodium

Chicken Artichoke Stew

The tangy flavours of dill, citrus and artichoke combine with tender chicken for a meal your dinner guests won't soon forget.

All-purpose flour	2 tbsp.	30 mL
Boneless, skinless chicken thighs, trimmed of fat, halved	1 1/2 lbs.	680 g
Canola oil	1 tbsp.	15 mL
Coarsely chopped onion	1 1/2 cups	375 mL
Sliced carrot (about 1/2 inch, 12 mm, pieces)	2 cups	500 mL
Can of artichoke hearts (14 oz., 398 mL), drained and quartered	1	1
Prepared chicken broth	2 cups	500 mL
Tomato paste (see Tip, page 83)	2 tbsp.	30 mL
Grated orange zest	1 tsp.	5 mL
Salt	1/4 tsp.	1 mL
Pepper	1/4 tsp.	1 mL
Water	1 tbsp.	15 mL
Cornstarch	2 tsp.	10 mL
Chopped fresh dill (or 3/4 tsp., 4 mL, dried)	1 tbsp.	15 mL

Put flour into large resealable freezer bag. Add chicken. Seal bag. Toss until coated. Remove chicken. Discard any remaining flour.

Heat canola oil in large frying pan on medium. Add chicken. Cook for about 10 minutes, stirring occasionally, until browned.

Layer next 3 ingredients, in order given, in 3 1/2 to 4 quart (3.5 to 4 L) slow cooker. Arrange chicken over top.

Stir next 5 ingredients in medium bowl until smooth. Pour over chicken. Do not stir. Cook, covered, on Low for 7 to 8 hours or on High for 3 1/2 to 4 hours. Transfer chicken and vegetables with slotted spoon to serving bowl. Cover to keep warm.

Stir water into cornstarch in small cup until smooth. Add to slow cooker. Add dill. Stir. Cook, covered, on High for about 15 minutes until boiling and thickened. Add to chicken mixture. Stir. Makes about 6 1/4 cups (1.5 L).

1 cup (250 mL): 269 Calories; 11.1 g Total Fat (4.6 g Mono, 2.7 g Poly, 2.6 g Sat); 71 mg Cholesterol; 19 g Carbohydrate; 6 g Fibre; 24 g Protein; 504 mg Sodium

Chicken Stew

For a family-friendly meal, nothing beats a simple yet hearty chicken stew with rich, comforting flavours—and don't forget biscuits for dipping!

Halved red (or yellow) baby potatoes	2 cups	500 mL
Boneless, skinless chicken thighs, cut into 1 inch (2.5 cm) pieces	1 1/2 lbs.	680 g
Poultry seasoning	1/2 tsp.	2 mL
Salt, sprinkle		
Pepper, sprinkle		
Envelopes of chicken gravy mix (1 oz., 31 g, each)	2	2
Water	2 cups	500 mL
Frozen pea and carrot mix, thawed	2 cups	500 mL

Put potatoes into 3 1/2 to 4 quart (3.5 to 4 L) slow cooker. Arrange chicken over top. Sprinkle with poultry seasoning, salt and pepper.

Combine gravy mix and water in medium bowl. Pour over chicken. Cook, covered, on Low for 6 to 8 hours or on High for 3 to 4 hours.

Add peas and carrots. Stir. Cook, covered, on High for about 30 minutes until vegetables are tender. Makes about 8 cups (2 L).

1 cup (250 mL): 207 Calories; 7.6 g Total Fat (2.4 g Mono, 1.5 g Poly, 1.8 g Sat); 56 mg Cholesterol; 16 g Carbohydrate; 2 g Fibre; 17 g Protein; 498 mg Sodium

Pictured on page 143.

Satay Chicken Stew

The flavours of peanut butter and tomato are a tasty combo in this mildly spicy chicken stew—great served over rice or mashed sweet potatoes.

Boneless, skinless chicken breast halves, cut into 1 inch (2.5 cm) cubes	1 1/2 lbs.	680 g
Pepper, sprinkle		
Quartered fresh white mushrooms	3 cups	750 mL
Hot salsa	1 1/2 cups	375 mL
Tomato paste	2 tbsp.	30 mL
Water	1/2 cup	125 mL
Crunchy peanut butter	1/2 cup	125 mL

Heat large greased frying pan on medium-high. Add chicken. Sprinkle with pepper. Cook for about 6 minutes, stirring occasionally, until browned. Transfer to 3 1/2 to 4 quart (3.5 to 4 L) slow cooker.

Add mushrooms to same greased frying pan. Cook for about 5 minutes, stirring occasionally, until starting to brown. Add to slow cooker.

Combine salsa, tomato paste and water in small bowl. Pour over mushrooms. Cook, covered, on Low for 6 to 7 hours or on High for 3 to 3 1/2 hours.

Add peanut butter. Stir well. Makes about 4 cups (1 L).

3/4 cup (175 mL): 349 Calories; 17.8 g Total Fat (2.4 g Mono, 1.4 g Poly, 3.5 g Sat); 75 mg Cholesterol; 13 g Carbohydrate; 2 g Fibre; 34 g Protein; 431 mg Sodium

Shiitake Ginger Chicken

This sweet and spicy sauce infuses chicken morsels and shiitake mushrooms with wonderful ginger flavour.

Thinly sliced fresh shiitake mushrooms	2 cups	500 mL
Boneless, skinless chicken thighs	2 lbs.	900 g
Ginger marmalade	3/4 cup	175 mL
Soy sauce	3 tbsp.	45 mL
Finely grated ginger root	2 tbsp.	30 mL
Water	1/3 cup	75 mL

Heat large greased frying pan on medium. Add mushrooms. Cook for about 5 minutes, stirring often, until mushrooms start to release their liquid. Transfer to 3 1/2 to 4 quart (3.5 to 4 L) slow cooker.

Arrange chicken over mushrooms.

Combine remaining 4 ingredients in small bowl. Pour over chicken. Cook, covered, on Low for 5 to 6 hours or on High for 2 1/2 to 3 hours. Transfer chicken and half of solids with slotted spoon to large serving platter. Cover to keep warm. Skim and discard fat from cooking liquid. Carefully process with remaining solids in blender until smooth (see Safety Tip, page 9). Pour sauce over chicken and mushrooms. Serves 8.

1 serving: 254 Calories; 9.2 g Total Fat (3.6 g Mono, 2.1 g Poly, 2.4 g Sat); 74 mg Cholesterol; 22 g Carbohydrate; 1 g Fibre; 22 g Protein; 582 mg Sodium

Sweet Chili Chicken

Tender, sweet chicken with a hint of chili will be a hit with the kids! Make it a meal with rice and steamed vegetables.

Boneless, skinless chicken thighs	2 lbs.	900 g
Salt, sprinkle		
Pepper, sprinkle		
Prepared chicken broth	2/3 cup	150 mL
Sweet chili sauce	1/4 cup	60 mL
Minute tapioca	3 tbsp.	45 mL
Soy sauce	1 tbsp.	15 mL
Sweet chili sauce	1/4 cup	60 mL

(continued on next page)

Heat large greased frying pan on medium-high. Add chicken. Sprinkle with salt and pepper. Cook for about 3 minutes per side until browned. Transfer to 3 1/2 to 4 quart (3.5 to 4 L) slow cooker.

Combine broth, first amount of chili sauce, tapioca and soy sauce in small bowl. Pour over chicken. Cook, covered, on Low for 6 to 7 hours or on High for 3 to 3 1/2 hours.

Add second amount of chili sauce. Stir. Serves 8.

1 serving: 213 Calories; 9.2 g Total Fat (3.6 g Mono, 2.1 g Poly, 2.4 g Sat); 74 mg Cholesterol; 10 g Carbohydrate; trace Fibre; 21 g Protein; 571 mg Sodium

---

Pineapple Chicken

This sweet and saucy chicken dish can be served over steamed rice with a simple veggie stir-fry.

Boneless, skinless chicken thighs, quartered	1 1/2 lbs.	680 g
Can of pineapple tidbits (with juice) (19 oz., 540 mL)	1	1
Thinly sliced carrot	2 cups	500 mL
Thick teriyaki basting sauce	1/2 cup	125 mL
Water	2 tbsp.	30 mL
Cornstarch	1 1/2 tbsp.	25 mL

Heat large greased frying pan on medium-high. Add chicken. Cook for 3 minutes per side until browned. Transfer to 3 1/2 to 4 quart (3.5 to 4 L) slow cooker.

Add pineapple to same frying pan. Heat and stir until boiling. Add to slow cooker.

Add carrot and teriyaki sauce to slow cooker. Stir. Cook, covered, on Low for 6 to 7 hours or on High for 3 to 3 1/2 hours.

Stir water into cornstarch in small cup until smooth. Add to chicken mixture. Stir. Cook, covered, on High for about 10 minutes until sauce is slightly thickened. Makes about 6 cups (1.5 L).

1 cup (250 mL): 268 Calories; 9.4 g Total Fat (3.7 g Mono, 2.2 g Poly, 2.4 g Sat); 74 mg Cholesterol; 25 g Carbohydrate; 2 g Fibre; 21 g Protein; 646 mg Sodium

Pictured on page 143.

Turkey-stuffed Peppers

Vibrant red peppers brimming with ground turkey and brown rice create a hearty, yet light meal with lean ingredients.

Large red peppers	6	6
Canola oil	2 tsp.	10 mL
Lean ground turkey	1 lb.	454 g
Chopped celery	1 cup	250 mL
Chopped onion	1 cup	250 mL
Garlic cloves, minced (or 1/2 tsp., 2 mL, powder)	2	2
Cooked long-grain brown rice (about 2/3 cup, 150 mL, uncooked)	2 cups	500 mL
Can of diced tomatoes (with juice) (14 oz., 398 mL)		
Chopped fresh parsley (or 1 1/2 tsp., 7 mL, flakes)	1/4 cup	60 mL
Sliced green onion	1/4 cup	60 mL
Grated lemon zest	1 tsp.	5 mL
Grated orange zest	1/2 tsp.	2 mL
Ground allspice	1/2 tsp.	2 mL
Salt	1/4 tsp.	1 mL
Pepper	1/4 tsp.	1 mL
Water	1 1/2 cups	375 mL

Cut 1/2 inch (12 mm) from top of each red pepper. Remove seeds and ribs. Trim bottom of each pepper so it will sit flat, being careful not to cut into cavity. Set aside. Dice tops of peppers surrounding stem. Discard stems.

Heat canola oil in large frying pan on medium-high. Add turkey. Scramble-fry for about 7 minutes until turkey is no longer pink.

Add next 3 ingredients. Cook for about 5 minutes, stirring often, until celery is softened. Remove from heat.

Add next 9 ingredients and diced red pepper. Stir. Spoon into prepared peppers. Arrange upright in 7 quart (7 L) slow cooker.

Pour water around stuffed peppers. Cook, covered, on Low for 4 to 5 hours or on High for 2 to 2 1/2 hours. Makes 6 stuffed peppers.

1 stuffed pepper: 262 Calories; 7.4 g Total Fat (1.2 g Mono, 1.0 g Poly, 1.7 g Sat); 43 mg Cholesterol; 31 g Carbohydrate; 6 g Fibre; 19 g Protein; 330 mg Sodium

Cranberry Turkey Roast

Moist, delicious turkey is always welcome on festive occasions—and with this recipe you won't have to deal with a whole bird! This low-fat offering also comes with plenty of tangy gravy flavoured with orange and cranberry.

Canola oil	1 tsp.	5 mL
Boneless, skin-on turkey breast roast	3 lbs.	1.4 kg
Salt	1/4 tsp.	1 mL
Pepper	1/4 tsp.	1 mL
Orange juice	1 cup	250 mL
Fresh (or frozen, thawed) cranberries	1/2 cup	125 mL
Prepared chicken broth	1/2 cup	125 mL
Minute tapioca	2 tbsp.	30 mL
Brown sugar, packed	1 tbsp.	15 mL
Ground allspice	1/2 tsp.	2 mL

Heat canola oil in large frying pan on medium-high. Sprinkle roast with salt and pepper. Add to pan. Cook for about 5 minutes, turning occasionally, until browned on all sides. Transfer to 4 to 5 quart (4 to 5 L) slow cooker.

Process remaining 6 ingredients in blender or food processor until smooth. Pour over roast. Cook, covered, on Low for 5 to 6 hours or on High for 2 1/2 to 3 hours until internal temperature reaches 170°F (77°C). Transfer roast to cutting board. Cover with foil. Let stand for 10 minutes. Remove skin from roast. Skim and discard fat from sauce. Slice roast and arrange on large serving plate. Serve with sauce. Serves 8.

1 serving: 224 Calories; 1.8 g Total Fat (0.6 g Mono, 0.5 g Poly, 0.4 g Sat); 112 mg Cholesterol; 8 g Carbohydrate; 1 g Fibre; 41 g Protein; 192 mg Sodium

Honey Mustard Turkey

A warming stew with tangy mustard and sweet honey. Best served over mashed potatoes or egg noodles.

Canola oil	1 tbsp.	15 mL
Chopped celery	1 1/2 cups	375 mL
Chopped onion	1 1/2 cups	375 mL
Chopped carrot	1 cup	250 mL
Chopped parsnip	1 cup	250 mL
Dry (or alcohol-free) white wine	1/2 cup	125 mL
Prepared chicken broth	1/2 cup	125 mL
Dijon mustard (with whole seeds)	2 tbsp.	30 mL
Liquid honey	2 tbsp.	30 mL
All-purpose flour	2 tbsp.	30 mL
Dried rosemary, crushed	1/2 tsp.	2 mL
Dried thyme	1/4 tsp.	1 mL
Salt	1/2 tsp.	2 mL
Pepper	1/4 tsp.	1 mL
Boneless, skinless turkey thighs, trimmed of fat, cut into 3/4 inch (2 cm) pieces	2 lbs.	900 g

Heat canola oil in large frying pan on medium-high. Add next 4 ingredients. Cook for about 8 minutes, stirring often, until celery starts to soften.

Add next 4 ingredients. Stir. Transfer to 3 1/2 to 4 quart (3.5 to 4 L) slow cooker.

Combine next 5 ingredients in large resealable freezer bag. Add turkey. Seal bag. Toss until coated. Remove turkey. Discard any remaining flour mixture. Arrange turkey over vegetable mixture. Cook, covered, on Low for 8 to 10 hours or on High for 4 to 5 hours. Skim and discard fat. Makes about 5 1/2 cups (1.4 L).

1 cup (250 mL): 358 Calories; 11.9 g Total Fat (3.6 g Mono, 3.4 g Poly, 3.1 g Sat); 101 mg Cholesterol; 22 g Carbohydrate; 3 g Fibre; 36 g Protein; 535 mg Sodium

Layered Turkey Enchilada

Layering this delicious Mexican dish is the key to its success. It's just as easy to make as lasagna (and as tasty). It makes a big batch—perfect to feed a crowd.

Extra-lean ground turkey	3 lbs.	1.4 kg
Salsa	1 1/2 cups	375 mL
Can of condensed cream of chicken soup	1	1
(10 oz., 284 mL)		
Water	1 1/2 cups	375 mL
Pepper	1/4 tsp.	1 mL
Flour tortillas (9 inch, 22 cm, diameter),	6	6
cut or torn into eighths		
Grated Mexican cheese blend	3 cups	750 mL

Scramble-fry turkey in greased Dutch oven on medium for about 15 minutes until no longer pink. Add salsa, soup and water. Sprinkle with pepper. Stir.

To assemble, layer ingredients in greased 5 to 7 quart (5 to 7 L) slow cooker as follows:

1. 1/6 of turkey mixture

2. 8 tortilla pieces, overlapping

3. 1/6 of turkey mixture

4. 1/2 cup (125 mL) cheese

Repeat steps 2, 3 and 4 four more times to make another 4 layers. Cook, covered, on Low for 7 to 8 hours or on High for 3 1/2 to 4 hours. Let stand, uncovered, for 10 minutes. Makes about 12 cups (3 L).

1 cup (250 mL): 362 Calories; 19.9 g Total Fat (0.6 g Mono, 0.6 g Poly, 7.9 g Sat); 92 mg Cholesterol; 15 g Carbohydrate; trace Fibre; 30 g Protein; 726 mg Sodium

Turkey Fajitas

Host a fajita party for a casual TV night! Just spoon the saucy turkey and peppers into whole wheat tortillas and dinner is made. Serve with shredded lettuce, grated cheese and pickled jalapeño peppers.

Sliced onion	2 cups	500 mL
Boneless, skinless turkey breast roast, trimmed of fat	2 lbs.	900 g
Salsa	1 1/2 cups	375 mL
Brown sugar, packed	2 tsp.	10 mL
Chili powder	2 tsp.	10 mL
Smoked (sweet) paprika	2 tsp.	10 mL
Ground cumin	1 tsp.	5 mL
Thinly sliced green pepper	1 cup	250 mL
Thinly sliced red pepper	1 cup	250 mL
Thinly sliced yellow pepper	1 cup	250 mL
Salsa	1/2 cup	125 mL
Lime juice	1 tbsp.	15 mL
Whole wheat flour tortillas (10 inch, 25 cm, diameter)	8	8

Put onion into 3 1/2 to 4 quart (3.5 to 4 L) slow cooker. Place roast over top.

Combine next 5 ingredients in small bowl. Pour over roast. Cook, covered, on High for 4 to 4 1/2 hours. Transfer roast to large plate. Shred turkey using 2 forks. Return to slow cooker.

Add next 4 ingredients. Stir. Cook, covered, on High for about 30 minutes until peppers are tender-crisp.

Add lime juice. Stir. Arrange turkey mixture down centre of each tortilla. Fold bottom ends of tortilla over filling. Fold in sides, slightly overlapping, leaving top ends open. Makes 8 fajitas.

1 fajita: 359 Calories; 3.1 g Total Fat (0.1 g Mono, 0.3 g Poly, 0.3 g Sat); 74 mg Cholesterol; 49 g Carbohydrate; 6 g Fibre; 34 g Protein; 751 mg Sodium

Tri-colour Turkey Roll

Turkey stuffed with cheesy spinach served with a light yet rich-tasting cream sauce. Cooking with the skin on helps to keep the turkey breast moist.

Fresh spinach leaves, lightly packed	10 cups	2.5 L
Boneless, skin-on turkey breast roast (about 2 1/2 lbs., 1.1 kg)	1	1
Sun-dried tomato pesto	8 tbsp.	120 mL
Grated Asiago cheese	3/4 cup	175 mL
Pepper, sprinkle		
Boiling water	1 cup	250 mL
Onion and chive cream cheese	1/2 cup	125 mL
Sun-dried tomato pesto	1 tbsp.	15 mL

Heat large greased frying pan on medium. Add spinach. Heat and stir until spinach is wilted. Cool.

To butterfly roast, cut horizontally lengthwise almost, but not quite, through to other side. Open flat. Place between 2 sheets of plastic wrap. Pound with mallet or rolling pin to 1/2 inch (12 mm) thickness. Spread first amount of pesto over roast. Arrange spinach over pesto. Sprinkle with Asiago cheese and pepper. Roll up from skinless short edge to enclose filling, making sure the skin is over top. Tie with butcher's string. Put an even layer (2 to 3 inches, 5 to 7.5 cm, thick) of crumpled foil into bottom of 5 to 7 quart (5 to 7 L) slow cooker (see Tip, below). Pour boiling water into slow cooker. Place roast on foil. Cook, covered, on High for about 3 hours until internal temperature reaches 170°F (77°C). Transfer roast to cutting board. Cover with foil. Let stand for 10 minutes. Remove and discard string and skin from roast. Cut into 10 slices.

Carefully remove crumpled foil from slow cooker. Skim and discard fat from cooking liquid. Add cream cheese and remaining pesto. Whisk until smooth. Makes about 2 1/4 cup (550 mL) sauce. Serve sauce with turkey. Serves 10.

1 serving with 3 tbsp (45 mL) sauce: 239 Calories; 6.9 g Total Fat (0.3 g Mono, 0.2 g Poly, 3.4 g Sat); 99 mg Cholesterol; 11 g Carbohydrate; 2 g Fibre; 33 g Protein; 1404 mg Sodium

Pictured on page 161.

 Instead of using crumpled foil to elevate pans and other items, you can use canning jar lids or a roasting rack that fits your slow cooker.

Festive Turkey Dinner

Treat your family to their favourite holiday flavours any time of the year with this festive dish of turkey and vegetables in a creamy sauce, with lots of crispy stuffing on top.

Baby potatoes, cut in half	1 lb.	454 g
Boneless, skinless turkey thighs (or breasts), cut into 1 1/2 inch (3.8 cm) pieces	1 1/2 lbs.	680 g
Frozen mixed vegetables, thawed	4 cups	1 L
Can of condensed cream of celery soup (10 oz., 284 mL)	1	1
Box of turkey cranberry stuffing mix (4 1/2 oz., 120 g)	1	1
Hot water	1/2 cup	125 mL

Layer first 3 ingredients, in order given, in greased 3 1/2 to 4 quart (3.5 to 4 L) slow cooker.

Whisk soup in small bowl until smooth. Spoon over vegetables.

Stir stuffing mix and hot water in same small bowl until moistened. Spoon over turkey mixture. Cook, covered, on Low for 8 to 9 hours or on High for 4 to 4 1/2 hours. Serves 6.

1 serving: 369 Calories; 7.4 g Total Fat (0.1 g Mono, 0.2 g Poly, 2.4 g Sat); 79 mg Cholesterol; 39 g Carbohydrate; 3 g Fibre; 34 g Protein; 904 mg Sodium

1. Irish Stew, page 155
2. Mushroom Pork Marsala, page 141
3. Mango Chutney Pork, page 134

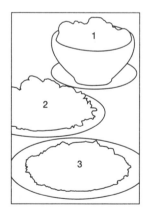

Cajun Turkey Stew

Tender turkey and potatoes in a spicy tomato sauce—with okra for Southern authenticity, but you can substitute corn or lima beans if you prefer.

Boneless, skinless turkey thighs, cut into 1 1/2 inch (3.8 cm) pieces	2 lbs.	900 g
Cajun seasoning	1 tbsp.	15 mL
Water	1/2 cup	125 mL
Red baby potatoes, quartered	2 lbs.	900 g
Can of diced tomatoes (with juice) (28 oz., 796 mL)	1	1
Chopped fresh (or frozen, thawed) okra	2 cups	500 mL
Cajun seasoning	1 tbsp.	15 mL
Cajun seasoning	1 tbsp.	15 mL

Put turkey into medium bowl. Sprinkle with seasoning. Stir until coated. Heat large greased frying pan on medium-high. Cook turkey, in 2 batches, for about 5 minutes, stirring occasionally, until browned. Transfer to 4 to 5 quart (4 to 5 L) slow cooker. Add water to same frying pan. Heat and stir, scraping any brown bits from bottom of pan, until boiling. Add to slow cooker.

Add next 4 ingredients. Stir. Cook, covered, on Low for 8 to 10 hours or on High for 4 to 5 hours.

Add remaining Cajun seasoning. Stir. Makes about 10 cups (2.5 L).

1 cup (250 mL): 211 Calories; 4.5 g Total Fat (1.2 g Mono, 1.3 g Poly, 1.4 g Sat); 63 mg Cholesterol; 21 g Carbohydrate; 2 g Fibre; 21 g Protein; 779 mg Sodium

Pictured on page 143.

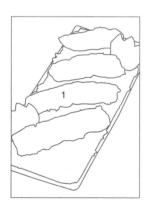

1. South Asian Steamed Salmon, page 117

Turkey and Wild Rice

This filling dish combines earthy wild rice and tender turkey pieces in a creamy sauce. Serve with a fresh veggie side like steamed asparagus.

Bacon slices, diced	3	3
Boneless, skinless turkey thighs, cut into 1 inch (2.5 cm) pieces	1 lb.	454 g
Can of condensed cream of wild mushroom soup (10 oz., 284 mL)	1	1
Prepared chicken broth	1 cup	250 mL
Wild rice	1 cup	250 mL
Water	2 cups	500 mL
Pepper, sprinkle		

Cook bacon in large frying pan on medium until crisp. Transfer with slotted spoon to paper towel-lined plate to drain. Drain and discard all but 1 tbsp. (15 mL) drippings.

Add turkey to same frying pan. Cook for about 10 minutes, stirring occasionally, until browned. Transfer to 3 1/2 to 4 quart (3.5 to 4 L) slow cooker. Scatter bacon over turkey.

Add remaining 5 ingredients to same frying pan. Heat and stir, scraping any brown bits from bottom of pan, until boiling. Add to slow cooker. Stir. Cook, covered, on Low for 6 to 7 hours or on High for 3 to 3 1/2 hours until rice is tender. Makes about 6 cups (1.5 L).

1 cup (250 mL): 186 Calories; 6.7 g Total Fat (1.7 g Mono, 0.7 g Poly, 2.0 g Sat); 7 mg Cholesterol; 26 g Carbohydrate; 2 g Fibre; 6 g Protein; 664 mg Sodium

Turkey Goulash

A hearty goulash, rich with flavourful turkey and paprika. Serve over egg noodles or spaetzle and garnish with a dollop of sour cream and a sprinkle of chopped fresh dill.

Can of tomato paste (5 1/2 oz., 156 mL)	1	1
Minute tapioca	3 tbsp.	45 mL
Envelope of onion soup mix (1 1/2 oz., 42 g)	1	1
Paprika	1 tbsp.	15 mL
Water	2 1/2 cups	625 mL
Salt, sprinkle		
Pepper, sprinkle		
Boneless, skinless turkey thighs, cut into 3/4 inch (2 cm) pieces	2 lbs.	900 g

(continued on next page)

Combine first 7 ingredients in 4 to 5 quart (4 to 5 L) slow cooker.

Add turkey. Stir. Cook, covered, on Low for 6 to 7 hours or on High for 3 to 3 1/2 hours. Makes about 7 cups (1.75 L).

3/4 cup (175 mL): 163 Calories; 4.5 g Total Fat (1.1 g Mono, 1.3 g Poly, 1.5 g Sat); 66 mg Cholesterol; 10 g Carbohydrate; 1 g Fibre; 2 g Protein; 554 mg Sodium

Classic "Baked" Beans

Cooking dry beans in a slow cooker is easy, healthy and inexpensive! Serve these beans with buttered biscuits. Freeze leftovers in small portions for lunches.

Dried navy beans	5 cups	1.25 L
Chopped onion	1 cup	250 mL
Water	5 cups	1.25 mL
Ketchup	1 1/2 cups	375 mL
Fancy (mild) molasses	1/3 cup	75 mL
Prepared mustard	2 tbsp.	30 mL
Salt	1/4 tsp.	1 mL
Pepper	1/4 tsp.	1 mL

Measure beans into large bowl or Dutch oven. Add water until 2 inches (5 cm) above beans. Soak overnight (see Tip, page 14). Drain. Rinse beans. Drain. Transfer to 5 to 7 quart (5 to 7 L) slow cooker.

Add onion and water. Cook, covered, on High for 4 to 4 1/2 hours until beans are tender (see Note, below).

Add remaining 5 ingredients. Stir. Cook, covered, on High for 30 minutes. Salt and pepper to taste. Stir. Makes about 12 cups (3 L).

1 cup (250 mL): 206 Calories; 0.5 g Total Fat (0.1 g Mono, 0.2 g Poly, 0.1 g Sat); 0 mg Cholesterol; 45 g Carbohydrate; 6 g Fibre; 8 g Protein; 939 mg Sodium

Pictured on page 233.

Note: Cooking beans on Low setting is not recommended as they may not cook fully.

Jamaican Rice and Beans

This creamy, mildly seasoned dish can be served as a vegetarian main course or as a side.

Chopped onion	1 cup	250 mL
Salt	1/4 tsp.	1 mL
Pepper	1/4 tsp.	1 mL
Cans of red kidney beans (14 oz., 398 mL each), rinsed and drained	2	2
Long-grain brown rice	2 cups	500 mL
Ground allspice	1 tsp.	5 mL
Can of coconut milk (14 oz., 398 mL)	1	1
Water	2 1/4 cups	550mL
Salt	1/4 tsp.	1 mL
Pepper	1/4 tsp.	1 mL

Heat medium greased frying pan on medium. Add onion, salt and pepper. Cook for about 5 minutes, stirring often, until softened. Transfer to 4 to 5 quart (4 to 5 L) slow cooker.

Add next 7 ingredients. Stir. Cook, covered, on Low for 6 to 7 hours or on High for 3 to 3 1/2 hours. Makes about 8 cups (2 L).

1 cup (250 mL): 363 Calories; 12.6 g Total Fat (1.3 g Mono, 0.8 g Poly, 9.7 g Sat); 0 mg Cholesterol; 54 g Carbohydrate; 8 g Fibre; 11 g Protein; 413 mg Sodium

Black Beans and Barley

Flavourful onion and a mild malt taste make this combination of black beans and tender barley a treat—serve with a crisp side salad.

Prepared vegetable broth	3 cups	750 mL
Pot barley	2 cups	500 mL
Can of beer (12 1/2 oz., 355 mL)	1	1
Envelope of onion soup mix (1 1/4 oz., 38 g)	1	1
Water	1 1/2 cups	375 mL
Cans of black beans (19 oz., 540 mL, each), rinsed and drained	2	2

Combine first 5 ingredients in 4 to 5 quart (4 to 5 L) slow cooker. Cook, covered, on Low for 5 to 6 hours or on High for 2 1/2 to 3 hours until barley is tender and liquid is absorbed.

Add beans. Stir. Cook, covered, on High for 10 minutes until heated through. Makes about 11 cups (2.75 L).

1 cup (250 mL): 246 Calories; 1.8 g Total Fat (0.1 g Mono, 0.8 g Poly, trace Sat); trace Cholesterol; 45 g Carbohydrate; 12 g Fibre; 10 g Protein; 723 mg Sodium

Vegetarian

Kale and Bean Rotini

A very appealing, colourful and flavourful vegetarian main course—complete with nutritious kale and plenty of kidney beans for protein.

Oil from sun-dried tomatoes	2 tsp.	10 mL
Chopped carrot	1 cup	250 mL
Chopped onion	1 cup	250 mL
Chopped celery	1/2 cup	125 mL
Garlic cloves, minced (or 3/4 tsp., 4 mL, powder)	3	3
Cans of white kidney beans (19 oz., 540 mL, each), rinsed and drained	2	2
Chopped kale leaves, lightly packed (see Tip, page 223)	3 cups	750 mL
Prepared vegetable broth	1 cup	250 mL
Finely chopped sun-dried tomatoes in oil, blotted dry	1/3 cup	75 mL
Chopped fresh rosemary (or 1/4 tsp., 1 mL, dried, crushed)	1 tsp.	5 mL
Pepper	1/4 tsp.	1 mL
Water	8 cups	2 L
Salt	1 tsp.	5 mL
Whole wheat rotini pasta	2 cups	500 mL
Frozen peas, thawed	1 1/2 cups	375 mL
Chopped yellow or orange pepper	1 cup	250 mL

Heat sun-dried tomato oil in large frying pan on medium. Add next 4 ingredients. Cook for about 10 minutes, stirring often, until onion is softened. Transfer to 3 1/2 to 4 quart (3.5 to 4 L) slow cooker.

Add next 6 ingredients. Stir. Cook, covered, on Low for 5 to 6 hours or on High for 2 1/2 to 3 hours.

Combine water and salt in large saucepan. Bring to a boil. Add pasta. Boil, uncovered, for 12 minutes, stirring occasionally.

Add peas and yellow pepper. Cook, uncovered, for about 2 minutes until pasta is tender but firm. Drain. Add to slow cooker. Stir. Makes about 9 1/3 cups (2.3 L).

1 cup (250 mL): 216 Calories; 2.9 g Total Fat (1.1 g Mono, 0.3 g Poly, 0.4 g Sat); 0 mg Cholesterol; 38 g Carbohydrate; 10 g Fibre; 12 g Protein; 253 mg Sodium

Pineapple Bean Bake

These smoky, sweet and tangy beans would make a great side dish at your next barbecue—
serve with a steak hot from the grill.

Cans of red kidney beans (19 oz., 540 mL, each), rinsed and drained	2	2
Cans of baked beans in tomato sauce (14 oz., 398 mL, each)	2	2
Can of crushed pineapple (with juice) (19 oz., 540 mL)	1	1
Finely chopped onion	1 cup	250 mL
Hickory barbecue sauce	1/2 cup	125 mL

Combine all 5 ingredients in 3 1/2 to 4 quart (3.5 to 4 L) slow cooker. Cook, covered, on Low for 8 to 9 hours or on High for 4 to 4 1/2 hours. Makes about 8 1/2 cups (2.1 L).

1 cup (250 mL): 294 Calories; 1.2 g Total Fat (0.1 g Mono, 0.1 g Poly, trace Sat); 0 mg Cholesterol; 58 g Carbohydrate; 17 g Fibre; 14 g Protein; 471 mg Sodium

Chunky Chipotle Chili

Hearty and warming like a good chili should be. Great with a slice of cornbread.

Can of diced tomatoes (with juice) (28 oz., 796 mL)	1	1
Can of red kidney beans (19 oz., 540 mL), rinsed and drained	1	1
Quartered fresh white mushrooms	2 cups	500 mL
Chopped celery	1 1/2 cups	375 mL
Chopped green pepper	1 1/2 cups	375 mL
Chopped onion	1 1/2 cups	375 mL
Coarsely chopped zucchini (with peel)	1 1/2 cups	375 mL
Frozen kernel corn, thawed	1 cup	250 mL
Tomato paste (see Tip, page 83)	3 tbsp.	45 mL
Chili powder	2 tbsp.	30 mL
Chopped chipotle peppers in adobo sauce (see Tip, page 56)	1 1/2 tsp.	7 mL
Ground cumin	1 tsp.	5 mL
Granulated sugar	1/2 tsp.	2 mL
Salt	1/4 tsp.	1 mL

Combine all 14 ingredients in 4 to 5 quart slow cooker. Cook, covered, on Low for 8 to 9 hours or on High for 4 to 4 1/2 hours. Makes about 8 1/2 cups (2.1 L).

1 cup (250 mL): 131 Calories; 0.8 g Total Fat (trace Mono, 1 g Poly, trace Sat); 0 mg Cholesterol; 24 g Carbohydrate; 6 g Fibre; 7 g Protein; 444 mg Sodium

Vegetarian

Sweet Potato Chili

Soft sweet potatoes make the base for this flavourful chili and help to create a great texture that works perfectly with black beans and kidney beans.

Chopped peeled orange-fleshed sweet potato	4 cups	1 L
Chopped onion	1 cup	250 mL
Can of white kidney beans (19 oz., 540 mL), rinsed and drained	1	1
Can of black beans (19 oz., 540 mL), rinsed and drained	1	1
Prepared vegetable broth	1 cup	250 mL
Chili powder	2 tbsp.	30 mL
Cocoa, sifted if lumpy	1 tbsp.	15 mL
Garlic powder	1/2 tsp.	2 mL
Salt	1/4 tsp.	1 mL
Pepper	1/4 tsp.	1 mL
Chopped tomato	1 1/2 cups	375 mL
Chopped fresh parsley	2 tbsp.	30 mL

Layer first 4 ingredients, in order given, in 3 1/2 to 4 quart (3.5 to 4 L) slow cooker.

Combine next 6 ingredients in small bowl. Pour over beans. Do not stir. Cook, covered, on Low for 7 to 8 hours or on High for 3 1/2 to 4 hours.

Add tomato and parsley. Stir. Makes about 6 1/2 cups (1.6 L).

1 cup (250 mL): 230 Calories; 1.0 g Total Fat (trace Mono, 0.7 g Poly, 0.1 g Sat); 0 mg Cholesterol; 44 g Carbohydrate; 11 g Fibre; 11 g Protein; 553 mg Sodium

Salsa Veggie Chili

This easy vegetarian chili always has delicious, crowd-pleasing results. Tasty with tortilla chips or crusty bread for dipping.

Can of kidney beans	1	1
(19 oz., 540 mL), rinsed and drained		
Chunky salsa	2 cups	500 mL
Tomato sauce	2 cups	500 mL
Package of veggie ground round	1	1
(12 oz., 340 g), (see Note, below)		
Chili powder	2 tsp.	10 mL

Combine all 5 ingredients in 3 1/2 to 4 quart (3.5 to 4 L) slow cooker. Cook, covered, on Low for 7 to 8 hours or on High for 3 1/2 to 4 hours. Makes about 6 cups (1.5 L).

1 cup (250 mL): 184 Calories; 0 g Total Fat (0 g Mono, 0 g Poly, 0 g Sat); 0 mg Cholesterol; 30 g Carbohydrate; 7 g Fibre; 16 g Protein; 1442 mg Sodium

Note: Veggie ground round is available in the produce section of your grocery store.

White Bean Vegetable Chili

This hearty bean chili is quick to put together, and can be used as a taco filling too! Add your favourite mixed veggies and serve with tortilla chips or corn bread.

Cans of white kidney beans (19 oz.,	2	2
540 mL, each), rinsed and drained		
Cans of stewed tomatoes	2	2
(14 oz., 398 mL, each), cut up		
Prepared vegetable broth	1 cup	250 mL
Envelope of chili seasoning mix	1	1
(1 1/4 oz., 35 g)		
Frozen mixed vegetables, thawed	3 cups	750 mL

Combine first 4 ingredients in 3 1/2 to 4 quart (3.5 to 4 L) slow cooker. Cook, covered, on Low for 6 to 8 hours or on High for 3 to 4 hours.

Add vegetables. Stir. Cook, covered, on High for about 30 minutes until vegetables are tender. Makes about 7 cups (1.75 L).

1 cup (250 mL): 206 Calories; 4.2 g Total Fat (0 g Mono, 0 g Poly, 1.0 g Sat); 4 mg Cholesterol; 34 g Carbohydrate; 7 g Fibre; 10 g Protein; 630 mg Sodium

Pictured on page 251.

Cranberry Chickpea Curry

This rich chickpea curry is filled with chewy wild rice and tangy cranberries. It goes great with plain yogurt, served on the side so everyone can mix in as much or as little as they like.

Canola oil	2 tsp.	10 mL
Chopped fresh brown (or white) mushrooms	2 cups	500 mL
Chopped onion	2 cups	500 mL
Chopped celery	1 cup	250 mL
Garlic cloves, minced (or 1/2 tsp., 2 mL, powder)	2	2
Curry powder	1 tbsp.	15 mL
Granulated sugar	1 tbsp.	15 mL
Ground cumin	1 tsp.	5 mL
Salt	1/4 tsp.	1 mL
Pepper	1/2 tsp.	2 mL
Dried crushed chilies	1/4 tsp.	1 mL
Wild rice	1/2 cup	125 mL
Can of chickpeas (garbanzo beans), (19 oz., 540 mL), rinsed and drained	1	1
Fresh (or frozen, thawed) cranberries	1 1/2 cups	375 mL
Prepared vegetable broth	1 1/2 cups	375 mL

Heat canola oil in large frying pan on medium. Add next 4 ingredients. Cook for about 10 minutes, stirring often, until celery is softened.

Add next 6 ingredients. Heat and stir for about 1 minute until fragrant. Transfer to 3 1/2 to 4 quart (3.5 to 4 L) slow cooker.

Add rice. Stir.

Add remaining 3 ingredients. Do not stir. Cook, covered, on Low for 6 to 7 hours or on High for 3 to 3 1/2 hours. Stir. Makes about 5 1/2 cups (1.4 L)

1 cup (250 mL): 227 Calories; 3.9 g Total Fat (1.5 g Mono, 1.5 g Poly, 0.2 g Sat); 0 mg Cholesterol; 42 g Carbohydrate; 8 g Fibre; 9 g Protein; 361 mg Sodium

Pictured on page 54.

Tofu Vegetable Curry

Serve this colourful and aromatic blend of veggies and browned tofu with brown rice or whole wheat naan bread.

Package of firm tofu (12 1/2 oz., 350 g), cut into 3/4 inch (2 cm) cubes	1	1
Mild curry paste	1 tsp.	5 mL
Canola oil	2 tsp.	10 mL
Canola oil	2 tsp.	10 mL
Sliced onion	2 cups	500 mL
Mild curry paste	1 tbsp.	15 mL
Garlic cloves, minced (or 1/2 tsp., 2 mL, powder)	2	2
Prepared vegetable broth	2 cups	500 mL
Cauliflower florets	2 cups	500 mL
Baby potatoes, larger ones halved	1 lb.	454 g
Sliced fresh (or frozen, thawed) okra (1/2 inch, 12 mm, pieces)	1 1/2 cups	375 mL
Sliced carrot	1 cup	250 mL
Water	1 tbsp.	15 mL
Cornstarch	1 tsp.	5 mL
Chopped fresh spinach leaves, lightly packed	1 1/2 cups	375 mL
Chopped tomato	1 cup	250 mL
Brown sugar, packed	2 tsp.	10 mL

Toss tofu and first amount of curry paste in medium bowl. Heat first amount of canola oil in large frying pan on medium-high. Add tofu. Cook for about 8 minutes, stirring occasionally, until browned. Transfer to large plate. Cool. Chill, covered.

Heat second amount of canola oil in same frying pan on medium. Add onion. Cook for about 8 minutes, stirring often, until softened. Add second amount of curry paste and garlic. Heat and stir for about 1 minute until fragrant. Add broth. Heat and stir, scraping any brown bits from bottom of pan, until boiling. Transfer to 4 to 5 quart (4 to 5 L) slow cooker.

Add next 4 ingredients. Stir. Cook, covered, on Low for 4 to 5 hours or on High for 2 to 2 1/2 hours.

Stir water into cornstarch in small cup until smooth. Add to slow cooker.

Add remaining 3 ingredients and tofu. Stir. Cook, covered, on High for about 15 minutes until boiling and thickened. Makes about 9 cups (2.25 L).

1 cup (250 mL): 127 Calories; 3.1 g Total Fat (1.4 g Mono, 1.1 g Poly, 0.3 g Sat); 0 mg Cholesterol; 20 g Carbohydrate; 3 g Fibre; 6 g Protein; 224 mg Sodium

Pictured on page 234.

Curried Cauliflower Paneer

The spinach contrasts beautifully with curry-coated cauliflower and paneer in this mild vegetarian dish. Serve over basmati rice and garnish with plain thick yogurt and cilantro.

Can of tikka masala curry sauce (10 oz., 284 mL)	1	1
Water	1 cup	250 mL
Cauliflower florets	4 cups	1 L
Cubed paneer	3 cups	750 mL
Salt	1/4 tsp.	1 mL
Fresh spinach leaves, lightly packed	4 cups	1 L
Chopped fresh cilantro (or parsley)	1 tbsp.	15 mL
Pepper, sprinkle		

Combine curry sauce and water in 3 1/2 to 4 quart (3.5 to 4 L) slow cooker. Add cauliflower, paneer and salt. Stir. Cook, covered, on Low for 5 to 6 hours or on High for 2 1/2 to 3 hours.

Add spinach, cilantro and a sprinkle of pepper. Stir. Makes about 6 cups (1.5 L).

1 cup (250 mL): 621 Calories; 50.5 g Total Fat (0 g Mono, trace Poly, 21.6 g Sat); 120 mg Cholesterol; 12 g Carbohydrate; 1 g Fibre; 29 g Protein; 2126 mg Sodium

Vegetable Curry

Serve this curry over coconut rice, and garnish with chopped cilantro for extra colour.

Chopped butternut squash (1 inch, 2.5 cm, pieces)	4 cups	1 L
Cauliflower florets	3 cups	750 mL
Baby potatoes, cut in half	1 lb.	454 g
Water	1/2 cup	125 mL
Jar of tikka masala cooking sauce (14 oz., 400 mL)	1	1
Can of diced tomatoes (with juice) (14 oz., 398 mL)	1	1

Combine first 4 ingredients in 3 1/2 to 4 quart (3.5 to 4 L) slow cooker. Cook, covered, on Low for 6 to 7 hours or on High for 3 to 3 1/2 hours until tender.

Add tikka masala sauce and tomatoes. Stir. Cook, covered, on High for about 30 minutes until heated through. Makes about 7 cups (1.75 L).

1 cup (250 mL): 407 Calories; 24.1 g Total Fat (trace Mono, 0.1 g Poly, 2.0 g Sat); 0 mg Cholesterol; 43 g Carbohydrate; 6 g Fibre; 7 g Protein; 2342 mg Sodium

Friendly Shepherd's Pie

Some shepherds are just too friendly to consume one of their flock! Here's a meatless
shepherd's pie made from lentils and veggies and colourfully topped with butternut squash.

Canola oil	2 tsp.	10 mL
Chopped onion	2 cups	500 mL
Garlic clove, minced (or 1/4 tsp., 1 mL, powder)	1	1
Prepared vegetable broth	2 1/4 cups	550 mL
Baby potatoes, quartered	1 lb.	454 g
Diced carrot	1 cup	250 mL
Diced parsnip	1 cup	250 mL
Dried green lentils	1 cup	250 mL
Frozen kernel corn, thawed	1 cup	250 mL
Diced celery	1/2 cup	125 mL
Tomato paste (see Tip, page 83)	2 tbsp.	30 mL
Dried thyme	1 tsp.	5 mL
Dried rosemary, crushed	1/2 tsp.	2 mL
Pepper	1/4 tsp.	1 mL
Mashed butternut squash (about 3 lbs., 1.4 kg, uncooked)	4 cups	1 L
Grated Italian cheese blend	2/3 cup	150 mL
Fine dry bread crumbs	1/3 cup	75 mL
Pepper	1/8 tsp.	0.5 mL

Heat canola oil in large frying pan on medium. Add onion and garlic. Cook for about
8 minutes, stirring often, until softened. Transfer to 4 to 5 quart (4 to 5 L) slow cooker.

Add next 11 ingredients. Stir. Cook, covered, on Low for 6 to 7 hours or on High for
3 to 3 1/2 hours. Stir.

Combine remaining 4 ingredients in medium bowl. Spread over potato mixture. Cook,
covered, on High for about 30 minutes until heated through. Serves 8.

1 serving: 368 Calories; 3.1 g Total Fat (0.7 g Mono, 0.5 g Poly, 0.5 g Sat); 2 mg Cholesterol; 77 g Carbohydrate;
13 g Fibre; 14 g Protein; 276 mg Sodium

Mushroom Quinoa

Quinoa, mushrooms and zucchini create an earthy combination of textures—serve this alongside slices of whole wheat baguette paired with olive oil and balsamic vinegar.

Canola oil	1 tbsp.	15 mL
Chopped portobello mushrooms	3 cups	750 mL
Chopped fresh white mushrooms	2 cups	500 mL
Chopped onion	2 cups	500 mL
Garlic cloves, minced (or 1/2 tsp., 2 mL, powder)	2	2
Basil pesto	2 tbsp.	30 mL
Red wine vinegar	1 tbsp.	15 mL
Pepper	1/2 tsp.	2 mL
Diced zucchini (with peel)	2 cups	500 mL
Prepared vegetable broth	1 1/2 cups	375 mL
Quinoa, rinsed and drained	1 cup	250 mL
Grated Parmesan cheese (optional)	2 tbsp.	30 mL
Red wine vinegar	2 tsp.	10 mL

Heat canola oil in large frying pan on medium. Add next 4 ingredients. Cook for about 12 minutes, stirring occasionally, until mushrooms start to brown.

Add next 3 ingredients. Stir. Transfer to 3 1/2 to 4 quart (3.5 to 4 L) slow cooker.

Add next 3 ingredients. Stir. Cook, covered, on Low for 4 to 5 hours or on High for 2 to 2 1/2 hours.

Add cheese and second amount of vinegar. Stir. Makes about 5 1/2 cups (1.4 L)

1 cup (250 mL): 227 Calories; 7.5 g Total Fat (2.0 g Mono, 1.5 g Poly, 0.9 g Sat); 1 mg Cholesterol; 34 g Carbohydrate; 4 g Fibre; 8 g Protein; 191 mg Sodium

Southern Italian Veggie Ragout

Fresh herb and Parmesan flavours stand out in this thick, spicy sauce, perfect for serving over whole wheat rigatoni, penne or macaroni. Store in an airtight container in the freezer for up to three months.

Canola oil	2 tsp.	10 mL
Chopped onion	1 1/2 cups	375 mL
Chopped celery	1 cup	250 mL
Tomato paste (see Tip, page 83)	2 tbsp.	30 mL
Dry (or alcohol-free) red wine	1 cup	250 mL
Can of diced tomatoes (with juice) (14 oz., 398 mL)	1	1
Chopped carrot	1 1/2 cups	375 mL
Chopped peeled orange-fleshed sweet potato	1 1/2 cups	375 mL
Package of veggie ground round (12 oz., 340 g), (see Note, page 206)	1	1
Prepared vegetable broth	1/2 cup	125 mL
Garlic cloves, minced (or 1/2 tsp., 2 mL, powder)	2	2
Dried crushed chilies	1/4 tsp.	1 mL
Salt	1/8 tsp.	0.5 mL
Pepper	1/4 tsp.	1 mL
Grated Parmesan cheese	1/4 cup	60 mL
Chopped fresh basil	3 tbsp.	45 mL
Chopped pine nuts, toasted (see Tip, page 267)	2 tbsp.	30 mL
Grated lemon zest	1 tsp.	5 mL

Heat canola oil in large frying pan on medium. Add onion and celery. Cook for about 10 minutes, stirring often, until onion is softened.

Add tomato paste. Heat and stir for 1 minute. Add wine. Heat and stir until boiling. Transfer to 3 1/2 to 4 quart (3.5 to 4 L) slow cooker.

Add next 9 ingredients. Stir. Cook, covered, on Low for 7 to 8 hours or on High for 3 1/2 to 4 hours.

Add remaining 4 ingredients. Stir. Makes about 6 1/2 cups (1.6 L).

1 cup (250 mL): 215 Calories; 4.7 g Total Fat (1.4 g Mono, 1.4 g Poly, 0.9 g Sat); 3 mg Cholesterol; 22 g Carbohydrate; 6 g Fibre; 14 g Protein; 615 mg Sodium

Onion Kale Barsotto

This creamy barley mixture combines the contrasting flavours of earthy kale and feta with delicate dill and lemon.

Canola oil	1 tsp.	5 mL
Chopped onion	2 cups	500 mL
Pot barley	1 cup	250 mL
Garlic cloves, minced	2	2
(or 1/2 tsp., 2 mL, powder)		
Finely chopped kale leaves, lightly packed	2 cups	500 mL
(see Tip, page 223)		
Prepared vegetable broth	2 cups	500 mL
Diced red pepper	1 1/2 cups	375 mL
Water	1 1/2 cups	375 mL
Crumbled feta cheese	3 tbsp.	45 mL
Chopped fresh dill	1 tbsp.	15 mL
(or 3/4 tsp., 4 mL, dried)		
Lemon juice	1 tbsp.	15 mL
Salt, sprinkle		
Coarsely ground pepper	1/2 tsp.	2 mL

Heat canola oil in large frying pan on medium. Add onion. Cook for about 8 minutes, stirring often, until softened.

Add barley and garlic. Heat and stir for about 1 minute until fragrant. Transfer to greased 3 1/2 to 4 quart (3.5 to 4 L) slow cooker.

Add next 4 ingredients. Stir. Cook, covered, on Low for 5 to 6 hours or on High for 2 1/2 to 3 hours.

Add remaining 5 ingredients. Stir. Makes about 5 1/2 cups (1.4 L).

1 cup (250 mL): 213 Calories; 3.2 g Total Fat (0.8 g Mono, 0.5 g Poly, 0.9 g Sat); 5 mg Cholesterol; 42 g Carbohydrate; 8 g Fibre; 7 g Protein; 241 mg Sodium

Veggie Shepherd's Pie

A hearty vegetarian dish with the comforting flavours of home, this slow cooker casserole has a nice blend of seasonings and a hint of spicy heat.

Packages of veggie ground round (12 oz., 340 g, each), see Note, page 206	2	2
Prepared bruschetta topping	1 1/2 cups	375 mL
Frozen peas, thawed	1 cup	250 mL
Can of kernel corn (7 oz., 199 mL), drained	1	1
Mashed potatoes (about 2 lbs., 900 g, uncooked)	4 1/2 cups	1.1 L
Salt, sprinkle		
Pepper, sprinkle		

Combine first 3 ingredients in 3 1/2 to 4 quart (3.5 to 4 L) slow cooker.

Scatter corn over ground round mixture. Do not stir. Sprinkle mashed potatoes with salt and pepper. Stir. Spread mashed potatoes over corn. Do not stir. Lay double layer of tea towels over slow cooker liner. Cover with lid. Cook on Low for 6 to 7 hours or on High for 3 to 3 1/2 hours. Makes about 10 cups (2.5 L).

1 cup (250 mL): 217 Calories; 2.9 g Total Fat (0 g Mono, trace Poly, trace Sat); 0 mg Cholesterol; 32 g Carbohydrate; 7 g Fibre; 15 g Protein; 902 mg Sodium

1. Café au Lait Custard, page 272
2. French Lamb Casserole, page 154

Barley Primavera

Creamy and appealing, this comfort food has a risotto-like texture and lots of colourful, tender-crisp vegetables, with the added nutritional value of barley.

Prepared vegetable broth	4 cups	1 L
Pot barley	2 cups	500 mL
Water	2 cups	500 mL
Frozen Italian mixed vegetables, thawed	4 cups	1 L
Alfredo pasta sauce	1 2/3 cups	400 mL
Prepared bruschetta topping	1 1/2 cups	375 mL

Combine broth, barley and water in 4 to 5 quart (4 to 5 L) slow cooker. Cook, covered, on Low for 5 to 6 hours or on High for 2 1/2 to 3 hours until barley is tender and liquid is absorbed.

Add vegetables and pasta sauce. Stir. Cook, covered, on High for about 30 minutes until vegetables are tender.

Add bruschetta topping. Stir. Makes about 12 cups (3 L).

1 cup (250 mL): 270 Calories; 12.7 g Total Fat (0 g Mono, 0 g Poly, 5.8 g Sat); 31 mg Cholesterol; 34 g Carbohydrate; 6 g Fibre; 6 g Protein; 577 mg Sodium

Pictured on page 233.

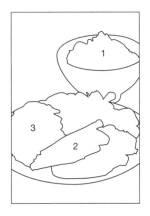

1. Strawberry Rhubarb Stew, page 279
2. Ale-sauced Pork Roast, page 127
3. Skinny Potato Vegetable Scallop, page 237

Veggie Lasagna

A rich and satisfying lasagna with plenty of vegetables and cottage cheese.

Canola oil	1 tsp.	5 mL
Chopped celery	1 cup	250 mL
Chopped onion	1 cup	250 mL
Finely chopped carrot	1 cup	250 mL
Garlic cloves, minced	3	3
(or 3/4 tsp., 4 mL, powder)		
Prepared vegetable broth	1 cup	250 mL
Tomato paste (see Tip, page 83)	2 tbsp.	30 mL
Grated zucchini (with peel)	2 cups	500 mL
Can of diced tomatoes (with juice)	1	1
(14 oz., 398 mL)		
Italian seasoning	1 tbsp.	15 mL
Large eggs, fork-beaten	2	2
Chopped fresh spinach leaves, lightly packed	3 cups	750 mL
2% cottage cheese	2 cups	500 mL
Pepper	1/2 tsp.	2 mL
Ground nutmeg (optional)	1/8 tsp.	0.5 mL
Oven-ready whole grain lasagna noodles, broken in half	9	9
Grated Italian cheese blend	1 cup	250 mL

Heat canola oil in large saucepan on medium. Add next 4 ingredients. Cook for about 10 minutes, stirring often, until onion is softened.

Add broth and tomato paste. Heat and stir for 1 minute.

Add next 3 ingredients. Heat and stir for about 5 minutes until boiling.

Combine next 5 ingredients in large bowl.

Layer ingredients in greased 5 to 7 quart (5 to 7 L) slow cooker as follows:

1. 1/3 tomato mixture

2. 6 noodle halves

3. Half spinach mixture

4. 1/3 tomato mixture

(continued on next page)

5. 6 noodle halves

6. Remaining spinach mixture

7. Remaining noodle halves

8. Remaining tomato mixture

Cook, covered, on Low for 5 to 6 hours or on High for 2 1/2 to 3 hours.

Sprinkle with Italian cheese blend. Let stand, covered, for about 3 minutes until cheese is melted. Let stand, uncovered, for 10 minutes. Serves 8.

1 serving: 204 Calories; 4.6 g Total Fat (1.2 g Mono, 0.5 g Poly, 1.7 g Sat); 60 mg Cholesterol; 25 g Carbohydrate; 4 g Fibre; 18 g Protein; 564 mg Sodium

---

Cauliflower Potato Scallop

This rich and creamy scallop is a decadent way to eat your vegetables. It's full of tender kale, potato and cauliflower.

Alfredo pasta sauce	2 cups	500 mL
Water	1 cup	250 mL
Thinly sliced peeled potato	5 cups	1.25 L
Chopped kale leaves, lightly packed (see Tip, page 223)	3 cups	750 mL
Cauliflower florets	3 cups	750 mL
Grated Parmesan cheese	1 cup	250 mL

Combine pasta sauce and water in small bowl.

To assemble, layer ingredients in well-greased 4 to 5 quart (4 to 5 L) slow cooker as follows:

1. Half of potato

2. Half of kale

3. Half of cauliflower

4. Half of sauce mixture

5. Half of cheese

6. Remaining potato

7. Remaining kale

8. Remaining cauliflower

9. Remaining sauce mixture

10. Remaining cheese

Cook, covered, on Low for 8 to 9 hours or on High for 4 to 4 1/2 hours. Makes about 10 cups (2.5 L).

1 cup (250 mL): 261 Calories; 11.9 g Total Fat (trace Mono, 0.2 g Poly, 5.3 g Sat); 32 mg Cholesterol; 31 g Carbohydrate; 4 g Fibre; 10 g Protein; 778 mg Sodium

Vegetarian

African Sweet Potato Stew

Primarily sweet with the flavours of peanut butter and sweet potato, this stew also has a bit of cayenne heat. Served on its own or with brown rice. Store in an airtight container in the freezer for up to three months.

Chopped peeled orange-fleshed sweet potato (1 inch, 2.5 cm, pieces)	5 cups	1.25 L
Halved fresh white mushrooms	2 cups	500 mL
Chopped fresh pineapple	1 1/2 cups	375 mL
Dried green lentils	3/4 cup	175 mL
Canola oil	2 tsp.	10 mL
Chopped onion	1 1/2 cups	375 mL
Tomato paste (see Tip, page 83)	2 tbsp.	30 mL
Curry powder	2 tsp.	10 mL
Finely grated ginger root (or 1/4 tsp., 1 mL, ground ginger)	1 tsp.	5 mL
Cayenne pepper	1/4 tsp.	1 mL
Garlic clove, minced (or 1/4 tsp., 1 mL, powder)	1	1
Prepared vegetable broth	3 cups	750 mL
Chopped fresh spinach leaves, lightly packed	1 cup	250 mL
Peanut butter	1/4 cup	60 mL
Lime juice	1 tbsp.	15 mL

Place first 4 ingredients in greased 4 to 5 quart (4 to 5 L) slow cooker.

Heat canola oil in large frying pan on medium. Add onion. Cook for about 5 minutes, stirring often, until softened.

Add next 5 ingredients. Heat and stir for about 1 minute until fragrant.

Add broth. Heat and stir until boiling. Transfer to slow cooker. Stir. Cook, covered, on Low for 6 to 7 hours or on High for 3 to 3 1/2 hours.

Add remaining 3 ingredients. Stir well. Makes about 9 1/2 cups (2.4 L).

1 cup (250 mL): 197 Calories; 5.0 g Total Fat (2.2 g Mono, 1.3 g Poly, 0.8 g Sat); 0 mg Cholesterol; 33 g Carbohydrate; 6 g Fibre; 7 g Protein; 223 mg Sodium

Pictured on page 234.

Vegetarian

Greek Eggplant Stew

Herbs, tomato and lemon give this dish a pleasant freshness. Serve over brown rice or with whole wheat pita bread, and don't forget a dollop of purchased tzatziki! Store in an airtight container in the freezer for up to three months.

Canola oil	1 tsp.	5 mL
Chopped onion	2 cups	500 mL
Can of tomato paste (5 1/2 oz., 156 mL)	1	1
Garlic cloves, minced (or 1/2 tsp., 2 mL, powder)	2	2
Cans of chickpeas (garbanzo beans), 19 oz. (540 mL) each, rinsed and drained	2	2
Chopped peeled eggplant	4 cups	1 L
Chopped zucchini (with peel)	3 cups	750 mL
Can of diced tomatoes (with juice) (14 oz., 398 mL)	1	1
Coarsely chopped green pepper	1 cup	250 mL
Coarsely chopped red pepper	1 cup	250 mL
Dried oregano	2 tsp.	10 mL
Liquid honey	1 tsp.	5 mL
Ground cinnamon	1/2 tsp.	2 mL
Salt	1/8 tsp.	0.5 mL
Pepper	1/2 tsp.	2 mL
Ground nutmeg	1/8 tsp.	0.5 mL
Chopped tomato	1 cup	250 mL
Chopped fresh parsley	1/4 cup	60 mL
Chopped fresh mint	2 tbsp.	30 mL
Lemon juice	2 tbsp.	30 mL

Heat canola oil in large frying pan on medium. Add onion. Cook for about 8 minutes, stirring often, until softened.

Add tomato paste and garlic. Heat and stir for 2 minutes. Transfer to greased 4 to 5 quart (4 to 5 L) slow cooker.

Add next 12 ingredients. Stir. Cook, covered, on Low for 7 to 8 hours or on High for 3 1/2 to 4 hours.

Add remaining 4 ingredients. Stir. Makes about 10 cups (2.5 L).

1 cup (250 mL): 161 Calories; 2.5 g Total Fat (0.7 g Mono, 1.1 g Poly, 0.1 g Sat); 0 mg Cholesterol; 29 g Carbohydrate; 8 g Fibre; 8 g Protein; 256 mg Sodium

Mediterranean Chickpea Stew

This comforting chickpea stew features the freshness of vegetables and a mild chili heat. Serve with whole grain garlic toast or goat cheese crostini. Store in an airtight container in the freezer for up to three months.

Water	4 cups	1 L
Dried chickpeas (garbanzo beans), soaked in water overnight, rinsed and drained	2 cups	500 mL
Sliced fennel bulb (white part only)	2 cups	500 mL
Sliced onion	1 cup	250 mL
Dried oregano	1/2 tsp.	2 mL
Garlic cloves, minced (or 1/2 tsp., 2 mL, powder)	2	2
Pepper	1/2 tsp.	2 mL
Dried crushed chilies	1/4 tsp.	1 mL
Chopped zucchini (with peel), about 1/2 inch (12 mm) pieces	2 cups	500 mL
Chopped red pepper	1 cup	250 mL
Chopped yellow pepper	1 cup	250 mL
Basil pesto	1 tbsp.	15 mL
Salt	1/2 tsp.	2 mL
Chopped fresh basil	2 tbsp.	30 mL

Combine first 8 ingredients in 3 1/2 to 4 quart (3.5 to 4 L) slow cooker. Cook, covered, on High for 5 to 6 hours until beans are tender. Stir. Transfer 2 cups (500 mL) to small bowl. Mash. Return to slow cooker.

Add next 5 ingredients. Stir. Cook, covered, on High for about 30 minutes until zucchini is tender.

Add basil. Stir. Makes about 8 2/3 cups (2.1 L).

1 cup (250 mL): 184 Calories; 3.4 g Total Fat (trace Mono, 0.1 g Poly, 0.2 g Sat); trace Cholesterol; 31 g Carbohydrate; 9 g Fibre; 10 g Protein; 173 mg Sodium

Pictured on page 72.

222   Vegetarian

Chickpea Lentil Stew

Come home to hearty lentils and chickpeas brightened with the fresh flavours of tomatoes, garlic and feta. Use fresh basil as an additional garnish.

Cans of chickpeas (garbanzo beans), 19 oz. (540 mL) each, rinsed and drained	2	2
Cans of lentils (19 oz., 540 mL, each), rinsed and drained	2	2
Diced peeled potato	2 cups	500 mL
Water	2 cups	500mL
Prepared bruschetta topping	2 cups	500 mL
Crumbled feta cheese	1 cup	250 mL

Combine first 4 ingredients in 4 to 5 quart (4 to 5 L) slow cooker. Cook, covered, on Low for 6 to 8 hours or on High for 3 to 4 hours. Mash mixture several times with potato masher to break up potato.

Add bruschetta topping and feta cheese. Stir. Makes about 11 cups (2.75 L).

1 cup (250 mL): 298 Calories; 8.3 g Total Fat (1.1 g Mono, 1.1 g Poly, 2.1 g Sat); 12 mg Cholesterol; 47 g Carbohydrate; 9 g Fibre; 16 g Protein; 620 mg Sodium

 To remove the centre rib from lettuce or kale, fold the leaf in half along the rib and then cut along the length of the rib. To store, place the leaves in a large freezer bag. Once they are frozen, crumble them in the bag.

Meatless Moussaka

Lentils replace meat in this comforting Greek dish with simple and distinct tastes. For less fuss and more flavour, the traditional béchamel topping was replaced by a quick and easy sprinkle of creamy goat cheese.

Cans of lentils (19 oz., 540 mL, each), rinsed and drained	2	2
Tomato pasta sauce	3 cups	750 mL
Ground cinnamon	1/4 tsp.	1 mL
Salt	1/4 tsp.	1 mL
Pepper	1/4 tsp.	1 mL
Medium eggplants (with peel), cut into 1/4 inch (6 mm) slices	2	2
Goat (chèvre) cheese, crumbled	8 oz.	225 g

Combine first 5 ingredients in large bowl.

To assemble, layer ingredients in greased 5 to 7 quart (5 to 7 L) slow cooker as follows:

1. 2 cups (500 mL) lentil mixture

2. Half of eggplant

3. 2 cups (500 mL) lentil mixture

4. Remaining eggplant

5. Remaining lentil mixture

Cook, covered, on Low for 8 to 9 hours or on High for 4 to 4 1/2 hours.

Sprinkle with cheese. Cook, covered, on High for about 10 minutes until cheese is softened. Makes about 9 cups (2.25 L).

1 cup (250 mL): 257 Calories; 6.5 g Total Fat (1.4 g Mono, 0.5 g Poly, 3.8 g Sat); 12 mg Cholesterol; 42 g Carbohydrate; 9 g Fibre; 18 g Protein; 386 mg Sodium

Ratatouille

Chunky, tender vegetables in a rich tomato herb sauce. Ratatouille can be served as a side dish or spooned over pasta as a main course.

Chopped peeled eggplant (1 inch, 2.5 cm, pieces)	2 cups	500 mL
Chopped seeded Roma (plum) tomato	2 cups	500 mL
Chopped zucchini (with peel), 1 inch (2.5 cm) pieces	2 cups	500 mL
Can of diced tomatoes (with juice) (14 oz., 398 mL)	1	1
Chopped yellow or green pepper	1 cup	250 mL
Chopped red pepper	1 cup	250 mL
Sliced onion	1 cup	250 mL
Tomato paste (see Tip, page 83)	2 tbsp.	30 mL
Dried oregano	1/2 tsp.	2 mL
Garlic cloves, minced (or 1/2 tsp., 2 mL, powder)	2	2
Granulated sugar	1/2 tsp.	2 mL
Salt	1/2 tsp.	2 mL
Basil pesto	1 tbsp.	15 mL
Chopped fresh basil	1 tbsp.	15 mL
Chopped fresh parsley	1 tbsp.	15 mL

Combine first 12 ingredients in greased 4 to 5 quart (4 to 5 L) slow cooker. Cook, covered, on Low for 6 to 7 hours or on High for 3 to 3 1/2 hours.

Add remaining 3 ingredients. Stir. Makes about 6 3/4 cups (1.7 L).

1 cup (250 mL): 69 Calories; 1.5 g Total Fat (trace Mono, 0.2 g Poly, 0.3 g Sat); 1 mg Cholesterol; 12 g Carbohydrate; 4 g Fibre; 3 g Protein; 341 mg Sodium

Pictured on page 233.

Simple Dhal

This South Asian dish goes easy on the spices and is delicious served with rice or flatbread.

Chopped onion	1 cup	250 mL
Dried red split lentils	2 1/2 cups	625 mL
Mild curry paste	3 tbsp.	45 mL
Water	5 1/2 cups	1.4 L
Can of diced tomatoes (14 oz., 398 mL), drained	1	1
Salt	1/4 tsp.	1 mL
Chopped fresh cilantro (or parsley)	1/2 cup	125 mL

Heat medium greased frying pan on medium. Add onion. Cook for about 5 minutes, stirring often, until softened. Transfer to 3 1/2 to 4 quart (3.5 to 4 L) slow cooker.

Add lentils, curry paste and water. Stir. Cook, covered, on Low for 6 to 7 hours or High for 3 to 3 1/2 hours.

Add tomatoes and salt. Stir. Cook, covered, on High for about 10 minutes until heated through.

Add cilantro. Stir. Makes about 8 cups (2 L).

1 cup (250 mL): 252 Calories; 3.0 g Total Fat (0.3 g Mono, 0.2 g Poly, 0.4 g Sat); 0 mg Cholesterol; 40 g Carbohydrate; 9 g Fibre; 17 g Protein; 467 mg Sodium

Cauliflower Dhal

Dinner's ready, DAHL-ings! Treat the ones you love to this spicy, traditional East Indian dish. Perfect with pappadum, *an East Indian flatbread.*

Cauliflower florets	4 cups	1 L
Chopped peeled potato	2 cups	500 mL
Yellow split peas, rinsed and drained	1 cup	250 mL
Chopped onion	1 cup	250 mL
Garlic clove, minced	1	1
Prepared vegetable broth	3 cups	750 mL
Balsamic vinegar	2 tbsp.	30 mL
Red curry paste	1 tsp.	5 mL
Turmeric	1/4 tsp.	1 mL
Ground ginger	1/4 tsp.	1 mL
Ground nutmeg	1/4 tsp.	1 mL
Salt	1/2 tsp.	2 mL
Pepper	1/2 tsp.	2 mL

(continued on next page)

Vegetarian

Combine first 5 ingredients in 4 to 5 quart (4 to 5 L) slow cooker.

Measure remaining 8 ingredients into medium bowl. Stir well. Pour over cauliflower mixture. Stir well. Cover. Cook on Low for 8 to 9 hours or on High for 4 to 4 1/2 hours. Makes about 7 1/2 cups (1.9 L).

1 cup (250 mL): 154 Calories; 0.5 g Total Fat, 0 g Mono, 0 g Poly, 0 g Sat; 0 mg Cholesterol; 28 g Carbohydrate, 4 g Fibre; 9 g Protein; 460 mg Sodium

Make Ahead: The night before, prepare and assemble all 13 ingredients, as directed, in slow cooker liner. Cover. Chill overnight. Cook as directed.

Squash and Couscous

The earthiness of squash and the sweetness of apricot are combined with an eastern Mediterranean flair.

Chopped dried apricot	2/3 cup	150 mL
Boiling water	1 1/2 cups	375 mL
Cubed butternut squash (1 inch, 2.5 cm, pieces)	6 cups	1.5 L
Butter (or hard margarine), melted	2 tbsp.	30 mL
Salt, sprinkle		
Pepper, sprinkle		
Box of lemon and spinach couscous (7 oz., 198 g)	1	1
Pine nuts, toasted (see Tip, page 267)	2 tbsp.	30 mL

Combine apricot and water in small bowl. Let stand for 10 minutes. Drain, reserving 1 cup (250 mL) water. Transfer apricot to greased 4 to 5 quart (4 to 5 L) slow cooker.

Add squash. Drizzle with melted butter. Sprinkle with salt and pepper. Stir well. Cook, covered, on Low for 6 to 7 hours or on High for 3 to 3 1/2 hours until tender.

Combine couscous and reserved water. Add to squash mixture. Stir gently. Cook, covered, on High for about 10 minutes until couscous is tender and liquid is absorbed.

Sprinkle with pine nuts. Makes about 7 cups (1.75 L).

1 cup (250 mL): 270 Calories; 5.7 g Total Fat (1.3 g Mono, 1.0 g Poly, 2.2 g Sat); 9 mg Cholesterol; 54 g Carbohydrate; 6 g Fibre; 7 g Protein; 375 mg Sodium

Stuffed Cabbage Wraps

An easy version of traditional cabbage rolls, these rice and bean wraps have great tomato taste. Try them as a side.

Large head of green cabbage	1	1
Chopped onion	3/4 cup	175 mL
Cooked long-grain brown rice (about 1/2 cup, 125 mL, uncooked)	1 1/2 cups	375 mL
Can of black beans (19 oz., 540 mL), rinsed and drained	1	1
Tomato pasta sauce	1/2 cups	125 mL
Salt, sprinkle		
Pepper, sprinkle		
Tomato pasta sauce	2 1/2 cups	625 mL

Remove core from cabbage. Trim about 1/2 inch (12 mm) slice from bottom. Place, cut side down, in 4 to 5 quart (4 to 5 L) slow cooker. Cover with boiling water. Let stand, covered, for 5 minutes. Drain. Let stand until cool enough to handle. Carefully remove 8 large outer leaves from cabbage (see Note, below). Cut "V" shape along tough ribs of leaves to remove. Discard ribs. Set leaves aside.

Heat medium greased frying pan on medium. Add onion. Cook for about 5 minutes, stirring often, until starting to soften. Transfer to medium bowl.

Add rice, beans, first amount of pasta sauce, salt and pepper. Stir. Place about 1/3 cup (75 mL) rice mixture on 1 cabbage leaf. Fold in sides. Roll up tightly from bottom to enclose filling. Repeat with remaining rice mixture and cabbage leaves.

Pour remaining pasta sauce into slow cooker. Arrange cabbage rolls in 2 layers, seam side down, over sauce. Cook, covered, on Low for 7 to 8 hours or High for 3 1/2 to 4 hours. Transfer rolls with slotted spoon to serving plate. Serve with sauce. Makes 1 1/2 cups (375 mL) sauce and 8 rolls.

1 cabbage roll with 3 tbsp. (45 mL) sauce: 263 Calories; 4.1 g Total Fat (0.7 g Mono, 1.1 g Poly, 0.3 g Sat); 0 mg Cholesterol; 46 g Carbohydrate; 7 g Fibre; 9 g Protein; 643 mg Sodium

Note: Discard any other outer leaves that are partially steamed. Save the remaining cabbage in the refrigerator for another use.

Vegetarian

Veggie Pasta Sauce

This easy-to-prepare pasta sauce has a hearty, meaty texture, but no meat. It's perfect on pasta and can be used to make lasagna.

Tomato basil pasta sauce	4 cups	1 L
Package of veggie ground round	1	1
(12 oz., 340 g), (see Note, page 206)		
Chopped carrot	1 cup	250 mL
Chopped onion	1 cup	250 mL
Chopped zucchini (with peel)	1 cup	250 mL

Combine all 5 ingredients in 3 1/2 to 4 quart (3.5 to 4 L) slow cooker. Cook, covered, on Low for 7 to 8 hours or on High for 3 1/2 to 4 hours. Makes about 6 cups (1.5 L).

3/4 cup (175 mL): 144 Calories; 2.6 g Total Fat (trace Mono, trace Poly, trace Sat); 0 mg Cholesterol; 17 g Carbohydrate; 3 g Fibre; 11 g Protein; 692 mg Sodium

Pictured on page 179.

Lentil Pasta Sauce

A pasta sauce that will satisfy the family and add a vegetarian meal option to your weekly menu. Complete the meal with a salad and garlic bread.

Diced zucchini (with peel)	2 cups	500 mL
Chopped onion	1 cup	250 mL
Grated carrot	1 cup	250 mL
Roasted garlic tomato pasta sauce	6 cups	1.5 L
Can of lentils (19 oz., 540 mL),	1	1
rinsed and drained		

Heat large greased frying pan on medium. Add first 3 ingredients. Cook for about 10 minutes, stirring often, until onion is softened and starts to brown. Transfer to 3 1/2 to 4 quart (3.5 to 4 L) slow cooker.

Add pasta sauce and lentils. Stir. Cook, covered, on Low for 6 to 8 hours or on High for 3 to 4 hours. Makes about 9 cups (2.25 L).

3/4 cup (175 mL): 114 Calories; 1.2 g Total Fat (0.3 g Mono, 0.2 g Poly, 0.1 g Sat); 0 mg Cholesterol; 23 g Carbohydrate; 2 g Fibre; 6 g Protein; 334 mg Sodium

Barbecue Beans

This barbecue staple has all the flavour and fibre with less fat and sodium than you'd normally find. A sweet, tangy sauce coats tender romano beans, raisins and tomatoes. This recipe makes a big batch to share at a potluck or BBQ, or it can be frozen in smaller portions.

Water	5 cups	1.25 L
Dried romano beans, soaked in water overnight, rinsed and drained	2 cups	500 mL
Chopped dark raisins	1 cup	250 mL
Chopped onion	1 cup	250 mL
Chili powder	2 tsp.	10 mL
Bay leaves	2	2
Garlic cloves, minced (or 1/2 tsp., 2 mL, powder)	2	2
Dried crushed chilies	1/4 tsp.	1 mL
Pepper	1/4 tsp.	1 mL
Can of diced tomatoes (14 oz., 398 mL), drained	1	1
Can of tomato paste (5 1/2 oz., 156 mL)	1	1
Hickory barbecue sauce	1/4 cup	60 mL
Brown sugar, packed	3 tbsp.	45 mL
Apple cider vinegar	2 tbsp.	30 mL
Salt	1/4 tsp.	1 mL

Combine first 9 ingredients in 3 1/2 to 4 quart (3.5 to 4 L) slow cooker. Cook, covered, on High for 5 to 6 hours until beans are tender. Remove and discard bay leaves.

Add remaining 6 ingredients. Stir. Cook, covered, on High for about 30 minutes until heated through. Makes about 9 cups (2.25 L).

1 cup (250 mL): 167 Calories; 0.5 g Total Fat (0 g Mono, trace Poly, trace Sat); 0 mg Cholesterol; 36 g Carbohydrate; 5 g Fibre; 6 g Protein; 448 mg Sodium

Bavarian Stuffing

Flavourful stuffing with cabbage, apple and tart raisins. Use dark rye for a pleasing visual contrast and serve with roast pork or ham.

Day-old rye bread cubes	5 cups	1.25 L
Day-old whole wheat bread cubes	5 cups	1.25 L
Chopped onion	1 1/2 cups	375 mL
Chopped peeled cooking apple (such as McIntosh)	1 1/2 cups	375 mL
Shredded green cabbage, lightly packed	1 1/2 cups	375 mL
Chopped dark raisins	1/2 cup	125 mL
Large egg, fork-beaten	1	1
Prepared chicken broth	1 cup	250 mL
Apple cider vinegar	2 tbsp.	30 mL
Canola oil	1 tbsp.	15 mL
Dry mustard	2 tsp.	10 mL
Caraway seed	1/2 tsp.	2 mL
Parsley flakes	1/2 tsp.	2 mL
Pepper	1/4 tsp.	1 mL
Chopped walnuts, toasted (see Tip, page 267)	1/2 cup	125 mL

Combine first 6 ingredients in greased 4 to 5 quart (4 to 5 L) slow cooker.

Combine next 8 ingredients in medium bowl. Add to slow cooker. Mix well. Cook, covered, on Low for about 4 hours or on High for about 2 hours until internal temperature reaches 165°F (74°C).

Add walnuts. Stir. Makes about 8 cups (2 L).

1 cup (250 mL): 240 Calories; 8.8 g Total Fat (2.4 g Mono, 4.4 g Poly, 1.0 g Sat); 26 mg Cholesterol; 35 g Carbohydrate; 7 g Fibre; 8 g Protein; 272 mg Sodium

Greek Potatoes

Deliciously tender potatoes are simmered in the slow cooker with Greek seasoning and broth. Purchased tzatziki adds the perfect finishing touch.

Baby potatoes, larger ones halved	2 lbs.	900 g
Prepared chicken broth	2 cups	500 mL
Greek seasoning	1 tbsp.	15 mL
Salt	1/8 tsp.	0.5 mL
Pepper	1/8 tsp.	0.5 mL
Chopped fresh dill (or 1 1/2 tsp., 7 mL, dried)	2 tbsp.	30 mL
Greek seasoning	1 tsp.	5 mL
Tzatziki	1 cup	250 mL

Combine first 5 ingredients in 3 1/2 to 4 quart (3.5 to 4 L) slow cooker. Cook, covered, on Low for 6 to 8 hours or on High for 3 to 4 hours. Transfer with slotted spoon to serving dish. Discard any remaining cooking liquid.

Sprinkle with dill and second amount of Greek seasoning. Stir until coated.

Serve with tzatziki. Serves 8.

1 serving: 109 Calories; 1.3 g Total Fat (0 g Mono, 0 g Poly, 1.0 g Sat); 0 mg Cholesterol; 21 g Carbohydrate; 1 g Fibre; 3 g Protein; 43 mg Sodium

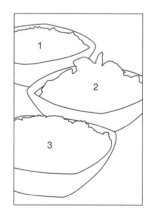

1. Classic "Baked" Beans, page 201
2. Ratatouille, page 225
3. Barley Primavera, page 217

Cranberry Apple Cabbage

A sweet and tangy mix of cabbage, with bites of tender cranberries and apple—serve this high-fibre dish alongside roast pork or poultry to infuse some colour into your meal.

Shredded red cabbage, lightly packed	6 cups	1.5 L
Chopped fresh (or frozen, thawed) cranberries	1 cup	250 mL
Diced peeled tart apple (such as Granny Smith)	1 cup	250 mL
Thinly sliced red onion	1 cup	250 mL
Bay leaves	2	2
Sparkling apple cider (with alcohol), or apple juice	2/3 cup	150 mL
Maple (or maple-flavoured) syrup	1/4 cup	60 mL
Apple cider vinegar	2 tbsp.	30 mL
Canola oil	1 tbsp.	15 mL
Salt	1/4 tsp.	1 mL
Pepper	1/4 tsp.	1 mL

Combine first 5 ingredients in 3 1/2 to 4 quart (3.5 to 4 L) slow cooker.

Combine remaining 6 ingredients in medium bowl. Add to slow cooker. Stir. Cook, covered, on Low for 5 to 6 hours or on High for 2 1/2 to 3 hours. Remove and discard bay leaves. Makes about 5 cups (1.25 L).

1 cup (250 mL): 131 Calories; 3.0 g Total Fat (1.7 g Mono, 0.9 g Poly, 0.2 g Sat); 0 mg Cholesterol; 27 g Carbohydrate; 5 g Fibre; 2 g Protein; 155 mg Sodium

Pictured on page 252.

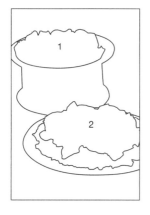

1. Tofu Vegetable Curry, page 208
2. African Sweet Potato Stew, page 220

Props: Lori Boutestein

Squash and Barley Pilaf

A mild and versatile side with a colourful autumn feel. This tender barley pairs well with the sweet, soft bites of butternut squash.

Chopped butternut squash (1 inch, 2.5 cm, pieces)	4 cups	1 L
Low-sodium prepared chicken broth	2 1/4 cups	550 mL
Chopped red pepper	1 cup	250 mL
Dried sage	1/2 tsp.	2 mL
Dried thyme	1/2 tsp.	2 mL
Salt	1/4 tsp.	1 mL
Pepper	1/4 tsp.	1 mL
Canola oil	1 tsp.	5 mL
Chopped onion	1 1/2 cups	375 mL
Diced celery	1/2 cup	125 mL
Pearl barley	1 cup	250 mL
Grated lemon zest	1 tsp.	5 mL

Combine first 7 ingredients in 3 1/2 to 4 quart (3.5 to 4 L) slow cooker.

Heat canola oil in large frying pan on medium-high. Add onion and celery. Cook for about 5 minutes, stirring often, until golden.

Add barley. Cook for about 3 minutes, stirring often, until barley starts to brown. Transfer to slow cooker. Stir. Cook, covered, on Low for 4 to 5 hours or on High for 2 to 2 1/2 hours until barley is tender and liquid is absorbed.

Add lemon zest. Stir gently. Makes about 6 cups (1.5 L).

1 cup (250 mL): 230 Calories; 1.8 g Total Fat (0.5 g Mono, 0.4 g Poly, 0.1 g Sat); 2 mg Cholesterol; 51 g Carbohydrate; 10 g Fibre; 6 g Protein; 341 mg Sodium

Pictured on page 252.

Skinny Potato Vegetable Scallop

Thinly sliced potatoes and an assortment of vegetables are complemented by savoury rosemary and a finishing touch of Parmesan cheese—everything you'd expect in a delicious scalloped potato dish, without being too rich or heavy.

Thinly sliced peeled waxy potato (see Note, below)	4 cups	1 L
Thinly sliced onion (see Note, below)	1 1/2 cups	375 mL
Thinly sliced yellow turnip (rutabaga), quartered lengthwise and sliced crosswise (see Note, below)	1 1/2 cups	375 mL
Thinly sliced carrot (see Note, below)	1 cup	250 mL
Chopped fresh rosemary (or 1/4 tsp., 1 mL, dried, crushed)	1 tsp.	5 mL
Garlic cloves, minced (or 1/2 tsp., 2 mL, powder)	2	2
Pepper	1/4 tsp.	1 mL
Prepared vegetable broth	2 cups	500 mL
All-purpose flour	2 tbsp.	30 mL
Grated Parmesan cheese	2 tbsp.	30 mL

Toss first 7 ingredients in large bowl. Transfer to well-greased 3 1/2 to 4 quart (3.5 to 4 L) slow cooker.

Whisk broth into flour in small bowl until smooth. Pour over potato mixture. Cook, covered, on Low for 8 to 9 hours or on High for 4 to 4 1/2 hours.

Sprinkle with cheese. Makes about 6 cups (1.5 L).

1 cup (250 mL): 124 Calories; 1.1 g Total Fat (trace Mono, 0.1 g Poly, 0.4 g Sat); 2 mg Cholesterol; 24 g Carbohydrate; 4 g Fibre; 5 g Protein; 235 mg Sodium

Pictured on page 216.

Note: Evenly sliced vegetables are one of the secrets to a good scallop. Use a mandolin or a food processor to ensure even thickness.

Wild Rice Pilaf

This rustic-looking mix has the great texture of wild rice and is flavoured with savoury hazelnuts, herbs and sweet dried cherries. Serve it with roast chicken or pork.

Canola oil	2 tsp.	10 mL
Sliced leek (white part only)	1 1/2 cups	375 mL
Thinly sliced celery	1 cup	250 mL
Prepared vegetable broth	3 cups	750 mL
Chopped carrot	1 cup	250 mL
Long-grain brown rice	1/2 cup	125 mL
Wild rice	1/2 cup	125 mL
Chopped dried cherries	1/4 cup	60 mL
Dried thyme	1/2 tsp.	2 mL
Coarsely ground pepper	1/4 tsp.	1 mL
Chopped flaked hazelnuts (filberts), toasted (see Tip, page 267)	2 tbsp.	30 mL
Chopped fresh parsley (or 3/4 tsp., 4 mL, flakes)	1 tbsp.	15 mL
White wine vinegar	2 tsp.	10 mL

Heat canola oil in large frying pan on medium. Add leek and celery. Cook for about 8 minutes, stirring often, until softened. Transfer to greased 3 1/2 to 4 quart (3.5 to 4 L) slow cooker.

Add next 7 ingredients. Stir. Cook, covered, on Low for 5 to 6 hours or on High for 2 1/2 to 3 hours.

Add remaining 3 ingredients. Stir. Makes about 6 cups (1.5 L).

1 cup (250 mL): 200 Calories; 4.1 g Total Fat (2.2 g Mono, 1.0 g Poly, 0.4 g Sat); 0 mg Cholesterol; 36 g Carbohydrate; 4 g Fibre; 5 g Protein; 271 mg Sodium

Peppy Mashed Potatoes

Textured, golden potatoes with a flavourful hint of horseradish. Leaving the peel on the baby potatoes gives an added dose of fibre.

Baby potatoes, halved	5 lbs.	2.3 kg
Prepared chicken broth	3/4 cup	175 mL
Butter, melted	2 tbsp.	30 mL
Salt	1/2 tsp.	2 mL
Pepper	1/2 tsp.	2 mL
Prepared horseradish	2 tbsp.	30 mL

Combine first 5 ingredients in 4 to 5 quart (4 to 5 L) slow cooker. Cook, covered, on Low for 7 to 8 hours or on High for 3 1/2 to 4 hours. Transfer with slotted spoon to large bowl. Mash.

Add horseradish and 1/2 cup (125 mL) cooking liquid. Mash well. Discard remaining cooking liquid. Makes about 9 cups (2.25 L).

1 cup (250 mL): 222 Calories; 1.3 g Total Fat (0.4 g Mono, 0.1 g Poly, 0.8 g Sat); 3 mg Cholesterol; 45 g Carbohydrate; 3 g Fibre; 6 g Protein; 131 mg Sodium

Harvest Turnip Mash

A refreshing change from mashed potatoes—these colourful mashed vegetables have a surprisingly tangy flavour from the apples.

Chopped yellow turnip (rutabaga)	5 cups	1.25 L
Chopped carrot	2 cups	500 mL
Chopped peeled cooking apple (such as McIntosh)	2 cups	500 mL
Prepared vegetable broth	1/2 cup	125 mL
Water	1/2 cup	125 mL
Butter, melted	1/4 cup	60 mL
Brown sugar, packed	2 tsp.	10 mL

Combine first 3 ingredients in 3 1/2 to 4 quart (3.5 to 4 L) slow cooker.

Combine remaining 4 ingredients in small bowl. Pour over turnip mixture. Cook, covered, on Low for 7 to 8 hours or on High for 3 1/2 to 4 hours. Mash well. Makes about 4 1/2 cups (1.1 L).

1 cup (250 mL): 192 Calories; 10.5 g Total Fat (2.6 g Mono, 0.6 g Poly, 6.4 g Sat); 27 mg Cholesterol; 25 g Carbohydrate; 6 g Fibre; 2 g Protein; 259 mg Sodium

Zucchini Couscous

This tomato-based couscous side boasts big, hearty pieces of zucchini and yellow pepper.
Garlic and herbs help to add a distinctly Italian influence.

Chopped zucchini (with peel), about 1/2 inch (12 mm) pieces	4 cups	1 L
Can of diced tomatoes (28 oz., 796 mL), drained	1	1
Chopped yellow (or orange) pepper	1 cup	250 mL
Prepared vegetable broth	1/2 cup	125 mL
Chopped green onion	1/4 cup	60 mL
Dried basil	1/2 tsp.	2 mL
Dried rosemary, crushed	1/2 tsp.	2 mL
Dried thyme	1/4 tsp.	1 mL
Garlic powder	1/4 tsp.	1 mL
Salt	1/4 tsp.	1 mL
Pepper	1/4 tsp.	1 mL
Whole wheat couscous	1 cup	250 mL

Combine first 11 ingredients in greased 3 1/2 to 4 quart (3.5 to 4 L) slow cooker. Cook, covered, on Low for 4 to 5 hours or on High for 2 to 2 1/2 hours.

Add couscous. Stir. Cook, covered, on High for about 10 minutes until couscous is tender and liquid is absorbed. Makes about 7 cups (1.75 L).

1 cup (250 mL): 104 Calories; 0.5 g Total Fat (trace Mono, 0.1 g Poly, trace Sat); 0 mg Cholesterol; 21 g Carbohydrate; 4 g Fibre; 4 g Protein; 389 mg Sodium

Asparagus Bake

The spears retain their shape and colour despite the long cooking time.

Fresh asparagus	1 lb.	454 g
All-purpose flour	1 1/2 tbsp.	25 mL
Salt	1/4 tsp.	1 mL
Pepper	1/8 tsp.	0.5 mL
Skim evaporated milk	3/4 cup	175 mL
Grated sharp Cheddar cheese	1/4 cup	60 mL

Cut off any tough ends of asparagus. Lay spears in 5 quart (5 L) slow cooker.

Stir flour, salt and pepper together in saucepan. Whisk in evaporated milk gradually until no lumps remain. Heat and stir until boiling and thickened.

Stir in cheese to melt. Pour over asparagus. Cover. Cook on Low for 3 to 4 hours. If you like your asparagus crunchy, check for doneness at 2 to 2 1/2 hours. Remove asparagus with slotted spoon. Serves 6.

1 serving: 70 Calories; 2.5 g Total Fat (0g Mono, 0 g Poly, 1.5g Sat); <5 mg Cholesterol; 8 g Carbohydrate, 2 g Fibre; 5 g Protein; 160 mg Sodium

Toasted Bulgur and Mushrooms

A few simple ingredients combine to create a versatile and nutritious side of fluffy bulgur with a nice, chewy texture and toasty flavour.

Bulgur (coarse grind)	2 cups	500 mL
Prepared chicken broth	2 cups	500 mL
Sliced fresh white mushrooms	2 cups	500 mL
Finely chopped onion	1/2 cup	125 mL
Butter, melted	2 tbsp.	30 mL
Dried dillweed	2 tsp.	10 mL

Combine all 6 ingredients in 3 1/2 to 4 quart (3.5 to 4 L) slow cooker. Cook, covered, on Low for 4 hours or on High for 2 hours. Stir well. Makes about 4 cups (1 L).

1 cup (250 mL): 326 Calories; 7.4 g Total Fat (1.9 g Mono, 0.7 g Poly, 4.0 g Sat); 15 mg Cholesterol; 57 g Carbohydrate; 13 g Fibre; 12 g Protein; 444 mg Sodium

Stuffed Sweet Potatoes

Delicious. Pineapple flavour comes through with pecans giving a nice crunch.

Medium sweet potatoes (or yams)	6	6
Canned crushed pineapple, with juice	1 cup	250 mL
Grated medium Cheddar cheese	1/4 cup	60 mL
Hard margarine (or butter), melted	1 tbsp.	15 mL
Salt	3/4 tsp.	4 mL
Pepper	1/8 tsp.	0.5 mL
Finely chopped pecans	2 tbsp.	30 mL
Paprika, sprinkle		

Place sweet potato, pointed ends up, in a 5 quart (5 L) slow cooker. Cover. Cook on Low for 7 to 8 hours. Cut thick slice from top lengthwise. Scoop out pulp into bowl, leaving shell 1/4 inch (6 mm) thick.

Add next 5 ingredients to potato pulp. Mash well. Spoon back into shells.

Sprinkle with pecans and paprika. Arrange on baking pan. Bake in 425°F (220°C) oven for 15 to 20 minutes until hot. Serves 6.

1 stuffed potato: 180 Calories; 5 g Total Fat (2 g Mono, 1 g Poly, 1.5 g Sat); <5 mg Cholesterol; 32 g Carbohydrate, 4 g Fibre; 3 g Protein; 420 mg Sodium

Glazed Carrots

These are best cooked on High to keep the great taste of carrot. Nicely glazed.

Peeled baby carrots	2 lbs.	900 g
Water	1/4 cup	60 mL
Cornstarch	1 tbsp.	15 mL
Brown sugar, packed	1/2 cup	125 mL
Hard margarine (or butter), melted	1 tbsp.	15 mL

Place carrot in 3 1/2 quart (3.5 L) slow cooker.

Stir water, cornstarch, brown sugar and margarine together in small bowl. Pour over carrot. Cover. Cook on High for 3 to 4 hours. Stir before serving. Makes 5 cups (1.25 L).

1/2 cup (125 mL): 90 Calories; 1.5g Total Fat (0.5 g Mono, 0 g Poly, 0 g Sat): 0 mg Cholesterol; 14 g Carbohydrate; 2 g Fibre; <1 g Protein; 90 mg Sodium

Herbed Barley Risotto

A flavourful risotto made with barley instead of rice.

Cooking oil	1 tbsp.	15 mL
Finely chopped onion	1 cup	250 mL
Sliced fresh white mushrooms	2 cups	500 mL
Garlic cloves, minced (or 1 tsp., 5 mL, powder)	4	4
Prepared vegetable broth	2 2/3 cups	650 mL
Medium tomatoes, peeled (see Tip, below), quartered, seeds removed	3	3
Pearl barley, rinsed and drained	1 cup	250 mL
Dry white (or alcohol-free) wine	1/2 cup	125 mL
Dried whole oregano	1/2 tsp.	2 mL
Dried rosemary, crushed	1/2 tsp.	2 mL
Salt	1/4 tsp.	1 mL
Pepper	1/4 tsp.	1 mL
Grated Parmesan cheese	1/3 cup	75 mL
Chopped fresh parsley (or 1 1/2 tsp., 7 mL, flakes)	2 tbsp.	30 mL

Heat cooking oil in medium frying pan on medium. Add onion. Cook for 5 to 10 minutes, stirring often, until softened.

Add mushrooms and garlic. Cook for 3 to 5 minutes, stirring occasionally, until mushrooms are softened. Transfer to 3 1/2 to 4 quart (3.5 to 4 L) slow cooker.

Add next 8 ingredients. Stir well. Cover. Cook on Low for 8 to 9 hours or on High for 4 to 4 1/2 hours.

Add Parmesan cheese and parsley. Stir well. Serves 4.

1 serving: 310 Calories; 7 g Total Fat (3 g Mono, 1.5 g Poly, 2 g Sat) 5 mg Cholesterol; 50 g Carbohydrate; 6 g Fibre; 11 g Protein; 810 mg Sodium

Make Ahead: The night before, slice mushrooms and prepare tomato mixture. Chill overnight in separate covered bowls. Assemble and cook as directed.

 To peel tomatoes, cut an "x" on the bottom of each tomato, just through the skin. Place tomatoes in boiling water for 30 seconds. Immediately transfer to a bowl of ice water. Let stand until cool enough to handle. Peel and discard skins.

Stuffed Baked Potatoes

Arrive home to hot baked potatoes. Prepare the stuffing while the oven heats.

Medium baking potatoes	6	6
Water	2 tbsp.	30 mL
Light cream cheese, softened	4 oz.	125 g
Non-fat sour cream	2/3 cup	150 mL
Onion salt	1 1/2 tsp.	7 mL
Chopped chives	1 tbsp.	15 mL
Salt	1/2 tsp.	2 mL
Pepper	1/8 tsp.	0.5 mL
Grated medium Cheddar cheese	1/3 cup	75 mL
Paprika, sprinkle		

Arrange potatoes in 3 1/2 quart (3.5 L) slow cooker, stacking if necessary. Add water. Cover. Cook on Low for 8 to 10 hours.

For stuffing, mash next 6 ingredients together in bowl. Cut lengthwise slice from top of each potato. Scoop hot potato into same bowl leaving shells intact. Mash well. Spoon back into shells.

Sprinkle with cheese and paprika. Arrange in single layer in 9 x 13 inch (22 x 33 cm) baking pan. Bake in 425°F (220°C) oven for about 15 minutes until hot. Makes 6 stuffed potatoes.

1 stuffed potato: 250 Calories; 4.5 g Total Fat (0.5g Mono, 0g Poly, 3g Sat); 15 mg Cholesterol; 41 g Carbohydrate, 3 g Fibre; 9 g Protein; 827 mg Sodium

Scalloped Potatoes

A breeze to make. Creamy and delicious.

Water	2 cups	500 mL
Cream of tartar	1 tsp.	5 mL
Medium potatoes, quartered lengthwise and thinly sliced	5	5
All-purpose flour	1/4 cup	60 mL
Salt	1 tsp.	5 mL
Pepper	1/8 tsp.	0.5 mL
Milk	1 1/2 cups	375 mL
Grated sharp Cheddar cheese	1/2 cup	125 mL

(continued on next page)

Combine water and cream of tartar in large bowl. Stir. Add potato. Stir well. This will help keep potatoes from darkening. Drain. Turn potato into 4 quart (4 L) slow cooker.

Stir flour, salt and pepper together in saucepan. Whisk in milk gradually until no lumps remain. Heat and stir until boiling and thickened.

Stir in cheese to melt. Pour over potato. Cover. Cook on Low for 6 to 8 hours. Makes 4 cups (1 L).

2/3 cup (150 mL): 220 Calories; 4 g Total Fat (1 g Mono, 0 g Poly, 2.5 g Sat); 10 mg Cholesterol; 39 g Carbohydrate, 3 g Fibre; 9 g Protein; 500 mg Sodium

Pumpernickel Bread

This dark-coloured, aromatic loaf is simple to make and requires no pre-rising.

Granulated sugar	1 tsp.	5 mL
Warm water	1 1/3 cups	325 mL
Envelope active dry yeast	1	1
(1/4 oz., 8 g), (1 scant tbsp., 15 mL)		
All-purpose flour	1 cup	250 mL
Rye flour	1 cup	250 mL
Molasses (not blackstrap)	2 tbsp.	30 mL
Cooking oil	2 tbsp.	30 mL
Cocoa	2 tbsp.	30 mL
Salt	1 tsp.	5 mL
Caraway seed (optional)	2 tsp.	10 mL
Rye flour	1 cup	250 mL

Stir sugar into warm water in large bowl. Sprinkle yeast over top. Let stand for 10 minutes. Stir to dissolve yeast.

Add next 7 ingredients. Beat on low to moisten. Beat on high for 2 minutes.

Stir in second amount of rye flour. Grease bottom of 3 1/2 quart (3.5 L) slow cooker. Turn dough into cooker. Lay 5 paper towels between top of slow cooker and lid. Put wooden match or an object 1/8 inch (3 mm) thick between paper towels and edge of slow cooker to allow a bit of steam to escape. Do not lift lid for the first 1 3/4 hours cooking time. Cook on High for about 2 hours. Loosen sides with knife. Turn out onto rack to cool. Cuts into 14 slices.

1 slice: 120 Calories; 2.5 g Total Fat (1.5 g Mono, 0.5 g Poly, 0 g Sat); 0 mg Cholesterol; 21 g Carbohydrate, 3 g Fibre; 3 g Protein; 170 mg Sodium

Herb Bread

Nicely rounded loaf. Herb-coloured with good flavour.

Granulated sugar	1 tsp.	5 mL
Warm water	1 1/3 cups	325 mL
Envelope active dry yeast	1	1
(1/4 oz., 8 g), (1 scant tbsp., 15 mL)		
All-purpose flour	2 cups	500 mL
Granulated sugar	1 tbsp.	15 mL
Cooking oil	2 tbsp.	30 mL
Dried whole oregano	1 tsp.	5 mL
Ground sage	1 tsp.	5 mL
Garlic powder	1/4 tsp.	1 mL
Onion powder	1/4 tsp.	1 mL
Salt	1 tsp.	5 mL
All-purpose flour	1 cup	250 mL

Stir first amount of sugar in warm water in large warmed bowl. Sprinkle with yeast. Let stand for 10 minutes. Stir to dissolve yeast.

Add next 8 ingredients. Beat on low to moisten. Beat on medium for 2 minutes.

Work in second amount of flour. Turn into greased 3 1/2 quart (3.5 L) slow cooker. Smooth top with wet spoon or hand. Place 5 paper towels between top of slow cooker and lid. Put wooden match or an object 1/8 inch (3 mm) thick between paper towels and edge of slow cooker to allow a bit of steam to escape. Do not lift lid for the first 2 hours cooking time. Cook on High for about 2 1/2 hours. Loosen sides with knife. Turn out onto rack to cool. Cuts into 14 slices.

1 slice: 120 Calories; 2 g Total Fat, 1 g Mono, 0.5 g Poly, 0 g Sat; 0 mg Cholesterol; 22 g Carbohydrate, <1 g Fibre; 3 g Protein; 170 mg Sodium

Banana Bread

Makes a large dark loaf. Tastes great plain or buttered.

Hard margarine (or butter), softened	6 tbsp.	90 mL
Granulated sugar	2/3 cup	150 mL
Large egg	1	1
Mashed banana (about 3 small)	3/4 cup	175 mL
All-purpose flour	1 1/2 cups	375 mL
Cocoa	1 tbsp.	15 mL
Baking powder	1 1/2 tsp.	7 mL
Baking soda	1/4 tsp.	1 mL
Salt	1/2 tsp.	2 mL
Chopped walnuts (optional)	1/2 cup	125 mL

Cream margarine and sugar together in bowl. Beat in eggs. Add banana. Mix.

Add remaining 6 ingredients. Stir to moisten. Turn into greased 9 x 5 x 3 inch (22 x 12 x 7.5 cm) loaf pan. Set pan on wire trivet in 5 quart (5 L) oval slow cooker. Place 5 paper towels between top of slow cooker and lid. Put wooden match or an object 1/8 inch (3 mm) thick between paper towels and edge of slow cooker to allow a bit of steam to escape. Do not lift lid for the first 2 hours cooking time. Cook on High for about 2 1/4 hours. A wooden pick inserted in centre should come out clean. Remove pan to wire rack to cool. Let stand for 20 minutes. Loosen sides with knife. Turn out onto rack to cool. Cuts into 18 slices.

1 slice: 130 Calories; 6 g Total Fat (2 g Mono, 3 g Poly, 1 g Sat); 10 mg Cholesterol; 18 g Carbohydrate, <1 g Fibre; 2 g Protein; 160 mg Sodium

Date Loaf

Sweet dates and crunchy walnuts pair perfectly in this large, moist loaf.

Boiling water	2/3 cup	150 mL
Baking soda	1 tsp.	5 mL
Chopped dates	1 cup	250 mL
Large egg, fork-beaten	1	1
Granulated sugar	2/3 cup	150 mL
Hard margarine (or butter), melted	2 tbsp.	30 mL
Vanilla	1/2 tsp.	2 mL
Salt	1/4 tsp.	1 mL
All-purpose flour	1 2/3 cups	400 mL
Chopped walnuts	1/2 cup	125 mL

Pour boiling water over baking soda in bowl. Stir. Add dates. Stir. Let stand until cool.

Combine egg, sugar, margarine, vanilla and salt in separate bowl. Beat. Add date mixture. Stir.

Add flour and walnuts. Stir. Turn into greased 9 x 5 x 3 inch (22 x 12 x 7.5 cm) loaf pan. Place pan on wire trivet in 5 quart (5 L) oval slow cooker. Place 5 paper towels between top of slow cooker and lid. Put wooden match or an object 1/8 inch (3 mm) thick between paper towels and edge of slow cooker to allow a bit of steam to escape. Do not lift lid for the first 2 hours cooking time. Cook on High for about 2 3/4 hours until wooden pick inserted in centre comes out clean. Remove pan to rack. Let stand for 20 minutes. Loosen sides with knife. Turn out onto rack to cool. Cuts into 18 slices.

1 slice: 130 Calories; 4 g Total Fat (1 g Mono, 2 g Poly, 0.5 g Sat); 10 mg Cholesterol; 24 g Carbs, 1 g Fibre; 2 g Protein; 120 mg Sodium

Cranberry Loaf

Lots of flavour and moist colourful slices.

Large egg	1	1
Prepared orange juice	2/3 cup	150 mL
Hard margarine (or butter), melted	2 tbsp.	30 mL
Granulated sugar	1 cup	250 mL
Salt	1 tsp.	5 mL
Vanilla	1/2 tsp.	2 mL
All-purpose flour	2 cups	500 mL
Baking powder	1 1/2 tsp.	7 mL
Coarsely chopped fresh (or frozen, thawed) cranberries	1 cup	250 mL

(continued on next page)

Beat egg in bowl. Add next 5 ingredients. Beat until smooth.

Add flour and baking powder. Stir just to moisten.

Add cranberries. Stir lightly. Turn into greased 9 x 5 x 3 inch (22 x 12 x 7.5 cm) loaf pan. Set pan on wire trivet in 5 quart (5 L) oval slow cooker. Place 5 paper towels between top of slow cooker and lid. Put wooden match between paper towels and edge of slow cooker to allow a bit of steam to escape. Do not lift lid for at least 2 hours. Cook on High for about 2 1/2 hours until wooden pick inserted in centre comes out clean. Remove pan from slow cooker. Let stand for 20 minutes. Loosen sides with knife. Turn out onto rack to cool. Cuts into 18 slices.

1 slice: 120 Calories; 1.5 g Total Fat (0.5 g Mono, 0 g Poly, 0 g Sat); 10 mg Cholesterol; 23 g Carbohydrate; <1 g Fibre; 2 g Protein; 180 mg Sodium

Tomato Herb Bread

This pretty loaf gets its colour from the tomato sauce.

Granulated sugar	1 tsp.	5 mL
Warm water	1/3 cup	75 mL
Envelope active dry yeast	1	1
(1/4 oz., 8 g), (1 scant tbsp., 15 mL)		
All-purpose flour	2 cups	500 mL
Granulated sugar	1 tbsp.	15 mL
Finely minced onion	1/4 cup	60 mL
Lukewarm tomato sauce, plus water	7.5 oz.	213 mL
to make 1 cup (250 mL)		
Grated sharp Cheddar cheese	1/4 cup	60 mL
Salt	1 tsp.	5 mL
Pepper	1/4 tsp.	1 mL
Dried whole oregano	1/2 tsp.	2 mL
All-purpose flour	1 cup	250 mL

Stir first amount of sugar into warm water in large warmed bowl. Sprinkle yeast over top. Let stand for 10 minutes. Stir to dissolve yeast.

Add next 8 ingredients. Beat on low to moisten. Beat on high for 2 minutes.

Work in second amount of flour. Turn into greased 3 1/2 quart (3.5 L) slow cooker. Smooth top with wet spoon or hand. Place 5 paper towels between top of slow cooker and lid. Put wooden match or an object 1/8 inch (3 mm) thick between paper towels and edge of slow cooker to allow a bit of steam to escape. Do not lift lid for the first 2 hours cooking time. Cook on High for about 2 1/2 hours. Loosen sides with knife. Turn out onto rack to cool. Cuts into 14 slices.

1 slice: 120 Calories; 1 g Total Fat (0 g Mono ,0 g Poly, 0 g Sat); < 5 mg Cholesterol; 23 g Carbohydrate, 1 g Fibre; 4 g Protein; 260 mg Sodium

White Bread

This bread has the same aroma and flavour as homemade bread
with a slightly more porous texture.

Granulated sugar	2 tsp.	10 mL
Warm water	1 1/4 cups	300 mL
Envelope active dry yeast	1	1
(1/4 oz., 8 g), (1 scant tbsp., 15 mL)		
All-purpose flour	2 cups	500 mL
Granulated sugar	2 tbsp.	30 mL
Cooking oil	2 tbsp.	30 mL
Salt	1 tsp.	5 mL
All-purpose flour	1 cup	250 mL

Stir first amount of sugar and warm water together in large bowl. Sprinkle with yeast. Let stand for 10 minutes. Stir to dissolve yeast.

Add first amount of flour, second amount of sugar, cooking oil and salt. Beat on low to moisten. Beat on high for 2 minutes.

Knead in second amount of flour until a stiff dough forms. Grease bottom of 3 1/2 quart (3.5 L) slow cooker. Turn dough into slow cooker. Lay 5 paper towels between top of slow cooker and lid. Put wooden match or an object 1/8 inch (3 mm) thick between paper towels and edge of slow cooker to allow a bit of steam to escape. Do not lift lid for the first 1 3/4 hours cooking time. Cook on High for about 2 hours. Loosen sides with knife. Turn out onto rack to cool. Cuts into 16 slices.

1 slice: 110 Calories; 2 g Total Fat (1 g Mono, 0.5 g Poly, 0 g Sat); 0 mg Cholesterol; 20 g Carbohydrate; <1 g Fibre; 3 g Protein; 150 mg Sodium

1. White Bean Vegetable Chili, page 206
2. Pineapple Cherry Cobbler, page 266

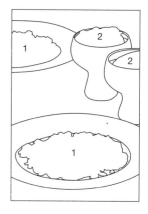

Brown Quick Bread

A porous biscuit-like mealtime or coffee break treat.

Whole wheat flour	2 cups	500 mL
All-purpose flour	1 cup	250 mL
Baking powder	1 tbsp.	15 mL
Salt	1 tsp.	5 mL
Molasses (not blackstrap)	2 tbsp.	30 mL
Cooking oil	2 tbsp.	30 mL
Water	1 1/3 cups	325 mL

Combine first 4 ingredients in bowl. Stir.

Add molasses, cooking oil and water. Mix until moistened. Turn into greased 5 quart (5 L) slow cooker. Place 5 paper towels between top of slow cooker and lid. Put wooden match or an object 1/8 inch (3 mm) thick between paper towels and edge of slow cooker to allow a bit of steam to escape. Do not lift lid for the first 1 3/4 hours cooking time. Cook on High for about 2 hours. Loosen sides with knife. Turn out onto rack to cool. Cuts into 14 wedges.

1 slice: 120 Calories; 2.5 g Total Fat (1 g Mono, 0.5 g Poly, 0 g Sat); 0 mg Cholesterol; 22 g Carbohydrate; 2 g Fibre; 3 g Protein; 240 mg Sodium

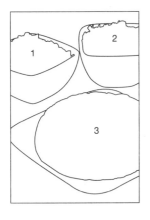

1. Squash and Barley Pilaf, page 236
2. Cranberry Apple Cabbage, page 235
3. Zucchini Cheddar Bacon Bread, page 254

Zucchini Cheddar Bacon Bread

A dense, moist bread with delicious bacon bites—another way to use up garden zucchini! Serve with soup for lunch or a light dinner.

All-purpose flour	1 cup	250 mL
Whole wheat flour	1 cup	250 mL
Grated sharp Cheddar cheese	1/4 cup	60 mL
Baking powder	2 tsp.	10 mL
Baking soda	1/2 tsp.	2 mL
Salt	1/4 tsp.	1 mL
Pepper	1/4 tsp.	1 mL
Large eggs, fork-beaten	2	2
Grated zucchini (with peel)	1 1/2 cups	375 mL
Buttermilk (or soured milk, see Tip, below)	3/4 cup	175 mL
Bacon slices, cooked crisp and crumbled	2	2
Canola oil	2 tbsp.	30 mL
Thinly sliced green onion	2 tbsp.	30 mL
Boiling water	2 cups	500 mL

Combine first 7 ingredients in large bowl. Make a well in centre.

Combine next 6 ingredients in medium bowl. Add to well. Stir until just moistened. Spread evenly in greased 8 inch (20 cm) springform pan. Put an even layer (2 to 3 inches, 5 to 7.5 cm, thick) of crumpled foil into bottom of 5 to 7 quart (5 to 7 L) slow cooker (see Tip, page 195). Pour boiling water into slow cooker. Place pan on foil, pushing down gently to settle evenly. Place double layer of tea towels over slow cooker liner. Cover with lid. Cook on High for about 2 1/2 hours until wooden pick inserted in centre comes out clean. Transfer pan to wire rack. Cool. Cuts into 12 wedges.

1 wedge: 129 Calories; 4.9 g Total Fat (2.2 g Mono, 1.0 g Poly, 1.3 g Sat); 40 mg Cholesterol; 17 g Carbohydrate; 2 g Fibre; 5 g Protein; 259 mg Sodium

Pictured on page 252.

 tip To make soured milk, measure 1 tbsp. (15 mL) white vinegar or lemon juice into a 1 cup (250 mL) liquid measure. Add enough milk to make 1 cup (250 mL). Stir. Let stand for 1 minute.

Fruity Chocolate Cake

A nice dark chocolate cake served up with saucy fruit—great for a winter dessert. Garnish with a dollop of whipped cream.

Package of chocolate cake mix (1 layer size)	1	1
Large eggs, fork-beaten	2	2
Melted butter (or hard margarine)	1/3 cup	75 mL
Water	1/3 cup	75 mL
Cans of fruit cocktail (14 oz., 398 mL, each), drained and juice reserved	2	2
Brown sugar, packed	1/2 cup	125 mL
Reserved fruit cocktail juice	2/3 cup	150 mL
Melted butter (or hard margarine)	3 tbsp.	45 mL
Boiling water	3/4 cup	175 mL

Beat cake mix, eggs, first amount of melted butter and water in medium bowl on high for about 3 minutes until smooth.

Add fruit. Stir gently until combined. Spread evenly in greased 3 1/2 to 4 quart (3.5 to 4 L) slow cooker.

Combine brown sugar, reserved juice and second amount of butter in small bowl. Carefully add boiling water. Stir until sugar is dissolved. Slowly pour over batter. Do not stir. Lay double layer of tea towels over slow cooker liner. Cover with lid. Cook on High for 1 1/2 to 2 hours until wooden pick inserted in centre comes out clean. Let stand, uncovered, for 10 minutes. Serves 8.

1 serving: 523 Calories; 22.8 g Total Fat (7.1 g Mono, 3.8 g Poly, 9.7 g Sat); 84 mg Cholesterol; 80 g Carbohydrate; 3 g Fibre; 6 g Protein; 649 mg Sodium

Raisin Bread Pudding

Bread pudding loaded with raisins, just like it should be! This pudding is especially nice drizzled with maple syrup.

Large eggs	4	4
Milk	2 cups	500 mL
Brown sugar, packed	1/2 cup	125 mL
Ground cinnamon	1/2 tsp.	2 mL
Raisin bread cubes (about 8 slices)	9 cups	2.25 L

Beat eggs in large bowl until frothy. Add next 3 ingredients. Beat well.

Add bread cubes. Toss. Transfer to well-greased 3 1/2 to 4 quart (3.5 to 4 L) slow cooker. Cook, covered, on High for about 2 hours until firm. Serves 6.

1 serving: 248 Calories; 5.4 g Total Fat (1.1 g Mono, 0.2 g Poly, 1.9 g Sat); 148 mg Cholesterol; 41 g Carbohydrate; 2 g Fibre; 10 g Protein; 229 mg Sodium

Maple Apple Bread Pudding

This high-fibre, lower-fat version of the comforting dessert has multi-grain bread, sweet bites of apple and the warm flavours of cinnamon and raisin.

Large eggs	4	4
Can of 2% evaporated milk (13 oz., 370 mL)	1	1
Milk	1 cup	250 mL
Brown sugar, packed	1/4 cup	60 mL
Maple (or maple-flavoured) syrup	3 tbsp.	45 mL
Vanilla extract	1 tsp.	5 mL
Ground cinnamon	3/4 tsp.	4 mL
Day-old multi-grain bread cubes	9 cups	2.25 L
Chopped dried apple	1 cup	250 mL
Chopped golden raisins	1/2 cup	125 mL

Whisk first 7 ingredients in large bowl.

Add remaining 3 ingredients. Stir. Transfer to well-greased 3 1/2 to 4 quart (3.5 to 4 L) slow cooker. Cook, covered, on Low for 3 to 3 1/2 hours until firm. Serves 8.

1 serving: 322 Calories; 4.7 g Total Fat (1.4 g Mono, 0.4 g Poly, 1.5 g Sat); 111 mg Cholesterol; 58 g Carbohydrate; 4 g Fibre; 12 g Protein; 417 mg Sodium

Chunky Spiced Applesauce

This fragrant applesauce is delicious whether served hot or cold. Pair it with gingerbread or sponge cake.

Chopped peeled tart apples (such as Granny Smith)	16 cups	4 L
Granulated sugar	1 cup	250 mL
Ground cinnamon	1 1/2 tsp.	7 mL
Ground nutmeg	1/2 tsp.	2 mL
Water	1 cup	250 mL
Dark raisins (optional)	1/2 cup	125 mL

Combine first 4 ingredients in 5 to 7 quart (5 to 7 L) slow cooker. Pour water over top. Cook, covered, on Low for 4 hours or on High for 2 hours.

Add raisins. Stir. Cook, covered, on High for about 1 hour. Stir to break up apples. Makes about 8 cups (2 L).

1/2 cup (125 mL): 131 Calories; 0.2 g Total Fat (trace Mono, 0.1 g Poly, 0.1 g Sat); 0 mg Cholesterol; 34 g Carbohydrate; 3 g Fibre; trace Protein; 3 mg Sodium

Apple Pecan Crisp

A casual, free-form dessert to spoon into bowls and enjoy! Not-too-tender fruit is topped with granola and toasty pecans for a naturally sweet treat perfect for serving with frozen yogurt.

Chopped peeled tart apple (such as Granny Smith)	5 cups	1.25 L
Fresh (or frozen, thawed) cranberries	1 cup	250 mL
Granulated sugar	1/3 cup	75 mL
Minute tapioca	2 tbsp.	30 mL
Orange juice	2 tbsp.	30 mL
Ground cinnamon	1/4 tsp.	1 mL
Crushed granola	1 1/2 cups	375 mL
Chopped pecans, toasted (see Tip, page 267)	1/2 cup	125 mL
Butter, melted	2 tbsp.	30 mL
Grated orange zest (see Tip, page 278)	1/4 tsp.	1 mL
Ground cinnamon	1/4 tsp.	1 mL

Combine first 6 ingredients in greased 3 1/2 to 4 quart (3.5 to 4 L) slow cooker. Cook, covered, on Low for 3 hours or on High for 1 1/2 hours.

Combine remaining 5 ingredients in small bowl. Spoon over apple mixture. Do not stir. Place double layer of tea towels over slow cooker liner. Cover with lid. Cook on High for about 30 minutes until browned and crisp. Serves 6.

1 serving: 319 Calories; 15.1 g Total Fat (5.0 g Mono, 2.3 g Poly, 3.0 g Sat); 10 mg Cholesterol; 48 g Carbohydrate; 9 g Fibre; 6 g Protein; 38 mg Sodium

Pictured on page 270.

Chocolate PB Brownies

Pour yourself a nice cold glass of milk to go with these delicious chocolate brownies. They look especially appetizing served with a scoop of vanilla ice cream, drizzled with chocolate sauce and sprinkled with peanuts.

Semi-sweet chocolate baking squares (1 oz., 28 g, each), chopped	5	5
Sweetened condensed milk (see Note, below)	2/3 cup	150 mL
Crunchy peanut butter	1/2 cup	125 mL
Large egg, fork-beaten	1	1
Biscuit mix	3/4 cup	175 mL
Boiling water	2 cups	500 mL

Heat chocolate in medium heavy saucepan on lowest heat, stirring often, until chocolate is almost melted. Remove from heat. Stir until smooth. Transfer to medium bowl.

Add condensed milk. Stir until smooth. Add peanut butter and egg. Stir until combined.

Add biscuit mix. Stir until no dry mix remains. Spread evenly in parchment paper-lined greased 8 inch (20 cm) round cake pan. Put an even layer (2 to 3 inches, 5 to 7.5 cm, thick) of crumpled foil into bottom of 5 to 7 quart (5 to 7 L) slow cooker (see Tip, page 195). Pour boiling water into slow cooker. Place pan on foil, pushing down gently to settle evenly. Lay double layer of tea towels over slow cooker liner. Cover with lid. Cook on High for 1 1/2 hours. Transfer pan to wire rack. Let stand for 10 minutes. Cuts into 12 wedges.

1 brownie: 207 Calories; 9.8 g Total Fat (0.6 g Mono, 0.1 g Poly, 3.2 g Sat); 22 mg Cholesterol; 26 g Carbohydrate; 1 g Fibre; 6 g Protein; 170 mg Sodium

Pictured on page 287.

Note: Store remaining sweetened condensed milk in the fridge and use it as a decadent addition to your morning coffee.

Saucy Brandied Apples

These aromatic stewed apples feature tart cranberries, sweet raisins and crunchy nuts—a great winter dessert when your oven is occupied! Serve with a scoop of vanilla ice cream or a dollop of whipped cream.

Brandy	1/2 cup	125 mL
Dried cranberries	1/2 cup	125 mL
Canned raisin pie filling	1 cup	250 mL
Peeled tart apples (such as Granny Smith)	6	6
Chopped pecans, toasted (see Tip, page 267)	1/4 cup	60 mL

Combine brandy and cranberries in small bowl. Let stand for 15 minutes.

Add pie filling. Stir. Transfer to 5 to 7 quart (5 to 7 L) slow cooker.

Cut apples in half. Remove cores (see Tip, below). Arrange apples, cut-side up, in slow cooker. Cook, covered, on Low for 6 to 7 hours or on High for 3 to 3 1/2 hours. Transfer fruit to large serving plate with slotted spoon. Makes about 1 cup (250 mL) sauce.

Sprinkle apples with pecans. Serve with sauce. Serves 12.

1 serving with 1 tbsp (15 mL) sauce: 111 Calories; 1.9 g Total Fat (1.0 g Mono, 0.6 g Poly, 0.2 g Sat); 0 mg Cholesterol; 18 g Carbohydrate; 2 g Fibre; trace Protein; 17 mg Sodium

 A melon baller is a very handy tool for coring an apple that is already peeled and halved.

Carrot Ginger Cake

No one will guess that this moist carrot cake was made in the slow cooker—or that it's a healthier take on tradition! Forego the icing and serve with vanilla yogurt instead.

All-purpose flour	1 cup	250 mL
Brown sugar, packed	2/3 cup	150 mL
Whole wheat flour	1/2 cup	125 mL
Baking powder	1 tsp.	5 mL
Baking soda	1/2 tsp.	2 mL
Ground ginger	1/2 tsp.	2 mL
Ground cinnamon	1/4 tsp.	1 mL
Salt	1/4 tsp.	1 mL
Large eggs	2	2
Apple juice	1/4 cup	60 mL
Canola oil	1/4 cup	60 mL
Vanilla extract	1 tsp.	5 mL
Grated carrot	1 1/2 cups	375 mL
Minced crystallized ginger	3 tbsp.	45 mL
Boiling water	2 cups	500 mL

Combine first 8 ingredients in large bowl. Make a well in centre.

Whisk next 4 ingredients in medium bowl.

Add carrot and ginger. Stir. Add to well. Stir until just moistened. Spread in greased 8 inch (20 cm) springform pan. Put an even layer (2 to 3 inches, 5 to 7.5 cm, thick) of crumpled foil into bottom of 5 to 7 quart (5 to 7 L) slow cooker (see Tip, page 195). Pour boiling water into slow cooker. Place pan on foil, pushing down gently to settle evenly. Place double layer of tea towels over slow cooker liner. Cover with lid. Cook on High for about 1 1/2 hours until wooden pick inserted in centre comes out clean. Transfer pan to wire rack. Cool. Cuts into 12 wedges.

1 wedge: 166 Calories; 5.6 g Total Fat (3.1 g Mono, 1.6 g Poly, 0.6 g Sat); 35 mg Cholesterol; 27 g Carbohydrate; 1 g Fibre; 3 g Protein; 170 mg Sodium

Marbled Yogurt Brownies

Nice, moist brownie wedges with vanilla marbling on top—they will delight and surprise because they're a healthier choice, and because of how they're made! Serve warm from the slow cooker with raspberry yogurt and fresh berries.

All-purpose flour	1/2 cup	125 mL
Cocoa, sifted if lumpy	1/3 cup	75 mL
Whole wheat flour	1/3 cup	75 mL
Baking powder	1/4 tsp.	1 mL
Baking soda	1/4 tsp.	1 mL
Salt	1/8 tsp.	0.5 mL
Egg whites (large)	2	2
Vanilla yogurt	2/3 cup	150 mL
Granulated sugar	1/2 cup	125 mL
Canola oil	2 tbsp.	30 mL
Egg white (large)	1	1
Vanilla yogurt	1/3 cup	75 mL
All-purpose flour	2 tbsp.	30 mL
Boiling water	2 cups	500 mL

Combine first 6 ingredients in medium bowl.

Whisk first amount of egg whites in large bowl until frothy. Add next 3 ingredients. Stir until smooth. Add cocoa mixture. Stir until no white streaks remain. Spread into parchment paper-lined greased 8 inch (20 cm) springform pan.

Whisk next 3 ingredients in small bowl until smooth. Drop spoonfuls randomly onto batter. Swirl wooden pick through top to create marbled effect. Cover pan with foil. Put an even layer (2 to 3 inches, 5 to 7.5 cm, thick) of crumpled foil into bottom of 5 to 7 quart (5 to 7 L) slow cooker (see Tip, page 195). Pour boiling water into slow cooker. Place pan on foil, pushing down gently to settle evenly. Cook, covered, on High for 1 1/2 hours. Transfer pan to wire rack. Let stand for 10 minutes. Cuts into 12 wedges.

1 brownie: 100 Calories; 3.0 g Total Fat (1.6 g Mono, 0.7 g Poly, 0.5 g Sat); 1 mg Cholesterol; 17 g Carbohydrate; 1 g Fibre; 3 g Protein; 90 mg Sodium

Pictured on page 288.

Fudgy Pudding Cake

This moist, saucy pudding is packed with oatmeal and nutty walnut bites. Delicious served warm—right from your slow cooker.

All-purpose flour	1 cup	250 mL
Brown sugar, packed	3/4 cup	175 mL
Chopped walnuts, toasted (see Tip, page 267)	1/4 cup	60 mL
Quick-cooking rolled oats	1/4 cup	60 mL
Cocoa, sifted if lumpy	3 tbsp.	45 mL
Baking powder	1 tsp.	5 mL
Salt	1/4 tsp.	1 mL
Large egg, fork-beaten	1	1
Milk	1/2 cup	125 mL
Butter, melted	2 tbsp.	30 mL
Vanilla extract	1 tsp.	5 mL
Brown sugar, packed	3/4 cup	175 mL
Cocoa, sifted if lumpy	1/4 cup	60 mL
Boiling water	1 1/4 cups	300 mL

Combine first 7 ingredients in large bowl. Make a well in centre.

Combine next 4 ingredients in small bowl. Add to well. Stir until just moistened. Spread evenly in greased 3 1/2 to 4 quart (3.5 to 4 L) slow cooker.

Combine second amounts of brown sugar and cocoa in medium bowl. Sprinkle over batter.

Carefully pour boiling water over top. Do not stir. Place double layer of tea towels over slow cooker liner. Cover with lid. Cook on High for 1 1/2 to 2 hours until wooden pick inserted in centre comes out clean. Serves 6.

1 serving: 366 Calories; 9.2 g Total Fat (2.1 g Mono, 2.6 g Poly, 3.6 g Sat); 47 mg Cholesterol; 71 g Carbohydrate; 3 g Fibre; 6 g Protein; 239 mg Sodium

Steamed Pumpkin Carrot Cake

This spicy snack cake is really easy to prepare. If desired, ice with prepared cream cheese frosting, drizzle with caramel sauce, or dust with icing sugar.

Carrot muffin mix	2 cups	500 mL
Ground cinnamon	1 tsp.	5 mL
Canned pumpkin pie filling	1 cup	250 mL
Large eggs	2	2
Water	2/3 cups	150 mL
Raisins	1/2 cup	125 mL

Combine muffin mix and cinnamon in large bowl. Make a well in centre.

Whisk pie filling, eggs and water in medium bowl until smooth. Add raisins. Stir. Add to well. Stir until just moistened. Pour into greased 8 inch (20 cm) springform pan. Put an even layer (2 to 3 inches, 5 to 7.5 mL, thick) of crumpled foil into bottom of 5 to 7 quart (5 to 7 L) slow cooker (see Tip, page 195). Place pan on foil, pushing down gently to settle evenly. Lay double layer of tea towels over slow cooker liner. Cover with lid. Cook on High for about 2 1/2 hours until wooden pick inserted in centre comes out clean. Transfer pan to wire rack. Cool completely. Cuts into 12 wedges.

1 wedge: 163 Calories; 6.7 g Total Fat (0 g Mono, 0 g Poly, 6.2 g Sat); 36 mg Cholesterol; 29 g Carbohydrate; 17 g Fibre; 7 g Protein; 536 mg Sodium

Toffee Pudding Cake

This soft, sponge-textured butterscotch cake has a tasty toffee layer on the bottom. Serve each slice with vanilla ice cream.

Large eggs	2	2
Package of white cake mix (1 layer size)	1	1
Box of instant butterscotch pudding powder (4-serving size)	1	1
Cooking oil	1/3 cup	75 mL
Water	1/2 cup	125 mL
Boiling water	2 cups	500 mL
Toffee bits	1/2 cup	125 mL

Beat first 5 ingredients on high in medium bowl for about 3 minutes until smooth. Pour into greased 8 inch (20 cm) springform pan. Put an even layer (2 to 3 inches, 5 to 7.5 cm, thick) of crumpled foil into bottom of 5 to 7 quart (5 to 7 L) slow cooker (see Tip, page 195). Pour boiling water into slow cooker (see Tip, page 195). Place pan on foil, pushing down gently to settle evenly.

Sprinkle toffee bits over top. Lay double layer of tea towels over slow cooker liner. Cover with lid. Cook on High for 2 hours until wooden pick inserted in centre comes out clean. Transfer pan to wire rack. Let stand for 15 minutes. Cuts into 12 wedges.

1 wedge: 325 Calories; 14.7 g Total Fat (5.6 g Mono, 3.6 g Poly, 3.1 g Sat); 43 mg Cholesterol; 46 g Carbohydrate; trace Fibre; 3 g Protein; 461 mg Sodium

Pictured on page 161.

Mango Blueberry Cobbler

A whole wheat, cinnamon-spiced biscuit tops a sweet blueberry and mango filling for an aromatic cobbler with an inviting and cozy look.

Chopped ripe (or frozen, thawed) mango	5 cups	1.25 L
Fresh (or frozen, thawed) blueberries	4 cups	1 L
Brown sugar, packed	1/4 cup	60 mL
All-purpose flour	2 tbsp.	30 mL
Grated lemon zest	1/2 tsp.	2 mL
All-purpose flour	3/4 cup	175 mL
Whole wheat flour	1/2 cup	125 mL
Brown sugar, packed	1/4 cup	60 mL
Baking powder	2 tsp.	10 mL
Ground cinnamon	1/2 tsp.	2 mL
Ground ginger	1/2 tsp.	2 mL
Salt	1/8 tsp.	0.5 mL
Milk	2/3 cup	150 mL
Canola oil	2 tbsp.	30 mL
Vanilla extract	1 tsp.	5 mL

Combine first 5 ingredients in greased 3 1/2 to 4 quart (3.5 to 4 L) slow cooker. Cook, covered, on Low for 4 to 5 hours or on High for 2 to 2 1/2 hours. Stir.

Combine next 7 ingredients in medium bowl. Make a well in centre.

Combine remaining 3 ingredients in small bowl. Add to well. Stir until just combined. Drop batter onto mango mixture, using about 1/4 cup (60 mL) for each mound. Cook, covered, on High for about 1 hour until wooden pick inserted in centre of biscuit comes out clean. Serves 8.

1 serving: 268 Calories; 4.4 g Total Fat (2.3 g Mono, 1.3 g Poly, 0.5 g Sat); 1 mg Cholesterol; 57 g Carbohydrate; 5 g Fibre; 4 g Protein; 188 mg Sodium

Pineapple Cherry Cobbler

This easy cobbler has sweet cherry and pineapple flavours underneath a cake-like biscuit layer.
Add a scoop of ice cream to each bowlful.

Can of cherry pie filling	1	1
(19 oz., 540 mL)		
Can of crushed pineapple (with juice)	1	1
(19 oz., 540 mL)		
Biscuit mix	1 1/2 cups	375 mL
Large egg, fork-beaten	1	1
Buttermilk (or soured milk),	1 cup	250 mL
(see Tip, page 254)		

Combine pie filling and pineapple in greased 3 1/2 to 4 quart (3.5 to 4 L) slow cooker.

Measure biscuit mix into medium bowl. Make a well in centre.

Add egg and buttermilk to well. Stir until just moistened. Spoon evenly over pineapple mixture. Cook, covered, on High for 2 1/2 to 3 hours until wooden pick inserted in centre comes out clean. Serves 8.

1 serving: 233 Calories; 3.9 g Total Fat (0.2 g Mono, trace Poly, 1.2 g Sat); 29 mg Cholesterol; 45 g Carbohydrate; 1 g Fibre; 5 g Protein; 354 mg Sodium

Pictured on page 251.

Winter's Day Compote

Gently cooked apple, apricot and raisins create a warm compote to serve alongside plain cheesecake or vanilla ice cream. Leftovers make a delicious addition to granola or oatmeal for breakfast.

Sliced peeled cooking apple (such as McIntosh)	3 cups	750 mL
Sliced peeled tart apple (such as Granny Smith)	3 cups	750 mL
Chopped dried apricot	1 cup	250 mL
Brown sugar, packed	1/3 cup	75 mL
Water	1 cup	250 mL
Can of raisin pie filling (19 oz., 540 mL)	1	1

Combine first 5 ingredients in 3 1/2 to 4 quart (3.5 to 4 L) slow cooker.

Spoon pie filling over top. Do not stir. Cook, covered, on Low for 5 to 6 hours or on High for 2 1/2 to 3 hours. Stir. Makes about 6 1/2 cups (1.6 L).

1/2 cup (125 mL): 115 Calories; 0.1 g Total Fat (0 g Mono, trace Poly, trace Sat); 0 mg Cholesterol; 29 g Carbohydrate; 2 g Fibre; trace Protein; 46 mg Sodium

 tip When toasting nuts, seeds or coconut, cooking times will vary for each type of nut—so never toast them together. For small amounts, place the ingredient in an ungreased shallow frying pan. Heat on medium for 3 to 5 minutes, stirring often, until golden. For larger amounts, spread the ingredient evenly in an ungreased shallow pan. Bake in a 350°F (175°C) oven for 5 to 10 minutes, stirring or shaking often, until golden.

Peaches à la Mode

This combination of sweet, syrupy peaches with pound cake and ice cream makes enough to please a crowd—no oven space required!

Cans of sliced peaches (28 oz., 796 mL, each), drained and juice reserved	2	2
Minute tapioca	2 tbsp.	30 mL
Ground cinnamon	1/2 tsp.	2 mL
Reserved peach juice	1/2 cup	125 mL
Frozen pound cake, thawed (10 1/2 oz., 298 g)	1	1
Butterscotch ripple ice cream	2 1/2 cups	625 mL

Combine first 4 ingredients in 3 1/2 to 4 quart (3.5 to 4 L) slow cooker. Cook, covered, on Low for 3 to 4 hours or on High for 1 1/2 to 2 hours.

Slice pound cake into 10 slices, about 3/4 inch (2 cm) thick. Top each slice with ice cream. Spoon peach mixture over top. Serves 10.

1 serving: 323 Calories; 11.2 g Total Fat (1.8 g Mono, 0.3 g Poly, 6.9 g Sat); 88 mg Cholesterol; 52 g Carbohydrate; 1 g Fibre; 4 g Protein; 184 mg Sodium

1. Danish Rice Pudding, page 280
2. Maple Orange Pears, page 277
3. Chocolate Hazelnut Cheesecake, page 274

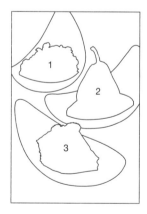

Rhuberry Sauce

This thick, delicious rhubarb and strawberry sauce is wonderful spooned over cakes, ice cream or even pancakes and waffles.

Chopped fresh (or frozen, thawed) rhubarb	6 cups	1.5 L
Container of frozen strawberries in light syrup (15 oz., 425 g), thawed	1	1
Granulated sugar	1 cup	250 mL
Minute tapioca	1 tbsp.	15 mL
Cinnamon stick (4 inches, 10 cm)	1	1

Combine all 5 ingredients in 3 1/2 to 4 quart (3.5 to 4 L) slow cooker. Cook, covered, on Low for 5 to 6 hours or on High for 2 1/2 to 3 hours. Remove and discard cinnamon stick. Makes about 5 cups (1.25 L).

1/2 cup (125 mL): 130 Calories; 0.2 g Total Fat (trace Mono, 0.1 g Poly, trace Sat); 0 mg Cholesterol; 33 g Carbohydrate; 2 g Fibre; 1 g Protein; 3 mg Sodium

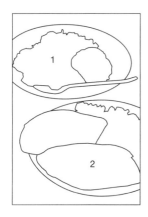

1. Apple Pecan Crisp, page 257
2. Fish Burritos, page 112

Café au Lait Custard

Rich, coffee-flavoured baked custard is a smooth, sweet ending to a meal. Whether you serve it warm or chilled, a dollop of whipped cream is the perfect garnish.

Large eggs	3	3
Granulated sugar	1/2 cup	125 mL
Vanilla extract	1 tsp.	5 mL
Salt, sprinkle		
Can of evaporated milk	1	1
(13 1/2 oz., 385 mL)		
Instant coffee granules	1 1/2 tbsp.	25 mL

Whisk first 4 ingredients in medium heatproof bowl until smooth.

Combine milk and coffee granules in medium saucepan on medium. Heat for about 5 minutes, stirring often, until coffee granules are dissolved and bubbles form around edge of saucepan. Slowly add to egg mixture, stirring constantly, until sugar is dissolved. Strain mixture through sieve back into pan. Pour mixture into 4 greased 3/4 cup (175 mL) ovenproof ramekins. Put an even layer (2 to 3 inches, 5 to 7.5 cm, thick) of crumpled foil into bottom of 5 to 7 quart (5 to 7 L) slow cooker (see Tip, page 195). Place ramekins on foil, pushing down gently to settle evenly. Pour hot water into slow cooker until halfway up side of ramekins. Lay double layer of tea towels over slow cooker liner. Cover with lid. Cook on High for about 1 1/2 hours until custard is set. Serves 4.

1 serving: 276 Calories; 9.5 g Total Fat (1.3 g Mono, 0.3 g Poly, 5.7 g Sat); 192 mg Cholesterol; 35 g Carbohydrate; 0 g Fibre; 11 g Protein; 286 mg Sodium

Pictured on page 215.

Chocolate Coconut Fondue

This deep, dark chocolate fondue has rich coconut flavour and tastes great with ripe fruit. It's perfect for parties because it doesn't require much attention! Just turn your slow cooker to Low to keep the fondue warm.

Dark chocolate bars (3 1/2 oz., 100 g, each), chopped	6	6
Can of coconut milk (14 oz., 398 mL)	1	1
Milk	1 cup	250 mL
Vanilla extract	1 tsp.	5 mL
Coconut extract	1/2 tsp.	2 mL
Chopped fresh pineapple (1 inch, 2.5 cm, pieces)	3 cups	750 mL
Fresh cherries	3 cups	750 mL
Halved fresh strawberries	3 cups	750 mL
Sliced banana (about 1 inch, 2.5 cm, pieces)	3 cups	750 mL

Combine first 5 ingredients in 3 1/2 to 4 quart (3.5 to 4 L) slow cooker. Cook, covered, on High for about 1 hour, stirring occasionally, until smooth.

Serve with remaining 4 ingredients for dipping. Serves 12.

1 serving: 431 Calories; 24.1 g Total Fat (0.4 g Mono, 0.2 g Poly, 16.9 g Sat); 5 mg Cholesterol; 53 g Carbohydrate; 8 g Fibre; 5 g Protein; 16 mg Sodium

Chocolate Hazelnut Cheesecake

This chocolatey cheesecake has rich flavour but a light texture—delicious! Top each slice with whipped cream and garnish with fresh berries.

Cream-filled chocolate cookies	10	10
Blocks of cream cheese (8 oz., 250 g, each), softened	2	2
Chocolate hazelnut spread	1 cup	250 mL
Large eggs, fork-beaten	3	3
Sour cream	1 cup	250 mL
Boiling water	2 cups	500 mL
Chocolate hazelnut spread	1/3 cup	75 mL

Process cookies in food processor until coarse crumbs form. Press firmly in greased 8 inch (20 cm) springform pan lined with parchment paper. Let stand in freezer for 10 minutes.

Beat cream cheese and first amount of chocolate hazelnut spread in large bowl, scraping down sides as necessary, until smooth.

Add eggs and sour cream. Beat well. Spread evenly over cookie crumbs. Put an even layer (2 to 3 inches, 5 to 7.5 cm, thick) of crumpled foil into bottom of 5 to 7 quart (5 to 7 L) slow cooker (see Tip, page 195). Pour boiling water into slow cooker. Place pan on foil, pushing down gently to settle evenly. Lay double layer of tea towels over slow cooker liner. Cover with lid. Cook on High for 1 1/2 hours. Transfer pan to wire rack. Cool completely. Chill, covered, for at least 6 hours or overnight.

Remove from pan. Spread remaining chocolate hazelnut spread over top and sides of cheesecake. Cuts into 12 wedges.

1 wedge: 361 Calories; 26.3 g Total Fat (4.1 g Mono, 1.7 g Poly, 13.3 g Sat); 105 mg Cholesterol; 24 g Carbohydrate; 2 g Fibre; 6 g Protein; 185 mg Sodium

Pictured on page 269.

PB Banana "Cheesecake"

Dessert tofu and bananas make for a dairy-free dessert that closely resembles cheesecake. A healthier after-dinner option for peanut butter lovers! Garnish with whipped cream, sliced banana and chocolate filigrees for a special presentation.

Graham cracker crumbs	1 cup	250 mL
Finely chopped unsalted peanuts	1/4 cup	60 mL
Brown sugar, packed	1 tbsp.	15 mL
Canola oil	1 tbsp.	15 mL
Overripe medium bananas, mashed	4	4
Packages of plain dessert tofu (5.35 oz., 150 g, each)	4	4
Large eggs	3	3
Liquid honey	1/4 cup	60 mL
Vanilla extract	1/2 tsp.	2 mL
All-purpose flour	1/4 cup	60 mL
Salt, just a pinch		
Boiling water	2 cups	500 mL
Icing (or confectioner's) sugar	1/2 cup	125 mL
Smooth peanut butter	1/2 cup	125 mL

Combine first 4 ingredients in small bowl. Press firmly into greased 8 inch (20 cm) springform pan lined with parchment paper. Let stand in freezer for 10 minutes.

Beat bananas and tofu in large bowl until smooth.

Add next 3 ingredients. Beat well.

Add flour and salt. Beat until combined. Pour over crumb mixture. Put an even layer (2 to 3 inches, 5 to 7.5 cm, thick) of crumpled foil into bottom of 5 to 7 quart (5 to 7 L) slow cooker (see Tip, page 195). Pour boiling water into slow cooker. Place pan on foil, pushing down gently to settle evenly. Place double layer of tea towels over slow cooker liner. Cover with lid. Cook on High for about 2 hours until firm. Transfer pan to wire rack. Blot top of cheesecake with paper towels. Cool. Chill, covered, for at least 6 hours or overnight. Remove from pan.

Beat icing sugar and peanut butter in medium bowl until fluffy. Spread over top of cake. Cuts into 12 wedges.

1 wedge: 237 Calories; 10.3 g Total Fat (4.7 g Mono, 2.8 g Poly, 2.0 g Sat); 53 mg Cholesterol; 32 g Carbohydrate; 2 g Fibre; 7 g Protein; 110 mg Sodium

Pictured on page 288.

Blue Cheese Pears

Poached pears are always a light, elegant dessert option. Here they are paired with a tangy blue cheese yogurt for a delightful sweet and savoury contrast.

White grape juice	2/3 cup	150 mL
Butter, melted	1 tbsp.	15 mL
Medium peeled firm pears	6	6
Plain Balkan-style yogurt	1 cup	250 mL
Crumbled blue cheese	3 tbsp.	45 mL
Liquid honey	2 tsp.	10 mL
Grated lemon zest	1/2 tsp.	2 mL
Salt, sprinkle		
Coarsely ground pepper	1/4 tsp.	1 mL
Chopped pecans, toasted (see Tip, page 267)	2 tbsp.	30 mL

Combine grape juice and butter in 4 to 5 quart (4 to 5 L) slow cooker.

Carefully remove cores from bottoms of pears using apple corer, leaving stems intact. Set upright in grape juice mixture. Cook, covered, on High for 2 hours. Transfer pears with slotted spoon to large plate. Cool. Cut pears into thin slices, leaving stem intact. Fan pears on 6 serving plates.

Combine next 6 ingredients in small bowl. Drizzle over pears.

Sprinkle with pecans. Serves 6.

1 serving: 162 Calories; 4.0 g Total Fat (1.3 g Mono, 0.6 g Poly, 0.9 g Sat); 4 mg Cholesterol; 31 g Carbohydrate; 4 g Fibre; 5 g Protein; 97 mg Sodium

Pictured on page 288.

Maple Orange Pears

These tender, golden pears are drizzled with delicate buttery sauce.
Serve with vanilla ice cream for a dinner party.

Maple syrup	1/2 cup	125 mL
Butter (or hard margarine), melted	2 tbsp.	30 mL
Water	2 tbsp.	30 mL
Medium firm peeled pears	6	6
Orange juice	2 tbsp.	30 mL
Cornstarch	2 tsp.	10 mL

Combine maple syrup, melted butter and water in 4 to 5 quart (4 to 5 L) slow cooker.

Carefully remove cores from bottom of pears using apple corer, leaving stems intact. Set upright in maple syrup mixture. Cook, covered, on High for 2 hours. Transfer pears with slotted spoon to serving plate.

Stir orange juice into cornstarch in small cup until smooth. Add to cooking liquid. Stir. Cook, covered, on High for about 20 minutes until thickened. Pour over pears. Serves 6.

1 serving: 205 Calories; 4.1 g Total Fat (1.0 g Mono, 0.2 g Poly, 2.4 g Sat); 10 mg Cholesterol; 45 g Carbohydrate; 5 g Fibre; 1 g Protein; 31 mg Sodium

Pictured on page 269.

Oatmeal Cookie Crisp

Choose your favourite fruit to cook up in this easy dessert—try strawberries and rhubarb in season for a special treat. Serve it warm with a dollop of whipped cream, or spoon some over vanilla ice cream.

Fresh (or frozen, thawed) mixed berries	4 cups	1 L
Minute tapioca	3 tbsp.	45 mL
Crushed crisp oatmeal cookies (about 12)	1 1/2 cups	375 mL
Chopped pecans	1/2 cup	125 mL
Butter (or hard margarine), melted	2 tbsp.	30 mL

Combine berries and tapioca in greased 3 1/2 to 4 quart (3.5 to 4 L) slow cooker. Cook, covered, on Low for 3 hours or on High for 1 1/2 hours.

Combine remaining 3 ingredients in small bowl. Spoon over berry mixture. Do not stir. Lay double layer of tea towels over slow cooker liner. Cover with lid. Cook on High for about 30 minutes until browned and crisp. Makes about 4 cups (1 L).

1/2 cup (125 mL): 257 Calories; 14.6 g Total Fat (6.2 g Mono, 2.4 g Poly, 4.4 g Sat); 12 mg Cholesterol; 30 g Carbohydrate; 4 g Fibre; 3 g Protein; 150 mg Sodium

Light Lemon Pudding

A low-fat pudding with full flavour! An aromatic whole wheat cake layer hides a saucy lemon pudding beneath. Dress it up with a fresh berry garnish.

All-purpose flour	3/4 cup	175 mL
Granulated sugar	1/2 cup	125 mL
Whole wheat flour	1/3 cup	75 mL
Baking powder	1 tsp.	5 mL
Grated lemon zest (see Tip, below)	1 tsp.	5 mL
Salt	1/4 tsp.	1 mL
Large egg, fork-beaten	1	1
Milk	1/2 cup	125 mL
Butter, melted	3 tbsp.	45 mL
Vanilla extract	1 tsp.	5 mL
Granulated sugar	1/2 cup	125 mL
Cornstarch	1 tbsp.	15 mL
Grated lemon zest (see Tip, below)	1 tsp.	5 mL
Boiling water	1 cup	250 mL
Lemon juice	1/4 cup	60 mL

Combine first 6 ingredients in large bowl. Make a well in centre.

Combine next 4 ingredients in medium bowl. Add to well. Stir until just moistened. Pour into greased 3 1/2 to 4 quart (3.5 to 4 L) slow cooker.

Combine next 3 ingredients in small bowl. Sprinkle over batter.

Carefully pour boiling water and lemon juice over batter. Do not stir. Cook, covered, on High for about 2 hours until wooden pick inserted in centre of biscuit comes out clean. Serve immediately. Serves 6.

1 serving: 236 Calories; 6.8 g Total Fat (1.9 g Mono, 0.4 g Poly, 4.0 g Sat); 52 mg Cholesterol; 44 g Carbohydrate; 1 g Fibre; 4 g Protein; 252 mg Sodium

 tip When a recipe calls for grated zest and juice, it's easier to grate the fruit first, then juice it. Be careful not to grate down to the pith (white part of the peel), which is bitter and best avoided.

Strawberries and Dumplings

Tender dumplings top scrumptious strawberries, all with a hint of lemon—like strawberry shortcake with a twist. Drizzle each serving with a bit of cream.

Small lemon	1	1
Frozen whole strawberries, thawed	4 cups	1 L
Granulated sugar	6 tbsp.	90 mL
Biscuit mix	1 cup	250 mL
Granulated sugar	2 tbsp.	30 mL
Milk	1/3 cup	75 mL

Grate 1 tsp. (5 mL) lemon zest into small bowl. Set aside. Squeeze 1 tsp. (5 mL) lemon juice into 3 1/2 to 4 quart (3.5 to 4 L) slow cooker.

Add strawberries and first amount of sugar to slow cooker. Stir. Cook, covered, on Low for 4 to 5 hours or on High for 2 to 2 1/2 hours until boiling.

Add biscuit mix and remaining sugar to reserved zest. Stir. Add milk. Stir until just moistened. Drop evenly over strawberry mixture in 6 mounds. Cook, covered, on High for about 30 minutes until wooden pick inserted in centre comes out clean. Serves 6.

1 serving: 282 Calories; 2.7 g Total Fat (0.1 g Mono, 0.1 g Poly, 0.6 g Sat); 1 mg Cholesterol; 66 g Carbohydrate; 3 g Fibre; 3 g Protein; 277 mg Sodium

Strawberry Rhubarb Stew

This thick, sweet-tart topping is deliciously fruity and can be served warm or cold over ice cream, frozen yogurt or angel food cake.

Chopped fresh (or frozen, thawed) rhubarb	4 cups	1 L
Peeled medium tart apples (such as Granny Smith), cut into 8 wedges each	2	2
Dried apricots, halved	2 cups	500 mL
Water	1 cup	250 mL
Liquid honey	1/4 cup	60 mL
Minute tapioca	2 tbsp.	30 mL
Cinnamon sticks (4 inches, 10 cm, each)	2	2
Fresh strawberries, quartered	3 cups	750 mL
Vanilla extract	1/2 tsp.	2 mL

Combine first 7 ingredients in 3 1/2 to 4 quart (3.5 to 4 L) slow cooker. Cook, covered, on Low for 5 to 6 hours or on High for 2 1/2 to 3 hours. Remove and discard cinnamon sticks.

Add strawberries and vanilla. Stir. Cook, covered, on High for about 20 minutes until strawberries are heated through. Makes about 7 cups (1.75 L).

1 cup (250 mL): 202 Calories; 0.4 g Total Fat (0.1 g Mono, 0.2 g Poly, 0.1 g Sat); 0 mg Cholesterol; 51 g Carbohydrate; 6 g Fibre; 2 g Protein; 30 mg Sodium

Pictured on page 216.

Desserts

Coconut Rice Pudding

Creamy and comforting, sweet coconut rice contrasts with the vibrant colour of fresh mango. This easy dessert goes well with a Thai or Vietnamese dinner.

Short-grain white rice	2 cups	500 mL
Granulated sugar	1 cup	250 mL
Water	3 cups	750 mL
Salt, sprinkle		
Can of coconut milk (14 oz., 398 mL)	1	1
Chopped ripe (or frozen, thawed) mango	1 1/2 cups	375 mL
Medium sweetened coconut, toasted (see Tip, page 267)	1/2 cup	125 mL

Put water into large bowl. Add water until rice is covered. Let stand for at least 6 hours or overnight. Drain.

Combine sugar and water in 3 1/2 to 4 quart (3.5 to 4 L) slow cooker. Add rice and salt. Stir. Cook, covered, on Low for 4 hours or on High for 2 hours.

Add coconut milk and mango. Stir.

Sprinkle coconut over individual servings. Makes about 7 cups (1.75 L).

1/2 cup (125 mL): 210 Calories; 7.1 g Total Fat (0.3 g Mono, 0.1 g Poly, 6.2 g Sat); 0 mg Cholesterol; 36 g Carbohydrate; 1 g Fibre; 2 g Protein; 32 mg Sodium

Danish Rice Pudding

This creamy pudding with tangy raspberry sauce is traditionally served at Christmas in Denmark. It's customary to hide a whole blanched almond in the pudding. Whoever finds the almond in their serving wins a prize.

Can of sweetened condensed milk (11 oz., 300 mL)	1	1
Arborio rice, rinsed and drained	1 cup	250 mL
Water	2 1/4 cups	550 mL
Slivered almonds, toasted (see Tip, page 267)	3/4 cup	175 mL
Whipping cream	1/4 cup	60 mL
Whipping cream	1 3/4 cups	425 mL
Container of frozen raspberries in syrup (15 oz., 425 g), thawed	1	1

(continued on next page)

Combine condensed milk, rice and water in well-greased 3 1/2 to 4 quart (3.5 to 4 L) slow cooker. Cook, covered, on Low for 4 hours or on High for 2 hours. Transfer rice mixture to large bowl. Let stand, uncovered, for 15 minutes.

Add almonds and first amount of whipping cream. Stir. Chill, covered, for about 45 minutes, stirring occasionally, until cooled completely.

Beat remaining whipping cream in medium bowl until stiff peaks form. Fold into rice mixture.

Put raspberries and syrup into medium saucepan. Cook, uncovered, on medium for about 10 minutes, stirring occasionally, until slightly reduced. Spoon over individual servings. Serves 8.

1 serving: 523 Calories; 30.2 g Total Fat (9.6 g Mono, 2.1 g Poly, 16.2 g Sat); 92 mg Cholesterol; 57 g Carbohydrate; 3 g Fibre; 8 g Protein; 82 mg Sodium

Pictured on page 269.

Indian Basmati Rice Pudding

The satisfying texture of brown basmati rice is paired with rich chai spices and flavourful bits of ginger. This rice pudding can be served warm or chilled, depending upon your preference.

Water	3 1/2 cups	875 mL
Brown basmati rice	2 cups	500 mL
Brown sugar, packed	1/2 cup	125 mL
Cinnamon sticks (4 inches, 10 cm, each)	2	2
Ground cardamom	1 tsp.	5 mL
Salt	1/8 tsp.	0.5 mL
Pepper	1/4 tsp.	1 mL
Large eggs	2	2
Milk	1 1/2 cups	375 mL
Minced crystallized ginger	3 tbsp.	45 mL
Vanilla extract	1/2 tsp.	2 mL

Combine first 7 ingredients in 3 1/2 to 4 quart (3.5 to 4 L) slow cooker. Cook, covered, on High for 3 hours. Remove and discard cinnamon sticks.

Whisk remaining 4 ingredients in medium bowl. Slowly add about 1 cup (250 mL) hot rice mixture, stirring constantly until combined. Slowly add mixture to slow cooker, stirring constantly. Cook, covered, on High for 15 minutes. Makes about 6 cups (1.5 L).

1 cup (250 mL): 325 Calories; 4.3 g Total Fat (0.9 g Mono, 0.2 g Poly, 0.9 g Sat); 74 mg Cholesterol; 67 g Carbohydrate; 3 g Fibre; 8 g Protein; 107 mg Sodium

Buttery Ginger Pineapple

This light dessert is simple yet exotic, with tangy bites of pineapple, buttery sauce with spicy ginger, and a sprinkling of toasted coconut.

Fresh (or frozen, thawed) pineapple chunks (1 1/2 inch, 3.8 cm, pieces)	6 cups	1.5 L
Ginger marmalade	1/4 cup	60 mL
Butter	3 tbsp.	45 mL
Water	1 tbsp.	15 mL
Cornstarch	1 tbsp.	15 mL
Flaked coconut, toasted (see Tip, page 267)	1/2 cup	125 mL

Put pineapple into 3 1/2 to 4 quart (3.5 to 4 L) slow cooker.

Combine marmalade and butter in small saucepan on medium-low. Heat and stir until butter is melted. Pour over pineapple. Stir until coated. Cook, covered, on Low for 3 to 4 hours or on High for 1 1/2 to 2 hours.

Stir water into cornstarch in small cup until smooth. Add to pineapple. Stir. Cook, covered, on High for 15 minutes until boiling and thickened.

Sprinkle individual servings with coconut. Makes about 4 cups (1 L).

1/2 cup (125 mL): 144 Calories; 5.9 g Total Fat (1.2 g Mono, 0.2 g Poly, 4.0 g Sat); 11 mg Cholesterol; 24 g Carbohydrate; 2 g Fibre; 1 g Protein; 49 mg Sodium

Vanilla Peach Tapioca Pudding

Use fresh peeled peaches while they're in season. This pudding is great served warm or chilled.

Water	2 cups	500 mL
Seed tapioca	1/2 cup	125 mL
Homogenized milk	3 cups	750 mL
Vanilla bean, split	1/2	1/2
Salt	1/8 tsp.	0.5 mL
Large egg	1	1
Brown sugar, packed	1/3 cup	75 mL
Reserved peach juice	1/3 cup	75 mL
White vinegar	1/2 tsp.	2 mL
Can of sliced peaches in juice (14 oz., 398 mL), drained and juice reserved, chopped	1	1

(continued on next page)

Combine water and tapioca in medium bowl. Let stand, covered, for 1 hour. Drain. Transfer to 3 1/2 to 4 quart (3.5 to 4 L) slow cooker.

Add next 3 ingredients. Stir. Cook, covered, on Low for 4 hours or on High for 2 hours, stirring once at halftime. Remove and discard vanilla bean.

Whisk next 4 ingredients in medium bowl. Slowly add about 1 cup (250 mL) hot tapioca mixture, stirring constantly until combined. Slowly add to slow cooker, stirring constantly. Cook, covered, on High for 15 minutes.

Add peaches. Stir. Makes about 4 2/3 cups (1.15 L).

1 cup (250 mL): 279 Calories; 6.2 g Total Fat (2.0 g Mono, 0.5 g Poly, 3.6 g Sat); 68 mg Cholesterol; 51 g Carbohydrate; 1 g Fibre; 7 g Protein; 162 mg Sodium

Orange Tapioca Pudding

This citrus-scented tapioca makes for rich and creamy comfort food when served warm, but it can be served up chilled as well.

Seed tapioca	1/2 cup	125 mL
Cold water	2 cups	500mL
Homogenized milk	3 cups	750 mL
Salt, sprinkle		
Medium orange	1	1
Large egg	1	1
Granulated sugar	1/3 cup	75 mL

Combine tapioca and cold water in medium bowl. Stir. Let stand, covered, for 1 hour. Drain. Transfer to 3 1/2 to 4 quart (3.5 to 4 L) slow cooker.

Add milk and a sprinkle of salt. Stir. Cook, covered, on Low for 4 hours or on High for 2 hours, stirring once at halftime.

Grate 1/2 tsp. (2 mL) orange zest into small bowl. Set aside. Squeeze 1/3 cup (75 mL) orange juice into separate medium bowl.

Add egg and sugar to orange juice. Whisk until smooth. Slowly add about 1 cup (250 mL) hot tapioca mixture, whisking constantly until combined. Slowly add mixture back to slow cooker, stirring constantly. Cook, covered, on High for 15 minutes. Add orange zest. Stir. Makes about 3 1/2 cups (875 mL).

1/2 cup (125 mL): 155 Calories; 4.1 g Total Fat (1.1 g Mono, 0.2 g Poly, 2.4 g Sat); 46 mg Cholesterol; 26 g Carbohydrate; trace Fibre; 4 g Protein; 146 mg Sodium

Graham Crumb Cake

This is such a neat cake. The graham crumbs take the place of flour. Chewy texture.

Hard margarine (or butter), softened	1/2 cup	125 mL
Granulated sugar	3/4 cup	175 mL
Large eggs	2	2
Graham cracker crumbs	2 1/4 cups	560 mL
Medium coconut	1/2 cup	125 mL
Baking powder	1 1/2 tsp.	7 mL
Salt	1/8 tsp.	0.5 mL
Milk	1/2 cup	125 mL
Vanilla	1 tsp.	5 mL
BUTTERSCOTCH ICING		
Brown sugar, packed	6 tbsp.	90 mL
Milk (or cream)	2 1/2 tbsp.	37 mL
Hard margarine (or butter)	3 tbsp.	45 mL
Icing (confectioner's) sugar	1 1/4 cups	300 mL

Cream margarine and sugar together in bowl. Beat in eggs, 1 at a time. Add graham crumbs, coconut, baking powder and salt. Stir well.

Add milk and vanilla. Stir. Line bottom of greased 5 quart (5 L) round slow cooker with foil. Pour batter over foil. Place 5 paper towels between top of slow cooker and lid. Put wooden match or an object 1/8 inch (3 mm) thick between paper towels and edge of slow cooker to allow a bit of steam to escape. Do not lift lid. Cook on High for 2 hours until wooden pick inserted in centre comes out clean. Remove slow cooker liner to rack or turn slow cooker off. Let stand for 20 minutes. Loosen sides of cake with knife. Invert cake onto plate, foil side up, then onto rack, foil side down, to cool. Remove foil before serving.

Butterscotch Icing: Combine brown sugar, milk and margarine in saucepan. Heat and stir until boiling. Boil for 2 minutes. Remove from heat. Cool.

Add icing sugar. Beat until smooth, adding more milk or icing sugar, if needed, to make proper spreading consistency. Makes about 1 cup (250 mL). Ice top and sides of cake. Cuts into 12 wedges.

1 wedge: 320 Calories; 14 g Total Fat, 4.5 g Mono, 3.5 g Poly, 3.5 g Sat; 35 mg Cholesterol; 46 g Carbohydrate, 1 g Fibre; 3 g Protein; 350 mg Sodium

Desserts

Marbled Cheesecake

A perfect dessert to make when your oven is already in use.

GRAHAM CRUST		
Hard margarine (or butter)	4 tsp.	20 mL
Graham cracker crumbs	1/3 cup	75 mL
Granulated sugar	1 tsp.	5 mL

FILLING		
Semi-sweet chocolate baking squares (1 oz., 28 g), cut up	3	3
Light cream cheese (12 oz., 375 g), softened	1	1
Granulated sugar	3/4 cup	175 mL
Non-fat plain yogurt	1/3 cup	75 mL
Vanilla	1 tsp.	5 mL
Large eggs	4	4
All-purpose flour	1/2 cup	125 mL

Graham Crust: Melt margarine in saucepan. Stir in graham crumbs and sugar. Press in ungreased 8 inch (20 cm) round cake pan.

Filling: Melt chocolate in saucepan over low, stirring often.

Beat cream cheese, sugar, yogurt and vanilla together in large bowl until smooth. Beat in eggs, 1 at a time. Add flour. Mix. Reserve 1 3/4 cups (425 mL) of cheese mixture. Pour remaining cheese mixture over bottom crust.

Stir melted chocolate into reserved 1 3/4 cups (425 mL) of cheese mixture. Stir. Drizzle over top of white layer. Cut through in a zig-zag motion to get a marbled look.

Tear off a 16 inch (40 cm) long piece of foil to make a foil strap. Fold lengthwise to make a strip 16 inches (40 cm) long and 4 inches (10 cm) wide. Set cake pan on center of foil strap. Put wire trivet in bottom of 5 quart (5 L) round slow cooker.

Using foil strap, carefully lower pan into slow cooker, leaving foil strap in the slow cooker to use to remove pan when baking is complete. Place 5 paper towels between top of slow cooker and lid. Cook on High for 3 hours. Remove pan. Cool. Refrigerate for several hours or overnight. Cuts into 12 wedges.

1 wedge: 220 Calories; 11 g Total Fat (1 g Mono, 0.5 g Poly, 6 g Sat); 90 mg Cholesterol; 25 g Carbohydrate, <1 g Fibre; 5 g Protein; 200 mg Sodium

Steamed Chocolate Pudding

No egg in this. Makes a chewy brownie-like dessert. Serve with ice cream and chocolate sauce.

Hard margarine (or butter), softened	1 tbsp.	15 mL
Granulated sugar	1/2 cup	125 mL
Cocoa	2 tbsp.	30 mL
Milk	1/2 cup	125 mL
Vanilla	1/2 tsp.	2 mL
All-purpose flour	1 1/2 cups	375 mL
Baking powder	2 tsp.	10 mL
Salt	1/2 tsp.	2 mL

Cream margarine, sugar, and cocoa together in bowl. Add milk and vanilla. Beat well.

Add flour, baking powder and salt. Mix well. Turn into greased 4 cup (1 L) bowl. Cover with greased foil, tying sides down with string. Place wire trivet in 5 quart (5 L) or 6 quart (6 L) slow cooker. Set bowl on top. Pour boiling water into slow cooker to reach halfway up bowl. Cover. Cook on High for 2 1/2 hours. Serves 6.

1 serving: 210 Calories; 2.5 g Total Fat (1 g Mono, 0.5 g Poly, 0.5 g Sat); 0 mg Cholesterol; 43 g Carbohydrate, 1 g Fibre; 5 g Protein; 330 mg Sodium

1. Chocolate PB Brownies, page 258
2. Chocolate Peanut Delight, page 32

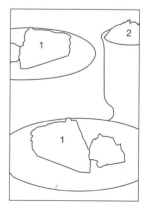

Dried Fruit Compote

A good breakfast dish or light dessert.

Dried pitted prunes	8 oz.	225 g
Dried apricots, halved	8 oz.	225 g
Canned sliced peaches, with juice (14 oz., 398 mL)	2	2
Maraschino cherries	12	12
Water	1 1/2 cups	375 mL
Granulated sugar	1/2 cup	125 mL

Combine all 6 ingredients in 3 1/2 quart (3.5 L) slow cooker. Stir. Cover. Cook on Low for 3 1/2 to 4 hours. Makes 6 3/4 cups (1.68 L).

1/2 cup (125 mL): 160 Calories; 0 g Total Fat (0 g Mono, 0 g Poly, 0 g Sat); 0 mg Cholesterol; 40 g Carbohydrate, 3 g Fibre; 2 g Protein; 15 mg Sodium

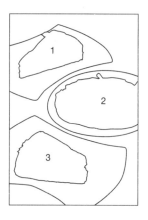

1. Marbled Yogurt Brownies, page 261
2. Blue Cheese Pears, page 276
3. PB Banana "Cheesecake," page 275

Recipe Index

Index

291

Index

Measurement Tables

Throughout this book measurements are given in Conventional and Metric measure. To compensate for differences between the two measurements due to rounding, a full metric measure is not always used. The cup used is the standard 8 fluid ounce. Temperature is given in degrees Fahrenheit and Celsius. Baking pan measurements are in inches and centimetres as well as quarts and litres. An exact metric conversion is given below as well as the working equivalent (Metric Standard Measure).

Spoons

Conventional Measure	Metric Exact Conversion Millilitre (mL)	Metric Standard Measure Millilitre (mL)
1/8 teaspoon (tsp.)	0.6 mL	0.5 mL
1/4 teaspoon (tsp.)	1.2 mL	1 mL
1/2 teaspoon (tsp.)	2.4 mL	2 mL
1 teaspoon (tsp.)	4.7 mL	5 mL
2 teaspoons (tsp.)	9.4 mL	10 mL
1 tablespoon (tbsp.)	14.2 mL	15 mL

Cups

Conventional Measure	Metric Exact Conversion Millilitre (mL)	Metric Standard Measure Millilitre (mL)
1/4 cup (4 tbsp.)	56.8 mL	60 mL
1/3 cup (5 1/3 tbsp.)	75.6 mL	75 mL
1/2 cup (8 tbsp.)	113.7 mL	125 mL
2/3 cup (10 2/3 tbsp.)	151.2 mL	150 mL
3/4 cup (12 tbsp.)	170.5 mL	175 mL
1 cup (16 tbsp.)	227.3 mL	250 mL
4 1/2 cups	1022.9 mL	1000 mL (1 L)

Oven Temperatures

Fahrenheit (°F)	Celsius (°C)
175°	80°
200°	95°
225°	110°
250°	120°
275°	140°
300°	150°
325°	160°
350°	175°
375°	190°
400°	205°
425°	220°
450°	230°
475°	240°
500°	260°

Dry Measurements

Conventional Measure Ounces (oz.)	Metric Exact Conversion Grams (g)	Metric Standard Measure Grams (g)
1 oz.	28.3 g	28 g
2 oz.	56.7 g	57 g
3 oz.	85.0 g	85 g
4 oz.	113.4 g	125 g
5 oz.	141.7 g	140 g
6 oz.	170.1 g	170 g
7 oz.	198.4 g	200 g
8 oz.	226.8 g	250 g
16 oz.	453.6 g	500 g
32 oz.	907.2 g	1000 g (1 kg)

Pans

Conventional Inches	Metric Centimetres
8x8 inch	20x20 cm
9x9 inch	23x23 cm
9x13 inch	23x33 cm
10x15 inch	25x38 cm
11x17 inch	28x43 cm
8x2 inch round	20x5 cm
9x2 inch round	23x5 cm
10x4 1/2 inch tube	25x11 cm
8x4x3 inch loaf	20x10x7.5 cm
9x5x3 inch loaf	23x12.5x7.5 cm

Casseroles

CANADA & BRITAIN		UNITED STATES	
Standard Size Casserole	Exact Metric Measure	Standard Size Casserole	Exact Metric Measure
1 qt. (5 cups)	1.13 L	1 qt. (4 cups)	900 mL
1 1/2 qts. (7 1/2 cups)	1.69 L	1 1/2 qts. (6 cups)	1.35 L
2 qts. (10 cups)	2.25 L	2 qts. (8 cups)	1.8 L
2 1/2 qts. (12 1/2 cups)	2.81 L	2 1/2 qts. (10 cups)	2.25 L
3 qts. (15 cups)	3.38 L	3 qts. (12 cups)	2.7 L
4 qts. (20 cups)	4.5 L	4 qts. (16 cups)	3.6 L
5 qts. (25 cups)	5.63 L	5 qts. (20 cups)	4.5 L

A new FOCUS on great taste!

Classic Curry

Bring a taste of the East into your home with these classic curries! Not in the mood for Indian? How about Malaysian, Thai or Vietnamese instead?

Eggceptional Eggs

Think eggs are just for breakfast? Think again! Salads, pasta, soups and desserts—all are "eggceptional" thanks to this humble little gem.

Going Bananas

Salads, stews, muffins, pies...with their sweet, creamy and healthy flesh, there is no limit to what you can do with this tasty fruit favourite—so go bananas!

Perfectly Pork

Ham, ribs, sausage, chops—no matter how you slice it, pork is perfect for family meals or entertaining!

Collect all of these FOCUS SERIES titles:

- *Apple Appeal*
- *Berries & Cream*
- *Burger Bravado*
- *Carrot Craze*
- *Charming Cupcakes*
- *Chicken Breast Finesse*
- *Chilled Thrills*
- *Chocolate Squared*
- *Christmas Cookies*
- *Classic Curry*
- *Coffee Cake Classics*
- *Cookie Jar Classics*
- *Cranberry Cravings*
- *Dip, Dunk and Dab*
- *Easy Roasting*

- *Eggceptional Eggs*
- *Fab Finger Food*
- *Fruit Squared*
- *Glorious Garlic*
- *Going Bananas*
- *Hearty Soups*
- *Hot Bites*
- *In A Nutshell*
- *Lemon Lime Zingers*
- *Mushroom Magic*
- *Pepper Power*
- *Perfectly Pork*
- *Salads to Go*
- *Scoops*
- *Shrimp Delicious*

- *Simmering Stews*
- *Simply Vegetarian*
- *Sips*
- *Skewered*
- *So Strawberry*
- *Splendid Spuds*
- *Squashed*
- *Steak Sizzle*
- *Sweet Dreams*
- *That's a Wrap*
- *Tomato Temptations*
- *Tossed*
- *Warm Desserts*
- *Zucchini Zone*